SCHOOLS MAKE A DIFFERENCE

Lessons Learned from a 10-Year Study of School Effects

SCHOOLS MAKE A DIFFERENCE

Lessons Learned from a 10-Year Study of School Effects

Charles Teddlie
Sam Stringfield

FOREWORD BY LARRY CUBAN

TEACHERS
COLLEGE
PRESS

Teachers College, Columbia University
New York and London

Published by Teachers College Press, 1234 Amsterdam Avenue,
New York, New York

Library of Congress Cataloging-in-Publication Data

Teddlie, Charles.
    Schools make a difference : lessons learned from a 10-year study
  of school effects / Charles Teddlie, Sam Stringfield.
        p.   cm.
    Includes bibliographical references and index.
    ISBN 0-8077-3237-0
    1. Schools—Louisiana—Evaluation—Longitudinal studies.
  I. Stringfield, Sam. II. Title.
  LA295.T43   1993
  370′.9763—dc20   92-44888

Printed on acid-free paper

Manufactured in the United States of America

99 98 97 96 95 94 93 8 7 6 5 4 3 2 1

To Our Wives and Mothers

Susan and Kathleen
Harriet and Blanche

Contents

Foreword

Had this study been available in the early 1980s rather than now, I suspect that the trajectory of "effective schools" research among academics might have been very different. The effective schools movement was anchored in the work of Ron Edmonds, who popularized the notion that in some schools with a predominantly low-income minority student body, students consistently performed on standardized tests well beyond what was expected of them. Policymakers and practitioners seized on the early research emerging from schools identified as "effective." On the basis of five or seven or ten correlates of effectiveness identified by researchers, districts constructed program after program in urban schools to put into practice these research findings.

By the mid-1980s, enough serious critiques of the faulty research methods used to investigate effective schools had been published to virtually push the subject off researchers' agendas. The use of skewed samples and flawed measures, the instability of test results, the lack of longitudinal studies, and the frequent ignoring of socioeconomic status were a mere sample of the charges contained in the withering criticism researchers unleashed on what was basically a small body of work. By the late 1980s, few academics took effective schools research seriously, and it had largely been banished to the netherworld of pop-research and exemplars of what-not-to-do for doctoral students.

But not for policymakers and practitioners. If ever a continental divide existed between researchers on the one side and policymakers and practitioners on the other, it is most clearly revealed over effective schools research. As researchers turned up their collective noses at this body of research, those who worked daily in improving schools embraced the findings with a relish bordering on passion in their efforts to create programs in urban and non-urban schools, districts, and states. A U.S. General Accounting Office report in 1989 found that 4 out of every 10 school districts in the nation had programs built on the findings of this small body of research that had been found irremediably flawed by academics.

Schools Make a Difference: Lessons Learned from a 10-Year Study of School

ix

Effects should do much to narrow the gap between researchers and those who work in schools. It is an important book for both researchers and practitioners for several reasons. Its authors take seriously the premise of the first generation of effective-schools researchers that there are schools with largely poor, minority students who can perform academically like their higher-income, nonminority peers, and they have carefully sought out the factors that are related to this success. To that end Teddlie and Stringfield systematically followed a careful research design, used both quantitative and qualitative methodologies, and, most crucially, included in their research a longitudinal study in which 16 Louisiana elementary schools were observed over an 8-year period. This is a first-rate study that avoids the lapses, outright errors, and lack of rigor that marked so many of the studies completed a decade or so earlier. Furthermore, Teddlie and Stringfield place their work—wisely, I believe—in the longer tradition of "school effects" studies. Thus, researchers cannot dismiss their work as just another "effective schools" study. To do so would be an error. Teddlie and Stringfield's rigorous design, their varied research methods, and the caution they apply in stating their findings give their work a stature that earlier studies lacked.

Some of their findings are significant because they provide solid support for ideas that have heretofore been believed more on the basis of intuition or faith than hard data. For example, their data clearly show that elementary schools can raise student achievement and that the improved achievement can persist over time. They also found that some schools initially identified as effective could deteriorate over time. Similarly, they found that the context—where students went to school, their background, and grade level—can have a large effect on which school improvement strategies are successful. Context matters.

Their research data also confirm the insight of the first generation of effective schools researchers and the practical intuition of administrators that the principal's leadership counts. Teddlie and Stringfield realized that school and classroom effects have to be studied together because they interact with one another and create school climates that in turn affect how teachers get socialized within a school and what teachers do with their students, and their data demonstrate these interactions. Finally, they found some surprising effects—for example, that district influence is modest to even negative on enhancing the effectiveness of schools, and that in four cases schools initially identified as ineffective were "naturally" improving, that is, local community impulses toward reversing ineffectiveness had prompted each school to begin improving.

These findings are important because they emerge from a careful, rigorous study. Will it influence researchers' agendas? Perhaps. It should, because it lays out a path to follow that could add stature to such studies. Will it influence the actions of policymakers and practitioners? Again, perhaps. It will strengthen the rationales for many existing programs aimed at elementary schools, and it may suggest different paths for districts to pursue. We shall see. In any even, Teddlie and Stringfield and Teachers College Press deserve our thanks for publishing this book.

Larry Cuban
Stanford University

Preface

The Louisiana School Effectiveness Study (LSES) has defined, to a large degree, a decade of professional growth for its two main authors. As such, a few notes and acknowledgments should precede the final work.

The LSES was begun in 1980, following the watershed period in school effects research marked by the works of Wilbur Brookover, Michael Rutter, and Ron Edmonds, and preceding the stern but productive criticism that was to engulf the field in the early to mid-1980s. At that point, we assumed that there were many other researchers across the United States busily working to follow up on the leads created by the aforementioned scholars.

We were quite surprised when only a handful of researchers, including Joe Murphy, Phil Hallinger, Steve Miller, and Larry Lezotte, attended the organizational session for the new American Educational Research Association (AERA) Special Interest Group (SIG) on School Effectiveness at the 1984 meeting in New Orleans. From small beginnings, the SIG has steadily grown to one of the largest and most active in AERA, but its emphasis over the years has swung to school improvement as well as the study of school effects. This occupation with school improvement describes the course of much of the American school effects work over the past decade.

While the number of American scholars studying school effects has increased only gradually over the past few years, our European colleagues have breathed new energy into the research area. Unfettered by the criticism of the American research, these scholars have consistently assumed school effects to be a viable area of research and have organized an annual congress and a journal to help institutionalize study in the field. In Chapter 12 of this book, it is the Europeans (such as Dave Reynolds, Bert Creemers, and Peter Mortimore) to whom we refer and hope to engage in a continuing dialogue.

It is heartening that the issues identified by the Europeans (e.g., magnitude of school effects, variance in school effects, context of school effects, multiple measures of school effects, theory development in school effects) are the same issues that have emerged from the LSES. As these topics within school effects are defined and explored, the area as a scientific field of study will develop more fully.

ACKNOWLEDGMENTS

There are a number of people whose contributions to the study should be acknowledged. First, thanks must go to the 94 anonymous schools, their superintendents, principals, teachers, and students who participated in various phases of the study. Special appreciation is extended to those 16 schools that allowed us to follow them over the course of the third and fourth phases of the study (LSES–III and –IV). It should be noted that pseudonyms have been substituted for actual school names throughout the book. Also, some identifying information (such as age, ethnicity, sex) has been changed to further protect the anonymity of the participants.

Our gratitude also goes to Bob Garvue and Hugh Peck at the Louisiana Department of Education (LDE) for their inspiration and financial support of the project. Garvue initiated the study by declaring that a school effects project couldn't get us in trouble, since "it was as American as apple pie." He apparently did not foresee the machinations of the fourth estate with regard to school effects research, as described in Chapter 12.

From an intellectual point of view, much of the LSES was a response to issues raised by Tom Good and Jere Brophy in their 1986 article on "School Effects." Their insights into the limitations of extant school effects research helped guide our efforts, especially during LSES–III and –IV.

Funding for the LSES came from a variety of sources, including the LDE, the University of New Orleans (UNO), and Louisiana State University (LSU). Funds from the Southeast Regional Council for Educational Improvement and the Center for the Social Organization of Schools at Johns Hopkins University have helped to sustain the project over the years. Funds were also provided through Chad Ellett and the LSU College of Education Teaching Internship and Statewide Evaluation for completion of the LSES–IV case studies.

During the course of the LSES, we have been fortunate to have assembled an excellent research team. More than 20 observers, testers, and other data gatherers have participated in the study, and four stand out as having made particularly significant contributions—Stephanie Desselle, Mary Ann Durland, Karen Soniat, and Sandy Suarez. The

LSES, and several ancillary investigations, have benefited from graduate students who have explored school effects in their dissertations—Debbie Heroman, Carol Scott Whelan, Irene Virgilio, Lynn Evans, Mic Lang, Carol Ter Haar, and Linda Crone. Thanks also go to Ruby Marchand, who provided stellar secretarial services during LSES-I, -II, and -III.

Perhaps the most enjoyable aspect of the project has been the creation of a research team that designed and conducted the study and then stayed around to write about it. This core team consisted of ourselves and Bob Wimpelberg and Peggy Kirby at UNO. Over the years the team has expanded to include Eugene Kennedy at LSU and Bob Slater at Texas A&M. Our often informal conversations with these colleagues have increased our understanding of the nature of school effects.

Finally, credit must go to those most responsible for actually getting this book produced. Thanks go to Ellen Albarado for her excellent organizational and word processing skills that kept the book on its timeline. A special thanks goes to Susan Liddicoat, our editor at Teachers College Press, for both her patience and light editorial touch.

PART I

Design and Initial Results from the LSES

The chapters in this part outline the rationale and four-phase design of the Louisiana School Effectiveness Study. Following an introduction in Chapter 1, Chapter 2 presents analyses of LSES-II data explaining variation in student achievement. In Chapter 3 contextual differences between effective and ineffective schools are described through further analyses of LSES-II data. Chapter 4 introduces a theoretical framework for conceptualizing results of the study and explains the methodology of LSES-III and -IV.

1 Introduction to a Multiphased Study of School Effects

Do some schools produce a higher level of student achievement than other schools that serve similar students? This question served as the initial focus for school effects research, one purpose of which is to provide direction for school improvement efforts.

A 1989 report by the U.S. General Accounting Office (GAO) illustrates how extensively American educators have embraced school effects research. In describing the extent of school improvement programs in the United States, the report stated:

> About 41 percent or 6,500 of the nation's school districts had effective schools programs in operation in approximately 38,000 elementary and secondary schools during school year 1987–88. . . . An additional 17 percent or about 2,600 of the nation's districts have plans to implement effective schools programs during school years 1988–89 or 1989–90. (GAO, 1989, p. 2)

Thus, more than 50% of American schools have undertaken school improvement efforts, according to the GAO report. The report also illustrates some rather basic contradictions within the school effects research area. For example, the school improvement programs cited were primarily based on a five-factor model derived from studies that are over a decade old. This five-factor model had a considerable impact on the Hawkins-Stafford Elementary and Secondary School Improvement Amendments of 1988 (Public Law 100-297), which specified that these characteristics should be stressed in improvement programs funded with Chapter 1 and 2 monies. The five factors are: strong principal leadership, a pervasive and broadly understood instructional focus, a safe and orderly school climate, high expectations for student achievement, and student achievement data used for evaluating program success (GAO, 1989).

This model was developed from research conducted primarily in lower-socioeconomic status (SES), urban elementary schools. The gener-

3

alization of this model to schools with different SES, urbanicity, and grade-level configurations had been widely questioned even prior to passage of the aforementioned law (e.g., Good & Brophy, 1986; Purkey & Smith, 1983; Rowan, Bossert, & Dwyer, 1983).

In reviewing school effects research, the GAO acknowledged this context problem and other criticisms.

> Criticism of the research is leveled against the (1) reduction of the findings to a set of specific characteristics, including the five just mentioned, to be used as a formula for school improvement; (2) generalization of the findings of studies conducted in urban elementary schools to all levels of schools . . . ; (3) notion that once aware of a set of specific characteristics, schools can simply . . . adopt them. (p. 14)

There is a rich irony here. Even as improvement programs based on early school effects research were being adopted nationwide and incorporated into federal law, a federal study acknowledged that the research findings that underpinned those programs might not be generalizable to, or productively implementable in, all schools. What's more, the list of unresolved school effects issues cited by the GAO is only partial. An earlier, comprehensive review by Good and Brophy (1986) listed 17 limitations of extant school effects research.

This book describes the Louisiana School Effectiveness Study (LSES), a decade-long project that attempted to address several of these issues. At the study's outset we decided that instead of developing a new taxonomy of effective schools characteristics (be they 5, 7, 9, 11, or whatever), we would concentrate on providing an expanded school effects research database. To the degree that LSES data shed light on school effects issues, they might inform future process-oriented school change.

We are not implying that *all* school improvement efforts based on the five-factor model are ill-conceived. In fact, the National Center for Effective Schools Research and Development recently published a series of case studies of successful intervention programs based on this model (Taylor, 1990). Three points, however, are clear about the current status of school effects research.

1. Many school improvement projects are based on overly simplified school effects models that may not be appropriate for the contexts in which they are being implemented.
2. Better conceptualized school effects research is needed in order to advance the area as a scientific discipline with separate domains cen-

tered around specific problem areas identified by Good and Brophy and others (e.g., Purkey & Smith, 1983; Ralph & Fennessey, 1983). As noted by Creemers and Reynolds (1990) in a general discussion of the school effects area, "In the early stages of a discipline there is much historical evidence that a problem solving approach is that which is most likely to generate intellectual advances" (p. 3).

3. Findings from these better conceptualized studies might then be used to more precisely inform school improvement models at particular schools with unique contexts and other important differences.

THE LIMITATIONS OF CURRENT RESEARCH

The Good and Brophy (1986) review in the *Third Handbook of Research on Teaching* presents a comprehensive list of limitations in existing school effects research. Several years have passed since the review, yet the list remains relevant for two reasons: (1) most of the issues have yet to be properly addressed; and (2) several issues that have been addressed have developed into separate research areas within school effects.

A brief review of eight of the limitations identified by Good and Brophy is appropriate at this point. These will serve as a backdrop for a discussion of major issues addressed by the LSES. The limitations are as follows:

1. *Independent Variables.* According to Good and Brophy, a wider range of variables should be included in school effects studies. For instance, not enough research has focused on how teachers from differentially effective schools vary on quantitative and qualitative measures (e.g., homework assignment, measures of classroom behavior).
2. *Validity.* Outcomes of school effectiveness should not be limited to student achievement on criterion-referenced tests (CRTs) and norm-referenced tests (NRTs). Other researchers have argued this point, suggesting that student attendance, student attitudes toward school, and other outcome measures be used as well (Cuban, 1983; Purkey & Smith, 1983; Ralph & Fennessey, 1983; Rowan, Bossert, & Dwyer, 1983).
3. *Stability.* More information is needed on the stability of school effects over time. A separate research area has developed around this issue of stability, with several recent studies (Lang, 1991; Mandeville, 1988; Mandeville & Anderson, 1987; Mandeville & Kennedy, 1991) expanding on earlier studies (Forsythe, 1973; Jencks et al., 1972; Reyn-

olds, Jones, & St. Leger, 1976; Rowan & Denk, 1982; Rutter, 1983; Rutter, Maughan, Mortimore, & Ouston, 1979).

4. *Multiple Criteria.* Related to the stability issue is the question of consistency: Are some schools generally effective or is their effectiveness limited to a few areas of achievement? More research is needed on the generalizability of school effects across multiple criteria at one point in time. For instance, a recent study by Lang (1991) found a moderate level of consistency within school effectiveness classifications when using both CRT and NRT scores from the same group of schools.

5. *Context.* Good and Brophy were among several authors who called for the study of school effects in settings more diverse than low-SES, urban elementary schools. A separate school effects research area has emerged with studies in more diverse SES contexts (e.g., Evans, 1988; Hallinger & Murphy, 1985, 1986; Teddlie & Stringfield, 1985; Teddlie, Stringfield, Wimpelberg, & Kirby, 1989); differing grade level configuration contexts (e.g., Levine & Eubanks, 1989; Levine, Levine, & Eubanks, 1984; Olthof & Lugthart, 1992; Rutter et al., 1979; Virgilio, Teddlie, & Oescher, 1991); and within various urbanicity contexts (e.g., Buttram & Carlson, 1983; Conklin & Olson, 1988; Stringfield & Teddlie, 1991b).

6. *Student/Teacher Perceptions.* Good and Brophy (1986) argued that better measures of student and teacher perceptions are needed. They asserted that studies need to "focus more closely on participants' reactions to specific events, especially events believed to be central to school effectiveness" (p. 589). They cited measures used by Brookover, Beady, Flood, Schweitzer, and Wisenbaker (1979) as good indices for assessing the general reactions of teachers and students to schools. An unanswered school effects question in this area might be: Why do some teachers have higher expectations for students than other teachers in the same school or in other schools serving similar populations?

7. *Conceptualization of School Effects.* More attention should be paid to conceptualizing and operationalizing school effects. According to Good and Brophy, many important school measures have not been examined because they have not been properly conceptualized.

8. *Independence of School Effects.* Good and Brophy noted that researchers need to more carefully isolate school effects from the effects of other levels of schooling (such as the teacher or district), noting that the "effects of all of these on achievement are confounded in reality" (p. 590). Recent school effects research studies have used hierarchical linear modeling (HLM) in an attempt to disentangle school effects

from student and teacher effects (e.g., Mandeville & Kennedy, 1991; Raudenbush & Bryk, 1986, 1989).

ISSUES ADDRESSED IN THE LOUISIANA
SCHOOL EFFECTIVENESS STUDY

Early in the LSES, we discovered that the study not only could provide insights into several of Good and Brophy's concerns, but could address some emerging issues as well. Reading a pre-press version of Good and Brophy's chapter in 1985, we were struck by how many of the issues raised there were either already being addressed or would be addressed in future phases of the study. The study's relevance to these issues was partially planned and partially serendipitous.

As for the "planned part," we were aware when we began our research in 1980 of several general areas of concern in the literature, such as context and stability. Consequently, we selected schools from different SES contexts (middle, low) to study in Phase Two (LSES-II), and deliberately studied schools across time in Phases Three and Four (LSES-III and -IV).

As for the "serendipitous part," our research design enabled us to study several unanticipated issues. For instance, during LSES-III and -IV we noted that some historically ineffective schools appeared to be improving without externally imposed plans. We labeled this phenomenon "naturally occurring school improvement" and contrasted it with externally imposed efforts along dimensions suggested by Huberman and Miles (1984).

The major issues addressed by the LSES are summarized on the following pages. References are made to chapters where results related to these issues are discussed. It is encouraging that some of our results, such as those related to differences in effective schooling for students from middle- and low-SES schools, have been replicated by others. We hope that LSES results may stimulate other investigators to more fully explore these emerging issues.

Are There School Effects?

The first question addressed by the LSES was the same question that initially defined the school effects area: Are there "school effects"? That is, are schools differentially effective in their ability to educate students?

The LSES was begun in the early 1980s, when evidence on school effects was just developing. At that point, the existence of school effects was widely debated, given the findings of Coleman and colleagues (1966) and Jencks and colleagues (1972). These reports were interpreted to conclude that schools had little effect on student achievement.

To date, four major process–product studies, including the LSES, have concluded that schools do have a definable impact on achievement (Brookover et al., 1979; Mortimore, Sammons, Stoll, Lewis, & Ecob, 1988a; Rutter et al., 1979; Teddlie, Falkowski, Stringfield, Desselle, & Garvue, 1984). Also, numerous outlier studies (e.g., Weber, 1971) have identified effective schools and have defined their most salient characteristics. Despite concerns about methodological weaknesses, literature reviews (e.g., Good & Brophy, 1986; Purkey & Smith, 1983) have concluded that the consistency of findings across studies provides strong evidence that differences exist among schools and that those differences are associated with differential achievement by students.

Chapter 2 reviews LSES-II evidence that supports the existence of school effects. Details of the statistical analysis, along with a comparison of LSES-II results with those reported by Brookover and colleagues (1979), using similar multiple regression techniques, and a reanalysis of the LSES-II results using HLM procedures, are provided in the Appendix.

The Stability of School Effects

Once the existence of school effects has been established, a second issue regarding their stability emerges. Good and Brophy concluded that it would be "disturbing" if effective schools did not have stable influences on achievement over consecutive years.

The stability of school effects was addressed directly in LSES-III and -IV, which involved following eight matched pairs of effective/ineffective schools over an 8-year period. Chapter 4 discusses issues regarding the stability of school effects, including why schools should or should not be expected to maintain their effectiveness status over time. A theoretical framework that addresses change in the effectiveness status of schools over time is introduced in this chapter.

Chapter 5 contains quantitative comparisons of the eight pairs of LSES-III and -IV schools on a number of dimensions, including student achievement, teacher behaviors, and student and faculty attitudes toward schooling. Chapters 6–8 present extensive case histories of three pairs of schools (one rural, one suburban, one urban) based on interviews and observations from LSES-III and -IV. Evidence of both stability and change in school effects is provided in these chapters.

The Context of School Effects

Contextual issues in school effects were addressed in LSES-II, -III, and -IV. Chapter 3 presents identified differences between effective middle-SES and low-SES schools. These results are derived from LSES-II, which involved the study of 76 schools throughout the state of Louisiana. These schools were divided into groups according to effectiveness status (effective, typical, ineffective) and student body SES (middle, low). Differential characteristics of schools in each of these categories are discussed in Chapter 3, which also compares the LSES-II results with those from a similar study conducted in California (Hallinger & Murphy, 1985, 1986).

Context was also studied in LSES-III and -IV, which compared schools specifically selected from urban, suburban, and rural areas. The effects that different urbanicity contexts have on school effectiveness processes are discussed in Chapters 6–8.

The issues of stability and context of school effects overlap. When following schools longitudinally, we were confronted with the question, What happens to school effects when contextual variables change over time? Effective schools must change to remain effective as their contexts change. Chapter 7 describes an effective principal who successfully adapted her school's educational practices to a changing student body. In this case, she correctly fit the best educational practices to existing conditions in the school as its community changed.

The Relationship of School and Teacher Effects

Good and Weinstein (1986) concluded that "researchers need to examine school and classroom processes simultaneously, identifying relationships that facilitate or hinder goals at each level" (p. 1096). The relationship between school and teacher effects is discussed in Chapter 10, which summarizes results from LSES-III and -IV plus another study (Virgilio, Teddlie, & Oescher, 1991). These studies involved the intensive investigation of teacher classroom behavior in both effective and ineffective schools. These studies revealed a consistent pattern of differences in both the mean rates and the variances of teaching behavior in differentially effective schools.

We also examined teacher perceptions within differentially effective schools. In LSES-II, teacher perceptions were assessed using a modified version of the Brookover and colleagues (1979) questionnaire. We built upon our findings in LSES-III and -IV by using both the modified Brookover questionnaire and teacher interviews. The teacher interviews allowed us to more fully explore such issues as, Do teachers in effective schools have more opportunities to learn from their fellow teachers? Perceptual questions at this level of complexity are best answered through one-on-one interviews with teachers.

Multilevel Issues Regarding School Effects

The degree to which school effects are independent of other levels of effect (such as district, teacher, and student effects) has concerned many researchers (e.g., Raudenbush & Bryk, 1986; Sirotnik & Burstein, 1985). This issue is directly addressed in the Appendix, which contains a reanalysis of LSES-II data using HLM models that statistically disentangle school effects from student and teacher effects. The multilevel issue is also addressed in Chapter 10, where we examine the interrelationship of school and teacher effects, and in Chapter 9, which discusses the effects that a district central office can have on educational processes and outcomes at the school level (Cuban, 1984).

Naturally Occurring School Change

One issue that emerged during the LSES was the identification of naturally occurring school improvement (Stringfield & Teddlie, 1990). At the time of our initial visits to eight historically ineffective schools in LSES-III, we found that four were engaged (with different degrees of success) in improvement efforts that were internally mandated.

As described in Chapter 4, we concluded that natural forces such as community discontent may lead to improvement at failing schools, and decline at formerly successful schools. Chapter 5 summarizes quantitative data gathered by observing eight pairs of schools over time, and classifies these schools as stable more effective, stable less effective, declining, or improving. The specific processes at work in improving, declining, or stable schools are then detailed in Chapters 6–8.

The Complementary Use of Quantitative and Qualitative Data

As the LSES developed, we found that both quantitative and qualitative data sources were useful and that results gleaned from one source often confirmed those from the other. For example, during LSES-III multiple observers correctly identified the effectiveness status of eight matched pairs of schools, even though the study involved a double blind design (Stringfield & Teddlie, 1991a).

Observers also correctly predicted improvement in some schools and detected inconsistencies in the classification of one school. These qualitative results were corroborated by quantitative sources, including student test scores and teacher classroom behavior. The resonance between the quantitative analyses (Chapter 5) and the qualitative analyses (Chapters 6–8) is reassuring, because it enhances the reliability of conclusions concerning school effects issues like stability and context (Miles & Huberman, 1984; Patton, 1990).

Theory Development

There is a need for more refined theories of school effects. Recent articles by Scheerens & Creemers (1989, 1990) have criticized the five-factor model and have postulated that a more comprehensive conceptualization of school effects should involve context or contingency theory. The five-factor model has also been criticized for being a static, taxonomic model of school effects. School improvement based on such a model may be conceptualized as the "transplant" of factors from effective schools into ineffective schools (Creemers & Reynolds, 1990). It is obvious that the activity of becoming an effective school is more complex than the mere transplanting of factors and that comprehensive models of school effects must include a description of the processes whereby schools improve or decline.

A preliminary model of school effects (Theory of School Effectiveness and Leadership), including both context and process variables, is presented in Chapter 4. Also, Chapter 9 utilizes Mitchell's (1990) cultural theory of leadership in drawing conclusions about the role played by principals in stable and changing schools. While neither of these theories provides a comprehensive framework, they represent attempts to move model development beyond taxonomic analyses.

The Use of Multiple Criteria in Longitudinal Studies

Most school effects research has focused on limited areas of student achievement as the only outcome variable. We used multiple outcomes in LSES-IV, as summarized in Chapter 5. While the results across some of these criteria are contradictory, a generally consistent pattern for each of the LSES-IV schools can be discerned. The issue of the independence of some of the outcome indicators is also discussed in Chapter 5.

Differences in Teacher Socialization Experiences

As part of LSES-IV, we surveyed beginning teachers regarding several aspects of socialization in effective and ineffective schools. Differences in the perceptions and behaviors of these beginning teachers are summarized in Chapter 11.

DESIGN OF THE LOUISIANA SCHOOL EFFECTIVENESS STUDY

The LSES was begun in 1980 and continued through final data collection in spring 1990. During that time, the study progressed through four phases of data collection, interspersed with periods of analysis and report writing. The four phases are summarized in Table 1.1. Chapters 2 and 3 contain more detailed descriptions of the design for LSES-II, while Chapter 4 details the LSES-III and -IV designs.

The pilot study (LSES-I) was conducted during the 1981–82 school year (Teddlie, Falkowski, & Falk, 1982). Two separate activities were accomplished during LSES-I: (1) the school climate questionnaires were field tested and modified; and (2) the entire methodology for LSES-II was pilot tested in a number of schools.

In the field test of the Brookover and colleagues (1979) student school climate questionnaire, we first surveyed third-grade students in regular classroom settings. We then interviewed small groups of students to determine if they understood the questions and to gather information on how to improve them. The student questionnaire was modified on the basis of findings from this pilot study. These modifications included minor changes in wording of questions that the students found hard to understand and the elimination of a few redundant items.

Data for LSES-II were collected during the 1982–83 school year (Teddlie, Stringfield, & Desselle, 1985). Altogether 76 schools with more than 250 third-grade teachers and more than 5,400 third-grade students were included in the sample. Twelve school districts participated in LSES-II. These districts were chosen from various parts of the state based on criteria related to availability of personnel data and willingness of the central office to participate. The LSES-II sample was highly representative of the statewide population of elementary schools (Bayless, 1983).

LSES-II was conceptualized as a large-scale process–product study similar to those conducted by Brookover and colleagues (1979) in Michigan and Rutter and colleagues (1979) in London. The emphases in the data analysis were twofold: (1) to determine the amount of variance in student achievement that was attributable to student SES and school

TABLE 1.1. Four Phases of the Louisiana School Effectiveness Study

Phase	Brief Description	Period
LSES-I Pilot study	Conceptualized project in 1980–81 Conducted pilot study in 1981–82, including field test of instruments Completed LSES-I *Report*	1980–82
LSES-II Macro level study (Process-product study)	Selected sample of 76 schools Collected school climate questionnaires and other instruments from 74 principals, 250 teachers and over 5400 students in 1982–83 Analyzed data LSES-II *Report* completed in 1984	1982–84
LSES-III Micro level longitudinal study (Case studies, first and second rounds of site visits)	Selected sample of eight matched pairs of schools Conducted over 700 hours of classroom observations and over 1,000 hours of on-site data collection in 1984–85 Analyzed data Prepared research reports and articles using LSES-III quantitative and qualitative data	1984–88
LSES-IV Micro level longitudinal study continued (Case studies, third and fourth rounds of site visits)	Designed LSES-IV during 1988–89 Conducted over 650 hours of classroom observations and over 950 total hours of on-site data collection in 1989–90 Analyzed data Prepared research reports and articles using both LSES-III and -IV data sources	1988–92

climate; and (2) to compare schools that varied in terms of effectiveness status and student SES characteristics.

The first set of analyses utilized both multiple regression and HLM techniques, as described in Chapter 2 and the Appendix. The second set of analyses enabled us to make the following comparisons: (1) differences among effective, typical, and ineffective schools; (2) differences between middle- and low-SES schools; and (3) differences among the six groups of schools generated by the design. The results of these analyses are detailed in Chapter 3.

LSES-III and -IV were designed to provide case studies of eight matched pairs of effective and ineffective schools over a 7-year time period. Schools for these two phases were purposefully selected to represent different geographic and urbanicity contexts within the state, as described in Chapter 4.

Data collection for LSES-III occurred in 1984–85, and the same schools were revisited in 1989–90 during LSES-IV. These phases of the study constitute a longitudinal examination of 16 schools. The study was designed to determine the degree to which individual schools retained their effectiveness status over time, despite natural changes in student body and staffing.

A major focus of LSES-III and -IV was the gathering of quantitative and qualitative classroom observational data on teachers in matched pairs of effective and ineffective schools. Therefore, over 700 hours of classroom observations were recorded in LSES-III, and some 600 hours were logged in LSES-IV. The results of these classroom observations constitute much of the results reported in Chapters 5–10.

In Chapter 2, data are presented from LSES-II that address two major issues in school effects research: the existence of school effects and multilevel issues regarding school effects. LSES-II provided additional confirmatory evidence concerning the existence of school effects. Data analyses described in Chapter 2 and the Appendix may be divided into two general approaches: one that replicates the Brookover and colleagues (1979) multiple regression approach, and a second approach that utilizes HLM in an attempt to disentangle school effects from student and teacher effects.

The LSES was designed to address a number of limitations of extant school effects research. The results of the study, and their relevance to those limitations, will be presented throughout the book. The results in this book have been reduced greatly from their original descriptions in various monographs, articles, and chapters cited throughout this book. The curious reader is urged to read the original sources in areas of interest.

2 Schools Do Make a Difference

*Eugene Kennedy, Sam Stringfield,
and Charles Teddlie*

The story of school effects is an evolving one. More is certainly known about school effects today than was known 25 years ago when Coleman and his colleagues bound the first volumes of the Equality of Educational Opportunity Study (EEOS). Looking back over the years since the much-contested conclusion that schools have little influence on student achievement independent of family background, it is clear that this work has been the impetus for much fruitful debate about school effects. The methodological and substantive developments over this period are such that little that was done then would be done now to address the same issues. In this chapter we trace some of these developments and attempt to place LSES-II within the evolving context that determined its distinct characteristics. Next we describe the design of LSES-II in some detail to provide a sense of the scope of this endeavor. This is followed by a reanalysis of the original data using recently developed statistical algorithms for modeling multilevel phenomena. Most of this reanalysis is located in the Appendix.

THE EVOLUTION OF PRODUCTION FUNCTION STUDIES

Historians note that the belief in education as an equalizer of the human condition is deeply ingrained in the American psyche, along with the principle that anyone with sufficient talent and motivation can succeed in America. Traditional thinking, amounting to a legend, holds that no other institution in society has served the function of equalizer as well as the public schools (Greer, 1976).

It was in this ideological environment and during a period of political upheaval that the 1964 Civil Rights Act directed the U.S. Office of Education (USOE) to undertake a study of public education institutions to document differences in educational opportunities based on race, religion, or national origin. This study was expected to document inequalities in educational opportunities and provide justification for legislation outlawing discrimination in access to educational resources.

Coleman and colleagues (1968) explained that while the general purpose of the project had been made clear by the USOE, the team had not been told how to model the problem. Had the task been to document racial differences in educational opportunity, a simple tabulation of resources would have sufficed. However, the directive seemed to require not only that differences in opportunity be documented, but that they be linked to differential student outcomes. Thus, the education process was modeled as a "production function" with inputs and outputs.

Initial Findings: Schools Don't Matter

The EEOS analysis sought to identify school characteristics that could explain between-school differences in achievement. The analysts estimated that the proportion of between-school variation in mean student achievement could be attributed to five groups of variables: student family background, student characteristics, peer group characteristics, teacher characteristics, and school characteristics. The EEOS authors wrote:

> That schools bring little influence to bear on a child's achievement that is independent of his background and general social context; that this very lack of an independent effect means that the inequalities imposed on children by their home, neighborhood, and peer environment are carried along to become the inequalities with which they confront adult life. (Coleman et al., 1966, p. 325)

These results were in such contrast to long held beliefs about American schools that challenges began almost immediately. Moynihan and others initiated a seminar of leading educational researchers at Harvard for the purpose of reanalyzing and reviewing the EEOS (see Mosteller & Moynihan, 1972). Entire editions of major journals (e.g., *Harvard Educational Review*) were devoted to this one topic (McIntosh, 1968). Other studies using the educational production function approach to studying school effects began to proliferate both here and abroad (e.g., Bridge, Judd, & Moock, 1979; Glasman & Biniaminov, 1981; Hanushek & Kain, 1972).

The majority of the emerging literature concurred with the Coleman conclusion that schools do not matter. For instance, Jencks and colleagues (1972) argued that most student achievement differences were due to factors that schools do not control. They concluded that if the total environment of individuals could be equalized, differences in test scores would fall by 25–40%. However, if the quality of elementary and high schools were equalized, differences in scores would fall only 1–3%.

Critics of these conclusions have raised two important questions about the utility of the production function as a mode of inquiry. The first concerns the appropriateness of this line of inquiry and focuses on alternative methods of studying school effects. The second issue concerns the adequacy of the model and focuses on the absence of school characteristics that affect student achievement.

Alternatives to the Production Function

In the 1970s a group of researchers led by Ron Edmonds began to question the logic of the production function. Edmonds and others noted that the EEOS regression-based results reflect normative patterns and would not detect the influence of schools on achievement if most schools were equally ineffective (Edmonds, 1979a; Klitgaard & Hall, 1974). An alternative approach would be to identify schools serving similar students, but differing significantly in student achievement. If such schools indeed exist, they would represent a refutation of the EEOS conclusion.

Edmonds (1979b, 1981) investigated city schools in the northeast and identified 55 effective schools. An effective school was defined as being one wherein there was essentially no relationship between family background and achievement. Study of these schools yielded a set of characteristics that separated effective from ineffective schools. This work and the work of others has become known as "school effects research."

Another challenge to the Coleman conclusions was a longitudinal study of London secondary schools (Rutter et al., 1979). Rutter and colleagues collected data on primary school students as they entered secondary schools. After 3 years, the schools that had accepted the majority of these students were studied. The results showed that schools in the sample differed widely in student achievement and other outcomes, even with statistical controls for differences in student background. These results indicated that schools have a substantial impact on student outcomes.

Expansion of the Production Function

A second criticism of the production function concerns the fact that only static school characteristics were included in the model. A significant attempt to address this issue was the inclusion of school climate measures in a study of elementary schools in Michigan by Brookover and colleagues (1978, 1979). Noting the static nature of the Coleman predictors, Brookover and colleagues argued that the normative climate of a school was an important determinant of attitudes and achievements. Their study was an attempt to identify those aspects of school climate that separate high- and low-achieving schools serving students with similar SES backgrounds.

Brookover and colleagues (1979) tested the importance of family SES background by entering it in a regression analysis to predict school mean achievement prior to climate measures and following climate measures. When SES and percent white were entered first, climate measures increased the percentage of explained variance by only 4%. When climate measures were entered first, they explained 73% of the variance in student achievement, while SES and percent white accounted for only an additional 10%. Brookover and colleagues concluded that much of the variance in school mean achievement attributed to student background variables might instead be due to the school social environment. These results illustrate the problem of multicollinearity among family background and school climate measures (that is, the correlation of these factors among themselves).

PHASE II OF THE LOUISIANA SCHOOL EFFECTIVENESS STUDY

Objectives

LSES-II built on the efforts of Brookover, Rutter, Edmonds, and others, and benefited from the critiques of the school effects research published in the early 1980s. Several methodological improvements were incorporated in this study.

Sampling. Representative sampling techniques were used, instead of sampling poor, urban schools exclusively. The focus of LSES-II analyses was on a stratified random sample of Louisiana elementary schools. While Brookover and colleagues (1979) discuss results from a random sample of elementary schools, they focused much of their attention on separate predominantly white and predominantly African-American samples. Purkey and Smith (1983) concluded that school effects research has too often focused on particular subsets of schools. LSES-II results do not—they are reported on a stratified random sample of schools from all SES backgrounds.

Testing. Norm-referenced tests, rather than criterion-referenced tests, were used as the major dependent variable. Critics (e.g., Good & Brophy, 1986; Rutter, 1983) have concluded that the effect of school climate on achievement may be underestimated due to lack of variability in the measures of student achievement. While both NRTs and CRTs were used in LSES-II, analysis focused on NRTs. Both the Brookover and Rutter studies used CRTs.

The LSES-II methodology required researchers to administer the NRTs, while prior studies had used only locally administered CRTs. The potentially misleading effect of nonstandard testing practices has been addressed elsewhere (e.g., Armor et al., 1976; Pechman, 1985; Stringfield & Hartman, 1985). By having all tests administered by the research team in all schools, LSES-II eliminated a potential source of error variance.

Analysis. In LSES-II, we directly addressed the problem of multicollinearity among SES and school climate variables. The Brookover technique of entering SES and school climate in alternating orders in separate analysis was useful in delineating the problem's scope; however, it did nothing to explain the nature of the relationship between SES and school climate. A reader inclined to believe that SES and school racial composition predate school climate might reason that the Brookover study demonstrated a limited effect of schools on achievement. In LSES-II, we utilized second-order factor analyses to reduce the dataset to a manageable and statistically independent set of predictors.

Despite these differences in methodology and analysis, our results replicate Brookover's major conclusion: Schools make a difference. The results of LSES-II are also similar to those of more recent input/output studies of school effects (e.g., Coleman, Hoffer, & Kilgore, 1982; Witte & Walsh, 1990), some of which use multilevel modeling techniques (Lee, 1986).

Sampling

LSES-II data were collected during the 1982–83 school year. Twelve school districts participated in the study, including urban, suburban, and rural areas from northern, central, and southern portions of the state. The sampling frame for LSES-II is as follows: The universe consisted of 795 Louisiana schools with third-grade classrooms; the study population consisted of 270 schools with third-grade classrooms in the 12 selected districts; and the study sample consisted of a stratified random sample of 76 schools. Schools were stratified on two dimensions, average percent correct on the language test of the Louisiana Basic Skills Test (BST) and average educational level of students' mothers. The final sample was highly representative of elementary schools in Louisiana (Bayless, 1983).

Instrumentation

The data gathered in LSES–II included

- Student SES and CRT information gathered from the 1982–83 administrations of the BST
- NRT data gathered by using a modified version of the Educational Developmental Series Lower Primary Tests (EDS), developed by Scholastic Testing Service (STS) (1978)
- Modified versions of the Brookover and colleagues (1979) climate questionnaires
- Other items used to assess social-psychological variables and faculty SES
- School structural characteristics gathered at the district central offices and the Louisiana Department of Education (LDE)

School Climate. The instruments for school climate assessment were modified versions of questionnaires developed by Brookover and colleagues (1979). Brookover's original climate questionnaires were composed of student scales, teacher scales, and principal scales, as follows:

Student

1. Student sense of academic futility
2. Future evaluations and expectations
3. Perceived present evaluations and expectations
4. Perception of teacher push and teacher norms
5. Student academic norms

Teacher

1. Ability, evaluations, expectations, and quality of education for college
2. Present evaluations and expectations for high school completion
3. Teacher–student commitment to improve
4. Perception of principal's expectations
5. Teacher academic futility

Principal

1. Parent concern and expectation for quality of education
2. Efforts to improve
3. Evaluations (principal and parents) of present school quality
4. Present evaluations and expectations of students

The LSES-II student school climate questionnaire was revised based on pilot testing from LSES-I (Teddlie, Falkowski, & Falk, 1982). Two types of questions measuring self-concept (Michael & Smith, 1976) and locus of control (Crandall, Katkovsky, & Crandall, 1965) were added to the student questionnaires.

Several items were inserted into the faculty school climate instruments. Examples of these include questions concerning the amount of time the principal spends in selected activities, and inquiries about the number of times during a day that class is interrupted by messages.

Items that measured teachers' SES were adapted from two sources. Data concerning the number of years of education completed by the teacher's father and mother and by the teacher himself or herself were gathered using the McDill and Rigsby (1973) technique. The occupations of teachers' parents were obtained with questions from the National Longitudinal Study of the High School Class of 1972.

A scale assessing self-concept of teachers and principals (Rosenberg, 1963) was also added. A locus of control scale (Taylor, Sadowski, & Peacher, 1981) was included in both the teacher and principal instruments.

Student Achievement. The NRTs were shortened versions of the EDS lower primary level achievement tests (STS, 1978). The instruments consist of a composite and subtests in the areas of reading, verbal skills, mathematics, and English. These analyses focused on the composite. An instrument review by the LDE found it to be consistent with the curriculum and instructional objectives of the state (Mills, Teddlie, & Falkowski, 1984).

Data Collection

Approximately 3½ hours were required to collect all information needed from students. Response rates were high for every aspect of LSES-II. Of the 250 third-grade teachers who were included in the study, 247 (98.8%) returned questionnaires. Seventy-four of the 76 principals (97.4%) returned their instruments. There were 5,829 children enrolled in third grade in the schools. Of these, 5,389 (92.5%) responded to the questionnaires and 5,402 (92.7%) took the NRT. The percentage of enrolled children for whom we have data is close to the percentage of students who are present in school on a given day (the state average percentage of attendance for 1982–83 was 93.2%).

Analysis Strategy

Aggregated to the school level, the datasets contained over 300 variables. Given the large number of variables and the number of schools involved (76), data reduction techniques were required. Several multivariate analysis methods were utilized, and five models were produced. While the models did not vary greatly, the one presented here was the most parsimonious and statistically rigorous.

A statistical procedure called factor analysis was used for data reduction (see Kim & Mueller, 1978). This technique reduced the numerous variables in the five nonachievement datasets to a smaller number of latent variables, called factors. Correlation coefficients (Pearson's r) were used to determine the extent to which these factors or latent variables were related to school mean achievement. Additionally, multiple regression was used to determine the extent to which all relevant factors could jointly predict school mean achievement.

The initial factor analysis resulted in a reduction from 300 variables to a smaller number of factors that were correlated among themselves. Because of the potential for problems with multicollinearity, these factors were themselves subjected to a factor analysis, called a second-order factor analysis (see Cattell, 1965; Rummel, 1970). As part of this additional step, the resulting second-order factors were forced to have zero intercorrelations among themselves. A more detailed description of the steps involved in these statistical analyses, and the results of the first- and second-order factor analyses, are found in the Appendix.

COMPARISON WITH BROOKOVER'S FINDINGS

The interest in school effects in the 1980s occurred despite a dearth of large-scale studies of predictors of school level achievement. LSES-II was an exception: a study that benefited from the measurement advances of Brookover and Rutter, plus the methodological concerns of the critics.

One goal of LSES-II was to produce a parsimonious model of school effects in which measures of principal, teacher, and student attitudes were not confounded by SES and race. Brookover and colleagues (1979) expressed well-founded concern about the multicollinearity problem in their analyses of 14 measures of school climate, SES, and school racial composition. Compounding this problem is the issue of conducting stepwise multiple regressions with extremely low ratios of cases to independent variables. Ratios under 10 to 1 often produce unstable and/or inflated estimates of r^2. Given research programs that call for the integration of background, principal, teacher, and student datasets, and in which school is the proper unit of analysis, this has caused extreme difficulty with sample sizes.

In this discussion, we note similarities and differences between results of our initial analyses and those of Brookover and colleagues (1979). While differences exist, we interpret our data, gathered in a different section of the nation during a later decade, to serve as a partial replication of the Brookover findings.

Factor selection and item inclusion rules varied between LSES–II and the Brookover study. Though the factor selection rules were not made explicit by Brookover and colleagues (1979), those used in LSES generated 30 climate factors, as contrasted with the 14 that Brookover reported. In LSES–II, a factor loading of .50 was required for an item to be deemed "associated" with a factor. The Brookover criterion was .30, which resulted in a smaller number of factors, each having many items associated with it.

Given the less than total item overlap, and the differences in inclusion rules, the data in Table A.1 (see Appendix) may be interpreted as supporting the generalizability of many of the factors first identified by Brookover. In both studies the highest non-SES correlates of achievement were factors measuring school climate as perceived by students.

In the Brookover study, Teacher Factor II (Present Evaluations and Expectations for High School Completion) is much more highly correlated with achievement ($r = .66$) than is the fairly comparable LSES–II T6 (High School Expectations), with an r of .23 (see Table A.1). Perhaps by fourth and fifth grade (Michigan study), that factor taps information more pertinent to current achievement than it does at third grade (Louisiana study).

The LSES–II first-order climate factors plus SES and race explained 77% of the variance (unadjusted) in student achievement. In the Brookover study, these factors accounted for 83% of the variance in student achievement. The difference in explained variance between these two studies appears attributable to the predictive power of race in the Michigan study, perhaps due to the racially bimodal nature of the sample of schools in the Michigan study.

Given the substantial multicollinearity and model stability problems, comparisons of stepwise regressions using the initial factors for the two studies would be problematic, and we believe results for both regressions to be somewhat suspect. However, the LSES–II second-order factor analysis undertaken to address these problems yielded an adjusted r^2 very close to the first-order results and also indicated that alterable variables (e.g., positive school climate) were important predictors of school mean student achievement. For more detail on these regression analyses, see the Appendix.

REANALYSIS OF LSES–II DATA USING
HIERARCHICAL LINEAR MODELING

Although the findings from Brookover and colleagues (1979) and LSES–II (Kennedy, Teddlie, & Stringfield, 1991) support the conclusion that schools make a difference, several reviews have been critical. In particular, this literature has been plagued by the multilevel analysis problem. Schools are inherently multilevel organizations: Students are nested within classrooms, which are nested within schools, which are nested within districts. Decisions made at one level constrain activities at other levels. Because the statistical tools needed to model this structure have only recently become available, both analysis and conceptualization have suffered (Raudenbush & Bryk, 1987).

Given the past statistical limitations, many school effects researchers have aggregated data to the school level. This strategy has a number of limitations: School effects may be underestimated because all within-school variation is lost; parameter estimates from this procedure tend to be unstable and inefficient (Aitkin & Longford, 1986); and conclusions about students risk cross-level inference problems (Knapp, 1977).

Under the general names of variance component models and hierarchical linear modeling (HLM), multilevel modeling procedures, which have become available in the last decade, allow researchers to explicitly model the hierarchical organization of schools. Thus, for example, not only can questions concerning correlates of student achievement be posed for student variables such as social background, but the impact of school characteristics (e.g., social climate, management practices) on achievement and its correlates can be modeled explicitly (e.g., Aitkin & Longford, 1986; Bryk & Raudenbush, 1992; Goldstein, 1986; Mason, Wong, & Entwisle, 1983; Raudenbush & Bryk, 1986). Using these recent statistical advances, we reanalyzed the original LSES–II data; these results are summarized in the Appendix.

The results of these more sophisticated analyses essentially replicated those using the regression approach. While SES and its correlates are significant predictors of student achievement, two composite school-climate variables were also (see SOF3 and SOF4 in Table A.3). Additionally, one composite climate variable (SOF4) significantly affected the SES-achievement slope.

These analyses indicate that, on average, students achieve more in schools in which they believe that their teachers and peers care about academics and hold high academic expectations for themselves. However, in both studies, most teacher and principal school-climate factors were more highly correlated with SES than with student achievement. By contrast, student perceptions of school climate were more highly correlated with achievement than with SES.

CONCLUSION: SCHOOLS MAKE A DIFFERENCE

Large-scale research on school effects in the United States has, we believe, gone through a full cycle. The Coleman report was widely interpreted as indicating that schools made little difference in student achievement. School effects studies of the 1970s (e.g., Brookover et al., 1979; Rutter et al., 1979), using more refined process measures at the school level, found substantial evidence of school effects. Reviews by Rutter (1983) and Good and Brophy (1986) have argued that methodological limitations have continued to cause underprediction of the amount of variance in learning that is affected by schools. Second-order factor analytic data from LSES-II substantiate Rutter's and Good and Brophy's assertion. In LSES-II, measures of potentially alterable school-related behaviors on the parts of principals, teachers, students, and parents were better predictors of student achievement than were second-order factors containing SES and racial data. The importance of these factors was supported in reanalyses of these data using HLM.

If there is a central conclusion to be drawn from LSES-II, it is that schools make a difference. Our replication of Brookover's results with regard to alterable school factors predicting school-level achievement leads us to that conclusion. Also, in our LSES-II analyses we found that 75% of the variation in individual student achievement (as opposed to school-level achievement) could be linked to student characteristics, 12% could be linked to teachers and experimental factors within classes, and fully 13% could be attributed to differences between schools. These estimates of school effects are very similar to those reported in other studies (e.g., Reynolds, 1992) and help confirm the conclusion that schools also play major roles in individual student achievement, especially when considered cumulatively over years.

Another conclusion from LSES-II and similar research is that the school attributes that make a difference are alterable. That is, they tend to reflect climatic and organizational characteristics that can be changed, such as teacher expectations or students' sense of academic futility.

In Chapter 3 we reconsider the approach to school effects that assumes that the process variables indicative of effectiveness are constant, irrespective of the population or setting of the school. This has important implications for those educators who accept that schools are important and permit their school improvement efforts to be influenced by this body of research.

3 School Context Is Important

For much of the history of school effects research, the varied contexts within which schooling occurs have been ignored. Levine and Lezotte (1990) included a brief chapter on context differences in school effects research. Of the 32 references in that chapter, 28 had been written since 1985. These recent studies had followed in the wake of the criticism from several authors (Cuban, 1984; Firestone & Herriott, 1982; Good & Brophy, 1986; Purkey & Smith, 1983) that results from earlier school effects studies conducted in urban, poor elementary schools couldn't be transferred to other types of schools.

This chapter will briefly address the historical reasons for the lack of early context studies and for the emergence of such studies in response to the criticism noted above. The chapter will then summarize the findings from the LSES on the context issue, with most of the focus on LSES-II, which explicitly studied the effect of the socioeconomic status of the student body. Brief portraits of effective and ineffective middle- and low-SES schools will be drawn.

The integration of results from LSES-II and -III with work done by Hallinger and Murphy (1985, 1986) will then follow. This integration has led to "contextually sensitive models for effective schools" (Teddlie et al., 1989).

THE EVOLUTION OF CONTEXT STUDY
IN SCHOOL EFFECTS RESEARCH

Why Context Was Initially Ignored

Several educational researchers saw the Coleman report conclusion that schools don't matter as a challenge and set out to find and describe schools that served low-SES students who performed well on standardized tests (Brookover et al., 1979; Brookover & Lezotte, 1979; Edmonds, 1979b; Glenn, 1981; Klitgaard & Hall, 1974; Venezky & Winfield, 1979). Weber (1971) identified and studied four low-SES, inner-city schools characterized by high achievement. He cited several characteristics of these schools, including strong leadership, high expectations, good atmosphere, individualization, and careful evaluation of pupil progress. His study emphasized school process, while the earlier studies by Coleman and Jencks had looked at static school characteristics.

These case studies typically involved inner-city elementary schools that serviced poor, primarily minority students. This emphasis on students from a particular economic and geographic subgroup was noted by Ron Edmonds (1979a), who wrote about effective schools for the "urban poor." Edmonds eloquently stated his opposition to the general conclusions of Coleman and Jencks: "Repudiation of the social science notion that family background is the principal cause of pupil acquisition of basic skills is probably prerequisite to successful reform of public schools" (p. 23).

Edmonds and others called for an equity orientation in school effects research. He wanted the children of the poor to attain those skills that described "minimally successful" middle class children. Due to this equity orientation, Edmonds did not address the issue of effective schooling for the middle class. In a discussion with Ron Brandt (1982), Edmonds asserted that middle class parents would intervene in any school in which a significant portion of students were not doing well.

How Context Came to Be Studied Directly

Case studies of urban, poor elementary schools resulted in the set of correlates of school effectiveness referred to in Chapter 1 as the five-factor model. As the five-factor model was popularized, several authors (Cuban, 1983; Good & Brophy, 1986; Ralph & Fennessey, 1983; Rowan, Bossert, & Dwyer, 1983) criticized school effects research for its sampling procedures. The conclusions about the characteristics of these effective schools did not fit the intuitive understanding that many people had about other types of schools (i.e., rural, suburban, middle-class, middle or high schools). It is at this point that a new phase of school effects research emphasizing the efficiency, rather than the equity, ideal began (Wimpelberg, Teddlie, & Stringfield, 1989).

This new phase of school effects research explicitly looks at schools from different contexts. In retrospect, it is surprising that context was not studied earlier, since it is widely recognized that factors such as SES have significant effects on human behavior. Sociologists, psychologists, and educators (e.g., Blumberg, 1972; Curtis & Jackson, 1977) have long recognized the importance of different SES groupings on human behavior.

The value shift from equity to efficiency of schooling (Wimpelberg et al., 1989) meant asking different questions. When researchers were interested in determining what produces effective schools for the urban poor, their value orientation was equity: How can we produce better schools for the disadvantaged? When researchers began studying schools in a variety of contexts, their value orientation shifted to efficiency: How can we produce better schools for all students? Levine and Lezotte (1990) concluded that three types of school contexts have been explicitly studied in school effects research: student body SES, grade level of schooling, and urbanicity (rural versus urban).

The next two sections of this chapter will describe in detail the methodology and results from the Louisiana study, emphasizing LSES–II but also including information from LSES–III. Consistent findings between the Hallinger and Murphy and the LSES studies will be emphasized in the section on contextually sensitive models of school effectiveness.

DESIGN OF THE LSES–II CONTEXT STUDY

Data collected for LSES–II were intended to be analyzed for two purposes: (1) they were to be used in regression-based analyses designed to replicate and extend similar analyses performed by Brookover and colleagues (1979); and (2) they were to be used in a multivariate analysis of variance (MANOVA) design intended to provide descriptions of schools varying by effectiveness status and SES of student body. Chapter 2 (and the Appendix) presented the results of the regression and HLM analyses, while this chapter will present the MANOVA results.

The design employed in this context study is an ex post facto criterion-group (Campbell & Stanley, 1966), and no effort should be made to interpret causality in our results. These analyses are intended to present descriptions of participants' perceptions of their schools grouped according to certain classifications. Throughout this chapter we will describe schools as effective or ineffective. This definition of effectiveness is a statistical one, not a summative statement regarding the quality of particular schools.

A factor analysis of the students' parents' SES data was performed to divide schools into middle- or low-SES groups. The average education of students' mothers, the average education of students' fathers, the percentage of students with fathers who had professional jobs, the percentage of students with mothers who had professional jobs, and the percentage of students who were white were determined for each school. The percentage of students who were white was considered to be an SES variable, since race and income level are so highly interrelated in Louisiana. These five variables were then factor analyzed, and one factor with an eigenvalue greater than 1.00 emerged. The 38 schools with an SES factor score greater than zero were considered to be middle-SES; the other 38 schools with an SES factor score less than zero were considered to be low-SES.

While a single score was used to categorize a school as middle or low socioeconomically, data on all five SES variables were used in a multiple regression model predicting how well a school should perform on the EDS third-grade test. The regression model allowed the investigators to predict how well each school should perform on the EDS based on the five SES characteristics. These predicted scores were then compared with the schools' actual scores, and a measure of the deviation from predicted score was made. This measure was the studentized residual (the difference between the predicted and actual scores divided by the standard error for the difference). Twenty-five schools were categorized as effective because their students scored above their predicted score, 27 were categorized as typical because their students scored at their predicted score, and 24 were categorized as ineffective because their students scored below their predicted score. This research design resulted in a fairly even distribution of schools, third-grade teachers, and third-grade students in each of the six types of schools, as indicated in Table 3.1.

TABLE 3.1. Numbers of Schools, Teachers, and Students in Six Types of Schools Studied in LSES-II

SES of Student's Parents	School Effectiveness (n's)		
	More Effective	Typical	Less Effective
Middle-SES			
Schools	12	15	11
Teachers	37	59	27
Students	808	1,244	594
Low-SES			
Schools	13	12	13
Teachers	35	50	40
Students	729	1,079	914

Note: The numbers of teachers and students are from the third-grade level only. The number of students indicates how many completed the EDS questionnaire.

RESULTS: DIFFERENCES AMONG SCHOOLS IN THE STUDY

Most of this section will present differences among the six types of schools in terms of the educational climate described by students, teachers, and principals on the Brookover questionnaires. Before turning to these school climate descriptions, however, it is informative to look at basic differences on variables such as test performance and SES of students. These differences will help set the stage for differences in the school educational climates that will be described later.

Differences on Basic Variables

The selected means on students' parents' SES characteristics presented in Table 3.2 confirm the large differences in backgrounds of students from the middle- and low-SES schools. The average score for each of the three middle-SES groups is higher than that for each of the three low-SES groups on mothers' education and fathers' occupation vari-

TABLE 3.2. Selected Means for Parents' Socioeconomic Characteristics for Six Types of Schools

School Effectiveness	Parents' SES Characteristics	
	Middle-SES	Low-SES
Average Education of Mothers[1]		
More Effective	3.35	2.70
Typical	3.38	2.74
Less Effective	3.28	2.87
Percentage of Students with Professional Fathers		
More Effective	33%	11%
Typical	43%	12%
Less Effective	33%	10%
Performance on EDS Basic Skills Tests		
More Effective	108.13	97.06
Typical	103.70	91.53
Less Effective	93.75	85.61

[1]Mother's educational level: 2 = attended high school; 3 = graduated from high school; 4 = attended college.

ables. These differences are quite large; for example, students in middle-SES schools were three times more likely to have professional fathers than those in low-SES schools.

Selected means on test performance (EDS Basic Skills Test, which has three subtests) for the six types of schools are also found in Table 3.2. The school effectiveness status independent variable had a highly significant effect on overall scores on this NRT [F (2,70) = 47.98, $p <$ .0001]. The most interesting aspect of this pattern of scores is that students from effective, low-SES schools actually outscored those from ineffective, middle-SES schools, even though they had less-educated parents employed in lower level professional jobs. This concurs with results reported by Mortimore and Sammons (1987) indicating that "on the average a student from a blue-collar worker's family attending an effective school achieved more highly than one from a white-collar family background attending one of the least effective schools" (p. 6). These results call into doubt Edmonds' assertion in the Brandt (1982) interview that middle class parents would intervene in any school in which a significant portion of students weren't doing well.

Differences in Educational Climate

Results from the analyses of these six types of differentially effective schools are detailed elsewhere (Teddlie et al., 1984; Teddlie & Stringfield, 1985; Teddlie et al., 1989). Data on over 225 educational climate and social psychological variables were included in these analyses. In this section, we will briefly highlight those analyses.

First, some general comments regarding the analyses of the student, teacher, and principal questionnaires are appropriate. The school SES characteristics had highly significant effects on responses from students, teachers, and principals. This was most significant on teacher and principal responses, indicating that adult perceptions were strongly affected by the SES characteristics of their students, regardless of the effectiveness status of their schools. While the students' SES characteristics also affected their perceptions, the magnitude of these effects were not as pronounced as for the adults.

The school effectiveness status had a significant effect on several of the students' responses, including their future educational expectations, perception of teacher push and teacher norms, and sense of academic futility. Students in more effective schools had higher future educational expectations than those from less effective schools. Students from more effective schools also felt less academic futility and perceived greater teacher push than did those from less effective schools. These results clearly indicate a more positive educational climate for students in more effective schools, as opposed to those in less effective schools. The characteristics of the six types of schools follow:

Effective Middle-SES Schools

1. Teachers were in frequent contact with parents and perceived them as being concerned with quality education.
2. Teachers reported having high present and future academic expectations for their students.
3. Teachers accepted responsibility for students' outcomes and actively worked with them to realize these high expectations. This attitude was reflected in student reports noting that teachers cared about them and pushed them to achieve.
4. These schools had the highest percentage of teachers teaching third grade exclusively.
5. The students apparently internalized the high expectations expressed by adults. Students in high-achieving, affluent schools had higher expectations than did their peers in equally affluent schools with lower student achievement. The general climate from the effective, affluent schools was one of concern for excellence from all the major participants.

Typical Middle-SES Schools

1. Compared with teachers in the effective middle-SES schools, the teachers in typical middle-SES schools took less responsibility for the academic achievement of their students.
2. Compared with students in the effective middle-SES schools, students perceived lower expectations from their teachers and parents; students also perceived less teacher push.

Ineffective Middle-SES Schools

1. Teachers had unrealistically high perceptions of their students' current level of academic achievement, expecting high achievement when it was only average. They appeared to base their perceptions on intrinsic student characteristics such as SES.
2. Students' future academic expectations were not as high as those of other middle-SES students.
3. The principals' academic expectations were lower than those of the teachers.

4. The principals stated that several aspects of student development (social skills, personal growth and development, occupational aspirations) were as important as teaching academic skills. The principals may have been expending too much of the schools' resources in nonacademic endeavors.
5. Principals' actions did not appear to effect changes in these schools.

Effective Low-SES Schools

1. While principals and teachers had modest long-term expectations for their students' achievement, particularly in regard to higher education, they held firm present academic expectations for their students.
2. Teachers reported spending more time on reading and math and assigning more homework than the other two low-SES groups.
3. Students perceived teachers as pushing them academically. They also reported receiving more teacher help than did students in less successful, low-SES schools.
4. Students perceived their teachers as having high present expectations for them.
5. Teachers reported that principals visited their classrooms frequently.
6. The teachers in this group were the youngest and least experienced of the low-SES groups.
7. The teachers in this group were the most likely of all the teachers to have teacher's aides.
8. Principals in these schools were the most likely to say that they had major input in hiring teachers. Twenty-three percent of the principals in the effective, low-SES schools said that they hired their teachers. No other group of schools had more than 9% of its principals report this power.

These less affluent, successful schools had principals who motivated teachers who, in turn, motivated students. The ability to instill in students a belief that they can learn is critical in effective low-SES schools. Apparently, students in effective middle-SES schools had this belief instilled at home and reinforced at school.

Typical Low-SES Schools

1. Teachers in this group perceived themselves as having more influence over student attitudes and held higher future expectations for their students than did other low-SES groups.
2. Parents were viewed by teachers as being more concerned and having higher expectations than in other low-SES groups.

3. Students viewed their teachers and parents as having positive perceptions of their schoolwork; students were viewed by teachers as having high expectations; students viewed their teachers as being less demanding and critical than did students in the effective low-SES schools.

It appeared that these overall positive perceptions, coupled with the belief that their teaching efforts were completely appropriate, resulted in less of a focus on student achievement. Faculty at these schools believed they were already doing a good job, so why should they push themselves or their students harder?

Ineffective Low-SES Schools

1. An overall negative academic climate in these schools appears to have contributed to the low student achievement. Of all the groups, teachers had the lowest expectations for students and rated them the lowest academically; the teachers accepted little responsibility for and perceived having little influence on student outcomes; they also appeared less satisfied with teaching and perceived themselves as unsuccessful in helping students attain goals.
2. When compared with students in other low-SES groups, students perceived their teachers as less praising, less caring, less helpful, and more critical. More than in the other groups, these students reported that their teachers did not consider learning important.
3. Principals, teachers, and pupils all perceived the lack of achievement within the schools.
4. Compared with the other groups, a higher percentage (21%) of teachers in these schools would rather teach in another school. By contrast, only 2% of the teachers in typical middle-SES schools wanted to teach elsewhere. Teachers in the low-SES, ineffective schools were absent an average of 3.51 days in the fall semester of LSES-II, while teachers in effective low-SES schools were absent only an average of 2.03 days.

CONTEXTUAL DIFFERENCES IN EFFECTIVE SCHOOLS MODELS

The remainder of this chapter will describe different characteristics associated with effectiveness in middle- and low-SES schools based on LSES-II and –III findings. The LSES-III methodology is detailed in Chapter 4 and involved the intensive study of eight matched pairs of effective/ineffective schools. The chapter will conclude with a discussion of the implications of contextually sensitive studies of school effects for the school improvement process.

Characteristics Associated with Effectiveness

Data from many studies indicate that there are a number of effective-school characteristics that should be found regardless of school SES. These include

1. Clear academic mission and focus
2. Orderly environment
3. High academic engaged time-on-task
4. Frequent monitoring of student progress

LSES results confirm that these attributes are characteristic of effective schools across SES groups.

While there are definite similarities between effective middle- and low-SES schools, there are a number of very interesting differences between the two groups of schools. Our research indicates that effective schools have implemented somewhat different strategies, depending on the SES context of the particular school under examination (Stringfield & Teddlie, 1988; Teddlie & Stringfield, 1985). Characteristics associated with effectiveness in middle- and low-SES schools are found in Table 3.3.

LSES results indicated a difference in future educational expectations by teachers in the two types of schools. Teachers in effective middle-SES schools held very high future and present educational expectations for their students, while teachers in effective low-SES schools held high present, but more modest future, expectations. While teachers in effective low-SES schools had modest long-term expectations for their students' achievement, they held firm present academic expectations for their students.

Results from research in California (Hallinger & Murphy, 1986) confirm these differences with regard to teacher expectations. The teacher expectations results are particularly interesting since some school effectiveness models (e.g., Brookover & Lezotte, 1979; Edmonds, 1979a) consider uniformly high expectations a prerequisite for effective schools.

To illustrate this point, the pattern of means for one question concerning teachers' expectations is presented in Table 3.4. There is an exaggerated difference in teacher expectations for the ineffective middle-SES group as opposed to the effective low-SES group. Compared with teachers from the effective low-SES group, teachers in the ineffective

**TABLE 3.3. Characteristics Associated with Effectiveness
in Middle- and Low-SES Schools**

Middle-SES Schools	Low-SES Schools
1. Promote both high present and future educational expectations.	1. Promote high present educational expectations. Ensure that students believe they can perform well at their current grade level. Allow high future educational goals to develop later.
2. Hire principals with good managerial abilities. Increase teacher responsibility for and ownership of instructional leadership.	2. Hire principals who are initiators, who want to make changes in the schools. Encourage a more active role for the principal in monitoring classrooms and providing overall instructional leadership.
3. De-emphasize visible external rewards for academic achievement (such rewards should be unnecessary if an adequate orientation is found at home).	3. Increase the external reward structure for academic achievement. Make high-achieving students feel special.
4. Expand curricular offerings beyond the basic skills.	4. Focus on basic skills first and foremost, with other offerings after basic skills have been mastered.
5. Increase contact with the community. Encourage parents with high educational expectations to exert pressure for school achievement.	5. Carefully evaluate the effect of the community on the school. If the community does not exert positive pressure for school achievement, create boundaries to buffer the school from negative influences.
6. Hire more experienced teachers.	6. Hire younger, possibly more idealist teachers. Give the principal more authority in selecting staff.

middle-SES group think their students will go much further in school. This occurs despite the fact that the effective low-SES group outachieved the ineffective middle-SES group.

Even though teachers from the effective low-SES group didn't believe their students would go as far in school as other groups believed about their students, low-SES teachers instilled the belief in their stu-

TABLE 3.4. Teacher Expectations for Likelihood of Students' Attending College

	Parents' SES Characteristics	
School Effectiveness	Middle-SES	Low-SES
More Effective	2.81	4.12
Typical	3.43	3.50
Less Effective	3.19	3.95

Note: Smaller numbers indicate a higher expectation for students. The specific values for the scale are as follows: 1 = 90% or more, 2 = 70%–89%, 3 = 50%–69%, 4 = 30%–49%, and 5 = less than 30%.

dents that they could learn. The students in the effective low-SES group believed not only that they could achieve well at the third-grade level, but also that they could do well in later schooling. When the students were told they could achieve at the third-grade level, they extrapolated that they could achieve in later schooling.

A second difference between effective low-SES and middle-SES schools concerns principals' characteristics. As was the case with teachers, principals in effective low- and middle-SES schools exhibited significantly different opinions regarding their students' academic future.

Compared with the other groups, principals in effective low-SES schools projected that a smaller percentage of their students would finish high school. They also indicated that fewer parents from their schools believed that their children would obtain college degrees. This occurred in spite of the facts that their students were scoring well above expectations and that the students believed they would go far in school.

The principals, like the teachers, see students in these effective low-SES schools making modest gains through the school's hard work, almost in spite of the parents and community. In contrast, the effective middle-SES principals projected that a larger percentage of their students would finish high school, and perceived that a higher percentage of the parents than in any of the other groups believed their children would graduate from college.

These differences in attitudes on the part of the middle- and low-SES principals were reflected in their behavior. Teachers reported that principals in effective low-SES schools observed their classes an average of 2.4 hours per semester, while teachers in effective middle-SES schools were observed only 1.4 hours. Additionally, teachers in effective low-SES schools reported the greatest frequency of principal assistance; teachers in effective middle-SES schools reported less assistance. Principals in effective middle-SES schools allowed teachers greater responsibility for and ownership of instructional leadership. Principals in effective low-SES schools tended to be initiators regarding school academic programs, while those in effective middle-SES schools tended to be managers of the academic programs, to use the terminology of Hall, Rutherford, Hord, and Huling (1984).

Hallinger and Murphy (1986) confirmed these context differences in instructional leadership. They concluded that effective low-SES principals "tended to take a very directive role in the selection, development and implementation of curriculum and instructional programs," while higher-SES principals "exercised less direct control over classroom instruction" (p. 341). Evans (1988) found that teachers in effective low-SES schools more frequently perceived their principals to be initiators than did teachers in ineffective low-SES schools.

The third difference between middle- and low-SES schools concerns the visibility and importance of the external reward structures. In several of the effective low-SES schools in LSES-III, public displays of individual academic achievement were omnipresent. The effective low-SES school principals spent a great deal of time developing and maintaining external rewards.

A major difference between effective low-SES and middle-SES schools on this reward structure dimension has to do with the overtness of the display. In one effective low-SES school observed in LSES-III, there were academic slogans on signs throughout the building. Examples included: "The smaller your education, the smaller your paycheck." Such overt symbols were typically not found in middle-SES schools, partially because principals and staff knew rewards for achievement were more likely to be found at home.

A fourth difference between effective low-SES and middle-SES schools has to do with curricular offerings. Hallinger and Murphy (1986) found a narrower focus on basic skills in the effective low-SES schools and a broader curricula emphasis in the effective higher-SES schools in their study. Observations from effective low- and middle-SES schools in LSES-II, -III, and -IV confirm these conclusions. On the other hand, our observations indicate that the narrow focus on basic skills in effective low-SES schools was also found at less effective low-SES schools. Emphasis on basic skills alone does not guarantee higher achievement in low-SES schools.

A fifth difference between effective low- and middle-SES schools has to do with contact with the community. In LSES-II, teachers in effective middle-SES schools were in frequent contact with parents and perceived the parents as being concerned with education. This was not the case in effective low-SES schools, where teachers and principals perceived parents not to be very involved with their children's education. The students in these effective low-SES schools saw their teachers as the adults pushing them to succeed.

Results from Hallinger and Murphy's (1986) research confirm this difference between effective low- and high-SES schools. The principals in effective low-SES schools in their study protected the boundaries of their schools from the intrusions of the less desirable elements in the community. On the other hand, principals in effective high-SES schools encouraged strong linkages with parents, resulting in a pervasive parental involvement.

A sixth difference between effective low- and middle-SES schools concerned the principals' authority in selecting staff and the characteristics of the staff selected. Principals in effective low-SES schools were the most likely of any group to say that they had major input in hiring their teachers. Twenty-three percent of the principals in this group said that they hired their teachers. Only 8% of the principals in effective middle-SES schools reported this authority, as did 9% of the principals in typical low-SES schools. No principals in the other groups of schools indicated that they had this power.

Additionally, the teachers in the effective low-SES schools were the least experienced of the groups of low-SES schools; that is, they had less experience teaching third grade and teaching in their school than did the typical low-SES or ineffective low-SES groups. This indicates that principals with hiring authority in low-SES schools might seek younger, possibly more idealistic teachers. The opposite holds true for the middle-SES schools, where the least experienced teachers were found in the ineffective schools.

Implications of Contextually Sensitive Studies

Staffs at effective schools implement different strategies for creating and maintaining effectiveness based on the schools' SES context. Important context issues could also include the school's geographic location or its grade-level configuration. All these factors should affect the particular school improvement plan that a given school adopts.

Elliot Eisner (1991) recently summarized his thoughts on this context issue and the role of the educational researcher:

> What is effective in one area of the country may be inappropriate in another. What some teachers can do others cannot. . . . The conditional quality of educational life, its high degree of context specificity is formidable.

. . . Researchers . . . offer considerations to be shared and discussed, reflected upon, and debated. (pp. 204–205)

The results of contextually sensitive studies have many implications at the school level. As a principal and staff develop overall school plans, they should take into account the school's context and make adjustments necessary to produce the best school possible. A simple listing of generic school effectiveness characteristics is not sufficient; the school plan should consider the entire social context of the school. The rest of this section will focus on school-level implications of the SES context differences discussed above.

Results from the LSES and from the Hallinger and Murphy (1986) study indicated that students in low-SES schools may need more basic skills instruction, especially in reading and mathematics, since many of these students are not academically ready when they first enter school. Principals and staff at middle- or high-SES schools may have greater flexibility in developing and implementing a broader curriculum, since their students are more likely to have mastered the basic skills.

Principals must take into account staff characteristics when formulating school plans. Effective low-SES schools are more likely to have a less-experienced faculty, while effective middle-SES schools are more likely to have a more-experienced faculty. In optimal circumstances, districts closely match principals with faculty characteristics, so that the leadership style of the principal is appropriate for his or her school. However, LSES results indicate that calculated assignment from the district level is rare, and individual principals may need training in adapting their style to best fit the needs of their teachers and students.

In most cases, principals in low-SES schools need to exercise more input into establishing school goals and more direct control over classroom instruction. Conversely, principals in middle-SES schools need to consider teacher norms for autonomy in the classroom and for shared decision making at the school level.

The degree of parental involvement at low-SES schools is another area where principal adaptability over time is important. Two distinct principal policies toward parental involvement in low-SES schools are described in Chapter 8. At a historically ineffective school, a new principal determined that community influence was negative and that he needed to establish a buffer zone between the community and the school. In an attempt to make the school more effective, this principal decided to buffer the school from some negative community influences; however, in the long run he planned to solicit more parental involvement as the school moved toward greater effectiveness.

At the historically more effective school, parental involvement was actively solicited, and the school became the center for community activities. The parents at this successful low-SES school were educated over time with regard to the principal's goals for the school and community expectations. As low-SES schools move toward effectiveness, principals should encourage greater parental interaction; this involvement can have a potentially powerful impact on student learning.

Principals and faculty might also consider SES characteristics when planning schoolwide reward programs and establishing procedures for promoting high expectations. Our data indicate that principals at low-SES schools might do well to expend more energy in developing tangible reward programs, since schools in these communities serve as the primary reinforcer of student achievement. LSES students at low-SES schools apparently needed more tangible rewards as they mastered basic skills. Principals at middle-SES schools typically did not have to develop such tangible reward programs.

With regard to educational expectations, principals and faculty at low-SES schools might consider focusing on schoolwide plans to promote high present educational expectations. Students might be given the message that they *can* master the materials they are currently studying and that their teachers and principal expect them to do that. LSES results indicate that students extrapolate these high present educational expectations into long-term goals. Principals and faculty at low-SES schools may let these future educational expectations develop naturally and concentrate their resources on promoting high present expectations.

The scenario at middle-SES schools is somewhat different. Results from the LSES and the Hallinger and Murphy study indicate that the teachers and principals at middle-SES schools promote both high present and future educational expectations. The promotion of high future expectations at middle-SES schools is seen as a reinforcer of parental expectations. Extensive efforts toward promoting high expectations is probably less necessary at middle-SES schools, since parents have already established rather high expectation levels for their children. The promotion of high present educational expectations appears to be absolutely necessary at low-SES schools.

The results reported in this chapter confirm that schools from different contexts require different strategies for success. Most of the findings described here came from LSES-II. LSES-III and -IV also involved the study of urbanicity as a context variable (see Chapters 6–8).

4 Rationale and Methodology for LSES–III and –IV

While LSES–II was a macro-level study of a relatively large representative sample of schools, LSES–III and –IV were designed as intensive case studies of a smaller number of schools over time. The design for LSES–III and –IV actually encompassed two major types of school effectiveness research approaches (Purkey & Smith, 1983): outlier studies and case studies. Outlier studies entail selecting highly effective schools (positive outliers) and unusually ineffective schools (negative outliers) and then assessing their characteristics. The case study approach involves the intensive study of school processes in a small number of schools, usually at one point in time.

The LSES–III and –IV design called for selecting pairs of effective and ineffective schools, matched on a number of demographic characteristics, and then following these schools over two points in time (1984–85 and 1989–90 school years). The longitudinal nature of this study distinguishes it from both case studies and outlier studies, which typically are conducted during a single year.

WHY A LONGITUDINAL STUDY OF SCHOOL EFFECTIVENESS?

Information from LSES–II and various literature reviews had led us (Stringfield & Teddlie, 1988) to conclusions about how effective and ineffective schools are created. In LSES–III, and especially LSES–IV, we wanted to follow schools that were already effective, or ineffective, and see how these outliers changed over time. We were interested in the processes whereby effective and ineffective schools retain their status or change.

In reviewing the school effectiveness literature, we were intrigued that so few longitudinal studies of this nature had been undertaken in the United States. While in a few instances investigators (e.g., Weber, 1971) returned to previously examined schools to see if they had retained their effectiveness status, these studies usually involved effective

43

schools only and were constrained to a very small number of schools. Even the most sophisticated U.S. studies tended to be cross-sectional, not longitudinal.

For instance, Hallinger and Murphy's (1986) case studies were based on 2 days of data collection plus an analysis of archived data. The Brookover and colleagues (1979) case studies of high- and low-achieving white and African-American schools in low-SES environments were based on data collected during 3 weeks to 3 months of observation. The LSES-II context study was based on data collected during 1 school year.

After examining these U.S. studies conducted over three waves of school effects research, we have concluded that there are three reasons why school process in differentially effective schools has not been studied longitudinally.

1. Early studies erroneously concluded that school process was not associated with positive school outcomes and, therefore, not necessary to study (e.g., Coleman et al., 1966; Jencks et al., 1972).
2. During the 1970s and early 1980s, there was an emphasis on the discovery of static correlates of effective schooling and too little emphasis on change processes.
3. Even after researchers understood that longitudinal studies of school processes were necessary, there was insufficient federal funding during the 1980s and early 1990s (Good, 1989) to conduct them.

The situation in the United Kingdom has been somewhat different, due partially to greater funding opportunities provided by the (now defunct) Inner London Education Authority (ILEA) and other agencies. Both the 3-year study of secondary schools (Rutter et al., 1979) and the 4-year study of primary or "junior" schools (Mortimore et al., 1988a) investigated school process variables and how they relate to student outcome variables over time with funds from the ILEA.

The major distinction between these British studies and what we proposed in LSES-III and -IV has to do with the level of description: the British studies describe school processes *in toto* aggregated across 12 secondary schools (Rutter et al., 1979) and 50 primary schools (Mortimore et al., 1988a), while the LSES-III and -IV studies involve detailed descriptions of school process at 16 different schools. The outlier/case study approach utilized in LSES-III and -IV allow us to describe in detail how individual schools, chosen for being particularly effective or ineffective, change over time.

Should We Expect Stability or Change or Both?

Several methodological critiques (Good & Brophy, 1986; Purkey & Smith, 1983; Rowan, Bossert, & Dwyer, 1983) indicated that instability in schools' effectiveness status over time could be a weakness of the research. As Good & Brophy (1986) stated, "It would be disturbing to go to the trouble and expense of identifying effective schools only to learn that these schools do not have stable effects on student achievement across consecutive years" (p. 586).

Evidence on school effectiveness stability across time has been contradictory, as indicated in reviews (Good & Brophy, 1986; Mandeville & Anderson, 1987). For example, Forsythe (1973) found low correlations among the residual values from regression analyses of data from two successive graduating classes for a sample of 50 high schools. Also, Rowan and Denk (1982) estimated that only about 10% of schools drawn from a large sample had consistent effectiveness status over consecutive years.

On the other hand, Weber (1971) concluded that two of his four effective schools maintained their effectiveness over several years. Similarly, Rutter and colleagues (1979) and Rutter (1983) reported that effective schools maintained their effectiveness over several consecutive years.

Part of this inconsistency in results may be due to differences in methodologies: Studies showing stable results were more likely to use extensive case history data, while those finding unstable results typically used regression analyses on archived data. Moreover, studies demonstrating unstable results looked at both effective and ineffective schools, while those that found greater stability investigated only effective schools.

After reviewing this contradictory literature, a simple question emerged: Why should we expect stable school effects, especially across lengthy time periods? As for ineffective schools, it is certainly undesirable to have a school consistently performing lower than expected. In fact, there may be pressures from the community and from local school boards to improve failing schools, as indicated by the extensive school improvement literature (Clark & McCarthy, 1983; King, 1992; Levine, 1991; Lezotte & Bancroft, 1985; McCormack-Larkin, 1985; Taylor, 1990). In cases where improvement is not imposed externally, there are documented cases of "naturally occurring" school improvement (Stringfield & Teddlie, 1990).

Just as there may be forces within the school, community, and governance structure to improve failing schools, there may also be forces leading to decline in successful schools. Slater and Teddlie (in press) referred to this process as entropy. Their Theory of School Effectiveness and Leadership (TSEL) postulates that it is easier for a school to deteriorate than to improve, and that it takes effort for a school to maintain its positive effectiveness status. To contend that there are natural forces propelling weaker schools to improve and stronger schools to decline assumes that effective schooling is a dynamic, ongoing process. The following section briefly describes the TSEL, which attempts to explain that process.

The Theory of School Effectiveness and Leadership

The TSEL (Slater & Teddlie, in press) is appropriate as a reference point for the discussion of school change over time, because it addresses two salient issues:

1. It describes schooling as an ongoing process whereby schools are continually getting better or worse (*stages*).
2. It incorporates contingency (or school *context*) into the description of effective schooling.

The TSEL contains three elements—administrative appropriateness, teacher preparedness, and student readiness—as shown in the model, briefly summarized in Figure 4.1.

The "stage" aspect of TSEL refers to the fact that schools are perpetually becoming more effective or less effective. A naive reader of the school effects literature might conclude that effective school status would be long lasting, or even permanent, once certain characteristics have been achieved. The TSEL, on the other hand, describes schools as existing within a cycle of several stages—ranging from chaos to excellent schools—through which they may pass in the course of their existence.

The "contingency" aspect of the TSEL refers to the fact that context affects the process whereby schools become more or less effective. Chapter 3 discussed context studies that examined the effect of student body SES, urbanicity, and grade level of schooling on school effectiveness processes. In the TSEL, context refers to the interaction between two or more of the theory's elements.

The three elements of the theory may be defined as follows:

FIGURE 4.1. Slater-Teddlie Typology of School Effectiveness and Leadership

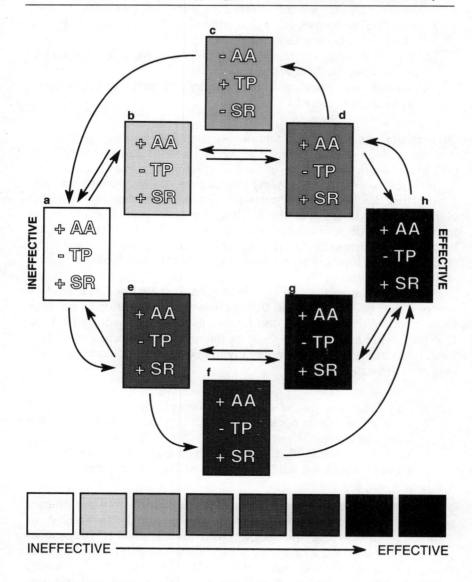

INEFFECTIVE ⟶ EFFECTIVE

KEY:
+ = High
- = Low

AA = Administrative Appropriateness
TP = Teacher Preparedness
SR = Student Readiness

1. *Administrative appropriateness* refers to whether or not the school administration, usually determined by the principal, is well matched to the particular characteristics of the student body and faculty that exist in the school.
2. *Teacher preparedness* refers to the skills and attitudes that collectively describe the teachers in a school.
3. *Student readiness* refers to the capacity and desire of the children in a school to learn.

On each of these elements, a school may be characterized as possessing positive or high characteristics (+) or negative or low characteristics (−), as shown in Figure 4.1.

Context issues arise whenever two or more of the elements interact. For instance, leadership appropriateness varies depending on the particular student readiness of a school. Thus, it is appropriate for a principal to stress "high present educational expectations" for students who are low on academic readiness. If students are already high on academic readiness, then it would be a waste of time to continually stress that all students can learn.

A valuable aspect of the TSEL is that an investigator can identify a school in terms of its type and then surmise what might occur in order for that school to improve or decline. For instance, in Figure 4.1 a Type D school with administrative appropriateness and teacher preparedness, but where students are not ready to maximize their learning, could evolve in three directions:

1. To a Type H school, if student readiness improved.
2. To a Type C school, if the principal or other leaders left the school or changed their approach.
3. To a Type B school, if many of the faculty retired or left the school, or suffered deteriorations in skills and attitudes.

The TSEL presents schooling as a collective function of the interaction of three types of players: leaders (the principal, the faculty, or a combination thereof); the faculty, who directly deliver educational services; and the student body, which consumes those services. A change in any of these elements, either naturally occurring or by human design, will change the school's effectiveness status. As Good and Brophy (1986) noted: "The conditions of effective schools may be only temporary, and as principals, teachers, and student cohorts change so too may the level of effectiveness" (p. 573).

METHODOLOGY FOR LSES–III AND –IV

Sample

The research design called for a matched-pair outlier sample for both LSES–III and –IV. The schools were to be selected based on data from two consecutive years of testing (1982–83, 1983–84) using the state basic skills test (BST). The same schools were to be visited in 1984–85 and 1989–90; thus, the sample selected for LSES–III was the same as that used for LSES–IV. Altogether we examined data for eight years (1982–90).

The final sample was to consist of nine pairs of schools—three rural pairs, three suburban pairs, and three urban pairs—representing all geographic regions of the state. Within these constraints, schools were selected that scored above (or below) achievement prediction for both years (1982–83, 1983–84).

The sampling pool consisted of 13 school districts, including the 12 districts in the LSES–II sample plus one large urban system. The urban system was added because it was largely composed of inner-city schools. Schools were chosen for LSES–III and –IV as follows:

1. Within the 13 school systems, third-grade school means on the total language arts section of the BST, a minimum-skills CRT, were computed. Mean scores were developed for both the 1982–83 and the 1983–84 school years.
2. Within each large school system and among contiguous rural systems, *separate* regression models were run in which mother's education, father's profession, and student body racial composition data were independent variables predicting mean BST language arts scores. A total of five separate regression models was used. This procedure is consistent with recommendations by Klitgaard and Hall (1974) and Purkey and Smith (1983) that regression-based analyses be repeated across years and schools be selected for study if they are consistent outliers.
3. A school was considered for inclusion in LSES–III and –IV if
   a. The school scored above (or below) achievement prediction for two consecutive years;
   b. The school scored substantially above (or below) prediction for at least one year; and
   c. A matching opposite directional outlier of similar economic and racial composition was identified within that system (or in a contiguous system in the rural models).

4. Among the potential pairs identified through steps 1–3c, pairs were chosen within the following constraints:
   a. Three would be rural, three suburban, and three urban;
   b. Pairs would be included from northern, central, and southern portions of the state;
   c. The sample would include pairs of predominantly minority, predominantly majority, and mixed student populations; and
   d. No system would contribute more than one pair to the sample (one exception was made to allow the study of a pair of extended-day programs).

Nine pairs of matched outlier schools were chosen using these criteria. The third-grade situation in one school proved to be anomalous within the school. Although the school had been matched on SES, the third graders were not socioeconomically similar to the other students in that school or to the matched-school third graders. This resulted from a local school desegregation settlement, which required that students be bused from one school to another for 1 year. In this case, students from other neighborhoods were bused to the school for their third-grade year. Because the pair of schools was clearly not well matched at third grade, it was dropped after the fall observation. Data summarizing characteristics of the retained eight pairs of schools are included in Chapter 5 (see Table 5.1).

Instrumentation for LSES–III

Data gathering in each of the schools included the use of several instruments plus extensive field notes during the 1984–85 school year. The specific instruments are described in more detail in Teddlie and colleagues (1984, 1989). They included parallel questionnaires for principals, teachers, and students that were derived from the Brookover and colleagues (1979) study; protocols for interviewing teachers and principals; a school observation checklist; an NRT; and high- and low-inference classroom observation systems. The Stallings (1980) Classroom Snapshot (CS), a low-inference measure of time-on-task and interactive teaching, provided basic classroom behavioral frequency data. The CS had been used previously in evaluation studies, studies of early childhood education, and studies of student teaching (Stallings & Freiberg, 1991; Stallings & Kaskowitz, 1974).

The Classroom Observation Instrument (COI) was developed for LSES–III to provide higher-inference classroom data. The COI was based on the teaching functions identified in Rosenshine's (1983) synthesis of teacher effectiveness research. Fifteen general indicators, each with specific cues, were used to guide qualitative data collection. Ten of these indicators were reported about in LSES-III; they are described in Chapter 5 (see Tables 5.3 and 5.4). Specific cues associated with "initial student practice," for example, included high frequency of questions, teacher-directed exchange, teacher prompts, opportunity for all students to respond, and success rate of 80% during initial learning.

A research version of the *3-R's Test, Level Nine* (Riverside, 1983) was administered to all third-grade students in the 16 schools during both the fall and spring semesters of LSES-III and -IV. These instruments were administered to provide NRT data (in addition to the CRT data from the BST) and to ensure standardization of testing procedures.

Procedure for LSES–III

During LSES-III, each school was visited by a two-person team for three full school days in both the fall and spring semesters. Principal and teacher questionnaires were administered during the 3-day fall visits, student questionnaires during the 3-day spring visits. The *3-R's Test* was administered to all third graders during the morning of the third day of each site visit.

During each visit, field teams devised an observation schedule that included 12 classroom visits per observer, so that each observer visited every third-grade class for at least one class period each day. Other classrooms were scheduled for observations as time permitted. Observations were scheduled so that at some point during the 3 days each class was observed during every hour listed as an academic period.

During each observation class, the majority of site visits included at least 24 full class period observations, 12 of them concentrated in the third grade. Over 700 hours of classroom observations and over 1,000 total hours of on-site data gathering were conducted.

The subjective impressions of observers are a central source of the data presented in later chapters. Therefore, the observers will be briefly described here. The project director and senior researcher had Ph.D.s in social and educational psychology, respectively. Both had participated in previous LSES phases, and one had engaged in classroom research. Neither had taught in the elementary or secondary grades.

The educational backgrounds of the five additional observers included a Ph.D. in educational administration, a bachelor's degree in nursing, a master's degree in experimental statistics, and doctoral studies in social psychology and education. One of the five had taught in the elementary grades; two had taught in secondary schools. One had been involved in previous phases of LSES and had gathered classroom observational data.

A double blind was built into the design. Neither the participants in the schools observed nor the visiting teams of researchers knew whether the schools were high or low outliers. To the extent possible, team membership was shifted on a school-to-school basis, and individuals who visited one school in a pair typically did not visit the other.

Audiotapes containing the impressions of observers regarding each school were made at the end of data gathering. Those audiotapes, observers' field notes, and our own notes from previous and subsequent interviews form the basis of the case studies in Chapters 6–8.

Instrumentation for LSES–IV

Most of the instruments administered during LSES–III were also administered in LSES–IV. The following changes and additions were made:

1. The CRT was changed by the state (Louisiana Department of Education, 1990) from the BST to a new test, known as the Louisiana Education Assessment Program (LEAP).
2. The higher-inference classroom observation instrument was changed from the COI to the Virgilio Teacher Behavior Inventory (VTBI).
3. A new instrument, the 12 Hierarchical Dimensions Instrument (12 HD), was added to quantitatively assess school-level climate factors.
4. An instrument designed to assess the social induction experiences of new teachers, the Beginning Teacher Questionnaire (BTQ), was added.

The LEAP test replaced the BST during the interim from LSES–III to LSES–IV. While the BST was a minimum-standards test, the LEAP test was designed as a grade-level assessment program using performance standards based partially on teachers' perception of whether or not their students would pass the test.

The VTBI, which consisted of 35 closed-ended items, replaced the open-ended COI as the higher-inference measure of teaching behavior. Satisfactory measures of internal consistency, interrater reliability, content validity, concurrent validity, and construct validity were obtained during a validation study (Teddlie, Virgilio, & Oescher, 1990). Five dimensions of teacher effectiveness are measured by the instrument: classroom management, instructional strategies, instructional presentation/questioning, classroom social psychological climate, and classroom physical climate.

The 12 HD (Stringfield & Teddlie, 1991a) consisted of observers' ratings of processes on school-, classroom-, and student-level dimensions, which had been found in LSES–III to be relevant to discriminations between high- and low-achieving schools. These dimensions included such factors as the students' ability to extract academic meaning from schooling, planned academic push, experimentation with new curricular and instructional techniques, coordination among programs, and systematic recognition and rewards.

The BTQ consisted of 14 items related to three areas of teacher socialization into new schools: assistance, monitoring, and team-building. These questionnaires were completed by all beginning teachers in fall 1989.

Procedure for LSES–IV

The procedure followed for LSES–IV was essentially the same as for LSES–III. Due to time constraints, the two-person teams visited sites for 3 days in the fall and 2 in the spring, rather than 6 days in total. In spite of this, the teams were able to observe around 600 hours in the classrooms and around 900 hours total on-site at the 16 schools.

The LSES–IV observers included four individuals from LSES–III (the project director, the senior researcher, the Ph.D. in educational administration, and a former doctoral student who by then had a Ph.D. in educational media), plus two new observers. One new observer, who also had a Ph.D. in educational administration, had taught in secondary schools and had conducted school effectiveness research previously. The other, a doctoral student in educational research methodology, had taught in elementary schools and had run her own day care center.

Since audiotapes of impressions about schools had proved so valuable in LSES–III, we extended their use in LSES–IV. During both the fall and spring 1989–90 visits, observers produced audiotapes of their impressions while still in the field.

Results from LSES–III and –IV are presented in Part II. The context differences found in school effectiveness processes between pairs of geographically distinct schools should add to the body of knowledge concerning school context.

Quantitative and Qualitative Results from LSES–III and –IV

The chapters in this part present results from LSES–III and –IV, a longitudinal study of 16 schools over an 8-year period. Chapter 5 discusses the quantitative results from analyses of a number of school effects indices and concludes with a taxonomy of schools that reflects stability and change in effectiveness status over time. Chapters 6–8 are case studies of three pairs of schools—one rural, one suburban, and one urban— with commentary on the processes whereby schools from different contexts evolve over time.

5 Quantitative Results from LSES–III and –IV

At the beginning of LSES–III, it was important that each school be similar to its matched school on student body SES characteristics, and that the overall set of effective schools be equally matched to the overall set of ineffective schools. It was also important that each school be different from its matched school on achievement, and that the set of effective schools be quite different from the overall set of ineffective schools. Tables 5.1 and 5.7 contain information on these issues.

COMPARISONS AT THE BEGINNING OF LSES–III

The data contained in Table 5.1 include the predicted, actual, and residual scores on the BST for all 16 schools for the 2 years preceding LSES–III. Five separate regressions were run to generate these predicted and residual values. Since selected schools were to be matched within district, it was necessary that a separate regression analysis be generated for each district. Some of the data from contiguous rural districts were combined in order to have a large enough sample size to produce stable regression equations. Average mothers' education, percentage of fathers with white-collar jobs, and student body racial characteristics were used to predict BST language arts scores in these regressions.

The predicted scores for all the positive and negative outliers are very similar for both years: 88.4 versus 88.8 for 1982–83, 88.8 versus 89.7 for 1983–84. The overall actual scores are quite different for the two years: 92.0 versus 84.2 for 1982–83, 93.7 versus 83.7 for 1983–84. These data indicate that the schools were well matched in terms of how well they were expected to score, but were quite different in terms of how they actually scored. Effective schools scored much better than their ineffective counterparts across both years, even though they had similar SES characteristics.

Again, throughout this chapter we will be describing schools as effective or ineffective. In doing this, we are using the term *effective* in a

TABLE 5.1. Criterion-Referenced Language Arts Data Used to Select LSES-III Schools, 1982–83 and 1983–84

Num.	Outlier Status	1982–83 Scores			1983–84 Scores		
		Predicted	Actual	Residual	Predicted	Actual	Residual
1	Negative	87.41	83.19	– 4.22	87.70	85.68	– 2.02
	Positive	88.77	93.77	+ 4.90	87.91	92.77	+ 4.86
2	Negative	90.35	87.39	– 2.96	92.05	86.79	– 5.26
	Positive	87.32	92.83	+ 5.51	86.98	93.05	+ 6.07
3	Negative	94.94	92.02	– 2.92	92.68	87.64	– 5.04
	Positive	91.49	95.61	+ 4.12	90.53	95.86	+ 5.33
4	Negative	87.15	80.84	– 6.31	88.12	81.08	– 7.04
	Positive	86.73	91.95	+ 5.22	87.92	92.50	+ 4.58
5	Negative	91.41	89.67	– 1.74	90.23	88.47	– 1.76
	Positive	91.64	93.48	+ 1.84	90.59	93.08	+ 2.49
6	Negative	80.33	71.69	– 8.64	84.75	67.71	– 17.04
	Positive	81.52	84.12	+ 2.60	85.10	93.09	+ 7.99
7	Negative	91.23	87.39	– 3.84	93.00	90.87	– 2.13
	Positive	92.24	92.47	+ 0.23	91.79	94.97	+ 3.18
8	Negative	87.23	81.61	– 5.62	88.81	80.99	– 7.82
	Positive	87.53	91.91	+ 4.33	89.51	94.05	+ 4.54
OUTLIER MEANS[a]	Negative	88.76	84.23	– 4.53	89.67	83.65	– 6.02
	Positive	88.42	92.02	+ 3.60	88.79	93.67	+ 4.88

Note: The predicted scores and residual values were based on five separate regressions predicting third-grade language arts scores. Regression one yielded outlier status for schools 1, 2, 3, and 4, which were in one school district. Regression two yielded outlier status for schools 5, 6, 11, and 12, which were from two contiguous districts. Regression three yielded outlier status for schools 7, 8, 13, and 14, which were from two contiguous districts. Regression four yielded outlier status scores for schools 9 and 10, while regression five yielded outlier scores for schools 15 and 16.
[a]Negative and positive outlier means are not weighted by number of observations per school.

statistical sense and are not making summative judgments about particular schools.

RESULTS FROM LSES–III

This chapter presents a great deal of quantitative data regarding the schools in LSES–III and –IV. Readers more interested in summary statements than detailed presentation of data may want to go to the section at the end of the chapter entitled "Summary of Results."

Criterion-Referenced Test Results

Data in Table 5.2 indicate that the eight matched pairs of schools retained their effectiveness status with regard to BST scores during 1984–85, the year of LSES–III. Effective schools outscored ineffective schools on both the language arts and mathematics BSTs: 91.6 versus 87.6 for language arts, 91.3 versus 85.6 for mathematics. Except for Pair 3, the effective school outscored the ineffective school on both tests.

With regard to Pair 3, it appears that there were slight, but consistent, differences in SES of student body between these two schools, such that the ineffective school was slightly more affluent. Many of the nonwhite students in the effective school were foreign-born children whose parents had just arrived in the United States. This difference in SES level may have contributed to the difference in performance status between LSES–III and the data from the previous two years. More information on this inconsistency will be presented in the following sections.

Teaching Behaviors

Data in Tables 5.3, 5.4, and 5.5 contain information on differences in teaching behaviors in LSES–III between effective and ineffective schools, as measured by the COI. These data were initially in the form of field notes. Due to some inconsistencies in data collection procedures for the COI in fall 1984, all data in Tables 5.3–5.5 are from spring 1985 visits.

COI field notes were analyzed by independent raters. Considering all notes for any given teacher, two raters scored each of the indicators of effective teaching as being "evident," "contradictory or weak," "not evident," or "not observable." All "not observable" ratings were eliminated. The remaining ratings were scaled from 1 (evident) to 3 (not evident) and averaged across raters by teacher and school. Five of the

TABLE 5.2. Criterion-Referenced Test Data (BST) for Third-Grade Students, LSES-III Schools, 1984–85

Number	Outlier Status	Language Arts Score	Math Score
1	Negative	85.98	82.76
	Positive	89.46	86.98
2	Negative	90.52	86.17
	Positive	93.29	93.87
3	Negative	94.05	91.63
	Positive	92.27	91.53
4	Negative	85.45	85.78
	Positive	94.29	94.02
5	Negative	88.35	87.20
	Positive	89.20	93.10
6	Negative	80.14	84.29
	Positive	92.90	91.91
7	Negative	89.75	85.87
	Positive	92.19	94.78
8	Negative	86.58	80.99
	Positive	88.97	84.07
OUTLIER MEANS[a]	Negative	87.60	85.59
	Positive	91.57	91.28

[a]The negative and positive outlier means are not weighted by number of observations per school.

15 characteristics were observable in less than three-fourths of the 116 classes visited. Because elementary school classes are typically divided into time blocks of more than 1-hour duration, deletion of those five items seemed prudent. "Daily review," "weekly and monthly review," and "initial student practice" would require that the lesson be observed from its actual beginning to end and not in 1-hour frames. Likewise, "systematic evaluation" and "lesson plans" would require consultation with the teacher, as these were, in most cases, not discerned from actual instruction. The conversion of field notes via the rating scale thus resulted in numerical indices for 10 of the 15 general indicators.

Pairs of independent raters converted the field notes to quantitative

TABLE 5.3. Comparison of Means by School Type on Several Dimensions of Effective Teaching, LSES-III Data

Variable	Effective Schools (n = 8)		Ineffective Schools (n = 8)		
	M	SD	M	SD	t
Time-on-task	1.33	.31	1.98	.65	2.55*
Presentation of new material	1.45	.34	2.01	.39	3.06**
Independent practice	1.65	.69	2.24	.49	1.97
High expectations	1.25	.18	1.84	.51	3.15**
Positive reinforcement	1.40	.28	1.71	.28	2.24*
Interruptions minimal	1.43	.56	2.06	.56	2.25*
Discipline	1.32	.28	1.76	.42	2.46*
Friendly ambience	1.29	.30	1.68	.41	2.22*
Student work displayed	1.54	.29	1.70	.61	.69
Appearance of room	1.35	.33	1.58	.30	1.47

Note: 1 = evidence of effective behavior; 2 = evidence of contradictory behavior; 3 = absence of effective behavior.
* $p < .05$
** $p < .01$

ratings using the described methods. The percentage of agreement between raters on the 10 indicators of effective teaching ranged from .71 to .85, with an average overall agreement of .80.

Data were analyzed at both the school level (Table 5.3) and the classroom level (Table 5.4). Sirotnik and Burstein (1985) and Hanson, Gardner, and McNamara (1986) have cautioned against analyses at only one level. Consistent results at both the school and classroom levels validate the results.

Schools classified as effective displayed more evidence of effective teaching than did schools classified as ineffective (see Table 5.3). Differences were statistically significant on 7 of the 10 indicators and approached statistical significance on two others. Effective schools do have teachers whose behavior differs from that of teachers in less effective schools.

TABLE 5.4. Comparison of Means by Classroom Type on Several Dimensions of Effective Teaching, LSES-III Data

Variable	Teachers in Effective Schools		Teachers in Ineffective Schools		
	M	SD	M	SD	F
Time-on-task	1.38	.58	2.03	.84	$F(1,115) = 23.44$****
Presentation of new material	1.54	.72	1.92	.77	$F(1,87) = 5.74$*
Independent practice	1.53	.74	2.10	.74	$F(1,90) = 13.78$***
High expectations	1.27	.50	1.82	.77	$F(1,87) = 16.36$****
Positive reinforcement	1.41	.56	1.73	.71	$F(1,105) = 6.88$**
Interruptions minimal	1.39	.58	2.11	.75	$F(1,102) = 30.48$****
Discipline	1.31	.59	1.85	.75	$F(1,111) = 17.88$****
Friendly ambience	1.27	.48	1.78	.71	$F(1,104) = 19.41$****
Student work displayed	1.63	.83	1.80	.87	$F(1,93) = 0.904$
Appearance of room	1.36	.49	1.65	.57	$F(1,111) = 8.88$**

Note: 1 = evidence of effective behavior; 2 = evidence of contradictory behavior; 3 = absence of effective behavior.
    * $p < .05$
    ** $p < .01$
    *** $p < .001$
    **** $p < .0001$

When the teacher rather than the school is used as the unit of analysis, consistently superior performance is again revealed in more effective schools. Teachers in these schools demonstrated better teacher behaviors on all 10 effectiveness indicators (see Table 5.4). These differences were statistically significant for 9 of the 10 categories.

A multivariate analysis of variance (MANOVA) was used to analyze the teacher-level data to ensure that the significant findings were not

TABLE 5.5. Teacher Means on Selected Dimensions of Effective Teaching for Eight Matched Pairs of Schools, LSES-III

		Effective Teaching Dimension							
Outlier		Time-on-Task		Presentation of New Material		High Expectations		Discipline	
No.	Status	M	SD	M	SD	M	SD	M	SD
1	Negative	2.91	.29	2.00	.88	1.56	.73	2.41	.73
	Positive	1.00	.00	1.07	.26	1.33	.49	1.13	.35
2	Negative	2.42	.72	2.24	.75	2.00	.77	2.07	.78
	Positive	1.58	.64	1.92	.86	1.36	.81	1.20	.41
3	Negative	2.46	.88	2.31	.75	2.64	.67	1.92	.67
	Positive	1.05	.23	1.70	.95	1.21	.58	1.15	.37
4	Negative	2.10	.88	2.16	.90	2.40	.83	1.84	.76
	Positive	1.59	.69	1.50	.53	1.46	.52	1.46	.81
5	Negative	1.31	.48	2.22	.83	1.64	.67	1.07	.27
	Positive	1.23	.44	1.11	.32	1.00	.00	1.07	.27
6	Negative	2.17	.72	2.33	.65	1.90	.88	1.58	.51
	Positive	1.88	.96	1.82	.81	1.43	.53	1.79	.97
7	Negative	1.18	.39	1.47	.72	1.06	.24	1.35	.49
	Positive	1.22	.65	1.33	.59	1.11	.32	1.67	.84
8	Negative	1.28	.46	1.33	.59	1.56	.62	1.82	.88
	Positive	1.10	.30	1.16	.50	1.05	.22	1.10	.30

Note: 1 = evidence of effective behavior; 2 = contradictory evidence; 3 = absence of effective behavior.

a result of multiple comparisons. When the school type (effective or ineffective) was used as the independent variable, the multivariate effect was significant ($F[10,48] = 2.5$, $p < .05$), indicating an overall effect for type of school on teacher behaviors.

The differences in classroom behavior according to school classification were also consistent within matched pairs of schools. Teacher means and standard deviations on four of the 10 effective-teaching dimensions are presented in Table 5.5 by matched pair. In Pair 7, the positive outlier school scored slightly poorer on three of the four chosen dimensions than did its negative match. One other pair tied in the discipline category, and the negative outlier in another pair outperformed its positive counterpart in this category. In all other cases teachers in the effective schools demonstrated superior teaching. These findings cannot be attributed to one or two particularly outstanding (or inept) teachers, since little variability was discovered on many teacher ratings. For example, there was no variability in time-on-task ratings in one school and no variability in teacher expectations in another. Standard deviations were less than 1.0 in all cases and less than .50 in one-third of the cases listed in Table 5.5.

Data in Table 5.6 are from the Stallings CS ratings from the LSES–III spring 1985 observations. These data show teachers in effective schools have higher rates of interactive and total time-on-task than those in ineffective schools. While the overall rates across all schools are higher for the effective schools, there are more discrepancies between paired schools than found on the COI.

Pairs 1 to 5 show consistent ratings in that effective schools had higher ratings than ineffective schools on measures of time-on-task. For Pair 7, the effective school had a higher rating on interactive time-on-task, but a lower rating on total time-on-task than the ineffective school. This finding replicates inconsistent results found on the COI for Pair 7, where the ineffective school had slightly higher ratings on some indicators of effective teaching. Since the Pair 7 effective school far outdistanced the ineffective school on CRT results for LSES–III (see Table 5.2), these teacher behavior inconsistencies had not had an immediate effect on achievement.

For Pairs 6 and 8, the ineffective schools outscored the effective schools on both interactive and total time-on-task. These results are inconsistent with the COI ratings, which indicated that the teachers in effective schools were performing better than those in ineffective schools. The COI data appear to be better predictors of CRT data, since the Pair 6 and 8 effective schools consistently outperformed their ineffective match on this test (see Table 5.2).

The time-on-task discrepancies are minimal for Pairs 7 and 8, while they are quite high for Pair 6. This indicates that something odd is going on in Pair 6, where the interactive time-on-task for the ineffective school is double that for the effective school. COI data also indicate that the Pair 6 effective school, while outscoring its ineffective match, had lower sores than any other effective school.

When considering all schools, the effective schools had 71% total time-on-task, while the ineffective schools had 64%. Using the school as the unit of analysis, this difference is not significant. However, when the teacher is used as the unit of analysis, the difference between effec-

TABLE 5.6. Time-on-Task Percentages of LSES-III Schools, Spring 1985

Outlier		Percentage Time-on-Task		
Number	Status	Interactive	Noninteractive	Total
1	Negative	25.2	25.5	50.7
	Positive	39.4	32.7	72.1
2	Negative	33.3	23.8	57.1
	Positive	31.5	37.8	69.3
3	Negative	34.5	23.7	58.2
	Positive	54.2	19.6	73.8
4	Negative	32.0	20.4	52.4
	Positive	46.0	22.8	68.8
5	Negative	41.0	28.4	69.4
	Positive	62.8	23.0	85.8
6	Negative	58.4	15.0	73.4
	Positive	27.7	31.8	59.5
7	Negative	49.4	27.6	77.0
	Positive	57.5	13.3	70.8
8	Negative	47.0	23.2	70.2
	Positive	35.3	30.0	65.3
ALL MEANS[a]				
	Negative	40.1	23.5	63.6
	Positive	44.3	26.4	70.7
MEANS WITHOUT PAIR 6[a]				
	Negative	37.5	24.6	62.1
	Positive	46.7	25.6	72.3

[a]Negative and positive means are not weighted by the number of observations per school.

tive and ineffective schools is significant $[F(1,129) = 4.96, p < .05]$, such that effective schools have higher time-on-task.

If Pair 6 is eliminated from the analysis, the effective schools had 72% total time-on-task, while the ineffective schools had 62%. This difference is significant at both the school $[t(12) = 2.23, p < .05]$ and the teacher level $[F(1,112) = 10.1, p < .005]$. Thus, with the exception of Pair 6, there is strong evidence that the effective schools *in toto* had higher time-on-task than the ineffective schools.

Demographic Changes

The predicted scores found in Table 5.1 indicate that the effective and ineffective schools considered altogether had similar characteristics. The data from Table 5.7 confirm this; for instance, average mothers' education across all effective schools for the two years (1982–83, 1983–84) used in the outlier analysis was 3.04 as compared with 3.14 for the ineffective schools (3 indicates completed high school, while 4 indicates attended college).

There are some schools where demographic changes were occurring. For instance, the student body in the Pair 2 ineffective school was becoming more affluent, and the student body in the Pair 7 effective

TABLE 5.7. SES **and Racial Characteristics of Third-Grade Students,** LSES-III **Schools, 1982–85**

	Outlier	1982–83		1983–84		1984–85	
Number	Status	Mothers' Education	% White	Mothers' Education	% White	Mothers' Education	% White
1	Negative	3.00	48.15	3.29	42.10	3.15	40.82
	Positive	3.30	52.11	3.02	52.17	3.38	37.31
2	Negative	3.49	45.83	4.06	56.41	3.87	44.44
	Positive	3.19	44.44	3.43	30.43	3.57	40.00
3	Negative	3.72	76.47	3.61	69.12	3.75	79.66
	Positive	3.26	68.42	3.21	59.52	3.57	64.86
4	Negative	2.69	01.14	2.87	03.61	2.92	02.35
	Positive	2.62	00.00	2.98	00.00	2.95	00.00
5	Negative	2.69	03.85	2.73	04.34	3.23	05.00
	Positive	2.43	04.76	2.22	03.70	2.26	09.68
6	Negative	2.93	00.00	3.58	00.00	3.17	00.00
	Positive	4.00	00.99	3.67	00.00	2.75	00.00
7	Negative	3.07	55.00	3.04	76.60	2.94	75.00
	Positive	3.07	68.97	2.63	62.50	2.34	71.88
8	Negative	2.64	55.39	2.76	58.57	2.74	63.89
	Positive	2.88	76.47	2.89	72.50	2.81	70.73

Note: Mothers' education: 2 = attended high school; 3 = finished high school; 4 = attended college; 5 = graduated from college.

school was becoming less affluent, over time. These trends continued through LSES–IV (see Table 5.11) and meant that the effective schools altogether were slightly lower in SES at the time of LSES–III than were the ineffective schools. Also, the mothers' education data for the Pair 6 effective school were unstable over time, as indicated in Tables 5.7 and 5.11. This instability is due to a large amount of missing data on this indicator for the Pair 6 effective school. Pair 6 observers indicated that the two schools appeared to be well matched on SES characteristics.

Norm-Referenced Test Results

Data in Table 5.8 are derived from student scores on an NRT (*3R's Test, Level Nine*) administered by the researchers during the fall and spring semesters. This test was not being administered by any school system in the state during LSES–III.

NRT data have some useful properties. They allow us to compute gain scores on the same cohort of students across time, without being overly concerned about ceiling effects. They also provide normally distributed data at the student, teacher, and school levels. This type of data is useful for conducting the analyses described in Chapter 2. It should be reiterated that the CRT data were our criterion for the initial classification of schools. If NRT data had been used instead, the schools in our LSES–III sample might have been different. Due to the different psychometric properties of CRTs and NRTs, a school classified as effective by one criterion might not be judged effective by the other. In fact, a recent study by Lang (1991) indicated only 50% agreement between CRTs and NRTs on classification of an effective school and 55% agreement between the two types of tests on classification of an ineffective school.

Data in Table 5.8 include the actual, predicted, and residual scores on the NRT for both the fall and spring testing in LSES–III, plus the gain index from fall to spring. Regression analyses were run predicting NRT scores from the 1984–85 mothers' education and ethnicity data found in Table 5.7. The two models were significant, with the fall model accounting for 50% of the variance in the NRT (42% adjusted) and the spring model accounting for 61% of the variance (55% adjusted). This regression analysis is different from those reported for the selection procedure on two dimensions:

1. The selection procedure utilized five separate district-level regression models run across 2 years, while the data reported in Table 5.8 were based on two regressions from the same year.

TABLE 5.8. Norm-Referenced Test Data for LSES-III, 1984–85

No.	Outlier Status	Fall Scores Actual	Predicted	Residual	Spring Scores Actual	Predicted	Residual	Raw Score Gain Index
1	Negative	20.5	22.5	-2.0	26.0	27.8	-1.8	24.4%
	Positive	23.6	22.6	1.0	29.1	28.1	1.0	28.4%
2	Negative	26.7	23.7	3.0	29.1	29.5	-0.4	14.7%
	Positive	23.9	23.0	0.9	28.0	28.7	-0.7	21.5%
3	Negative	23.6	25.2	-1.6	31.6	31.1	0.5	41.8%
	Positive	23.7	24.2	-0.5	32.0	30.0	2.0	43.0%
4	Negative	17.6	20.3	-2.7	23.0	25.3	-2.3	21.3%
	Positive	21.6	20.3	1.3	28.2	25.2	3.0	30.8%
5	Negative	21.3	20.9	0.4	27.4	26.1	1.3	28.1%
	Positive	22.6	19.7	2.9	26.9	24.3	2.6	21.1%
6	Negative	20.2	20.6	-0.4	23.8	25.7	-1.9	15.8%
	Positive	17.6	20.0	-2.4	23.2	24.8	-1.6	22.0%
7	Negative	23.5	23.7	-0.2	28.7	29.2	-0.5	26.7%
	Positive	23.5	23.7	0.8	26.9	27.7	-0.8	17.4%
8	Negative	21.6	22.9	-1.3	27.6	28.2	-0.6	28.0%
	Positive	24.1	23.3	0.8	29.0	28.7	0.3	25.9%
OUTLIER MEANS								
	Negative	21.9	22.5	-0.6	27.2	27.9	-0.7	24.6%
	Positive	22.6	22.0	0.6	27.9	27.2	0.7	26.0%

Note: The norm-referenced test data are from the research version of the *3R's Test, Level Nine* (Riverside, 1983). There were a total of 43 items on the test. The gain index is computed by dividing the gain score from fall to spring by the number of items missed in the fall testing.

2. All 16 schools in the study were included in the regression predicting the NRTs, while the schools were segregated into separate district-level analyses during the selection process.

At both the fall and spring testings, the total NRT score for the effective schools was higher than the total NRT score for the ineffective schools. The average residual score for the effective schools was higher than that for the ineffective schools at both points in time (see Table 5.8). The ineffective schools were predicted to score slightly higher than the effective schools due to their having somewhat higher SES scores for

Pairs 3, 5, and 7. If one adjusted the actual NRT scores based on the difference in predicted values by adding that difference to the actual score of the effective schools, then they would outscore the ineffective schools 23.1 to 21.9 in the fall and 28.6 to 27.2 in the spring on the 43-item test.

While the overall pattern of results on the NRTs supported the original classification system, there were two pairs (Pairs 2 and 6) where the ineffective school had a more positive residual than the effective school. For Pair 2, this may be a result of different academic emphases at the schools. The ineffective school in this pair changed both demographically and in school philosophy over the course of the study. Its student body became more affluent and its curriculum offerings more broad-based due to its unique designation as a school for the children of commuters to a downtown government/business complex.

The disparity in results for Pair 6 is more problematic, since it echoes earlier COI and time-on-task disparities. We began to be concerned that the effective school was a false positive (Stringfield & Teddlie, 1990), that is, a school designated as effective due to irregularities in CRT testing. These suspicions were confirmed in 1990 when the positive outlier was identified as one of a handful of schools with irregular erasure patterns on state tests. In the LSES–IV analyses, several comparisons will be made dropping Pair 6, since there appears to be no effective school in that pair.

RESULTS FROM LSES–IV

It is appropriate to call the schools historically effective or ineffective during LSES–IV, since all the schools had undergone changes in staff and student body since LSES–III. Their continued participation was based on data that would not have indicated a current outlier status. The criteria on which schools were designated as effective or ineffective was between six and seven years old when LSES–IV occurred.

Teaching Behaviors

The high-inference teacher behavior instrument used in LSES–IV was the VTBI. The data in Table 5.9 are the mean scores by school for the more than 550 classroom observations conducted in LSES–IV. Mean scores across all historically effective and ineffective schools are presented for all eight pairs, and also for seven pairs excluding problematic Pair 6.

TABLE 5.9. Teacher Means on the Virgilio Teacher Behavior Instrument
for LSES-IV Schools, 1989–90

No.	Outlier Status	Classroom Management	Presentation & Questioning Skills	Instructional Strategies Skills	Social Psychological Climate	Physical Climate
1	Negative	3.24	3.23	3.49	3.46	3.66
	Positive	3.78	3.55	3.99	4.00	3.72
2	Negative	3.36	3.28	3.44	3.59	4.13
	Positive	4.02	3.92	4.09	4.21	4.11
3	Negative	2.91	2.11	2.84	3.02	2.69
	Positive	3.30	2.60	3.58	3.40	3.39
4	Negative	3.48	3.23	3.53	3.54	3.07
	Positive	3.39	3.14	3.36	3.46	2.79
5	Negative	3.33	2.95	3.23	3.37	3.35
	Positive	3.43	2.86	3.29	3.73	2.98
6	Negative	2.93	2.27	2.81	2.84	3.03
	Positive	2.38	1.94	2.74	2.56	3.33
7	Negative	3.51	3.45	3.55	3.56	3.58
	Positive	3.59	3.41	3.41	3.55	3.92
8	Negative	3.26	3.01	3.55	3.48	3.44
	Positive	3.64	3.35	3.77	3.63	2.92
OUTLIER MEANS						
	Negative	3.25	2.95	3.31	3.36	3.37
	Positive	3.45	3.11	3.54	3.57	3.41
OUTLIER MEANS WITHOUT PAIR 6						
	Negative	3.30	3.04	3.38	3.43	3.42
	Positive	3.61	3.28	3.66	3.72	3.42

Note: A score of 1 indicates low performance; a score of 5 indicates high performance.

Historically effective schools had better scores on the five VTBI indicators of teacher behavior than historically ineffective schools. If classroom observation is used as the unit of analysis, these differences are significant on three dimensions: (1) classroom management, (2) instructional strategies skills, and (3) social psychological climate. Additionally, there was a marginal significance for presentation and questioning skills. When Pair 6 is dropped from the analysis, the differences between historically effective and ineffective schools increase on the first four VTBI indicators, and all four differences are statistically significant. (See Teddlie, 1992, for specific ANOVA F values and probability levels.)

Having such a large number of observations could have inflated the statistical significance of the results, so parallel analyses were run using the teacher and the school as the units of analysis. With the teacher as the unit of analysis and eliminating Pair 6, the historically effective schools again outscored the ineffective ones on four VTBI dimensions: (1) classroom management, (2) presentation and questioning skills, (3) instructional strategies skills, and (4) social psychological climate. When the school is used as the unit of analysis, there was a significant effect for classroom management and a marginal effect for social psychological climate.

Thus, there is evidence from high-inference instruments for the persistence of more positive teaching behaviors within historically effective schools. Looking at individual pairs, there is evidence of these effects in Pairs 1, 2, 3, 5, and 8. For Pair 6, there had already been contradictory evidence during LSES-III. Both Pair 6 schools appear to have relatively ineffective teaching again in LSES-IV.

This leaves Pairs 4 and 7 as having changed from LSES-III to -IV. The LSES-III scores on the high-inference COI instrument for Pair 7 were very close (see Table 5.5), as they are in LSES-IV (see Table 5.9). There were negative changes in student body SES over time at the historically effective school, accompanied by faculty loss. These changes appear to have equalized the two schools in terms of effective teaching behaviors.

For Pair 4, there was a more dramatic change, with the historically ineffective school improving greatly from LSES-III to LSES-IV, while the historically effective school stayed the same. This was due to a dynamic principal taking over at the historically ineffective school and making wholesale changes in the faculty. More detail on these changes can be found in the case study in Chapter 8.

While there is evidence for the persistence of teaching effects using high-inference data, the low-inference, time-on-task indices show no difference overall between historically effective and ineffective schools in LSES-IV, as indicated in Table 5.10. For four pairs (Pairs 1, 3, 7, and 8), the historically effective schools have higher overall time-on-task, but there are no differences, or differences in the other direction, for the remaining four pairs. It is postulated below that school effectiveness changes have a more direct effect on time-on-task, which can be greatly affected by school policies, than on indices like instructional presentation and classroom social psychological climate, which are more under the control of teachers.

TABLE 5.10. Time-on-Task Percentages of LSES-IV Schools, 1989–90

Outlier		Time on Task (%)		
No.	Status	Interactive	Noninteractive	Total
1	Negative	44.1	21.7	65.8
	Positive	56.3	14.6	70.9
2	Negative	56.1	21.5	77.6
	Positive	53.6	20.7	74.3
3	Negative	43.1	19.0	62.1
	Positive	46.4	17.3	63.7
4	Negative	61.2	23.1	84.3
	Positive	56.6	16.1	72.7
5	Negative	57.8	17.1	74.9
	Positive	46.0	17.0	63.0
6	Negative	37.3	20.3	57.6
	Positive	30.5	24.7	55.2
7	Negative	58.2	14.8	73.0
	Positive	58.4	22.5	80.9
8	Negative	46.4	23.9	70.3
	Positive	44.0	31.1	75.1
ALL OUTLIER MEANS[a]				
	Negative	50.5	20.2	70.7
	Positive	49.0	20.5	69.5
OUTLIER MEANS WITHOUT PAIR 6[a]				
	Negative	52.4	20.2	72.6
	Positive	51.6	19.9	71.5

[a]Negative and positive outlier means are not weighted by the number of observations per school.

Demographic Changes

The demographic trends noted in LSES–III continued in LSES–IV, as can be seen in Table 5.11. While most of the pairs of schools stayed relatively well matched over time, there were changes for Pairs 2 and 7 that persisted through LSES-IV.

For Pair 2, the historically ineffective school continued to attract a student body with higher SES levels than the historically effective

TABLE 5.11. SES and Racial Characteristics of Third-Grade Students,
LSES-IV Schools, 1988–90

Outlier		1988–89		1989–90	
Num.	Status	Mothers' Education	% White	Mothers' Education	% White
1	Negative	3.58	17.77	3.72	17.40
	Positive	3.60	24.60	3.39	18.20
2	Negative	4.17	51.06	4.18	34.70
	Positive	3.48	16.67	3.55	18.20
3	Negative	3.14	72.73	3.35	68.50
	Positive	3.45	60.66	3.46	60.87
4	Negative	3.11	1.60	2.74	0.00
	Positive	3.20	0.00	3.12	1.40
5	Negative	3.02	5.70	2.98	9.30
	Positive	2.78	0.00	3.05	4.80
6	Negative	3.20	0.00	3.56	0.00
	Positive	3.43	0.90	2.66	0.00
7	Negative	3.46	77.20	3.44	84.60
	Positive	2.22	55.90	2.75	52.00
8	Negative	2.92	60.20	2.96	50.00
	Positive	3.18	74.48	2.98	81.00

Note: Mother's education: 2 = attended high school; 3 = finished high school; 4 = attended college;
5 = graduated from college.

school. This was due to the school serving the children of commuters,
who had higher educational levels than those parents in the other
school. Also, the historically effective school was now part of a school
cluster designed to further racial integration.

For Pair 7, the historically ineffective school was now serving a
student body with more positive SES characteristics than its historically
effective matched school. In LSES-III, this trend was solely a function of
changes in the historically effective school caused by the closure of a
local industrial plant. With this plant's closure, many of the more affluent parents left the area, thus lowering the school's SES characteristics.
In LSES-IV, the historically ineffective school was attracting a student
clientele higher in SES status than had been the case earlier. The school

had added a new building through the passage of a local tax referendum, developed a more active parent teacher association (PTA), hired a staff member to coordinate the school's academic programs, and seen its standardized test results rise over time. All of these changes had a positive impact on the school's image, thus increasing the influx of students from higher-SES families.

For Pair 6, the instability in mothers' education data for the historically effective school continued through LSES–IV. Again, observers noted that the schools seemed well matched on SES characteristics. Nevertheless, such unstable data could potentially cause problems for regression analyses predicting scores on standardized tests.

Due to the demographic changes in Pairs 2 and 7, the historically ineffective schools had higher scores on the measure of mothers' education over the 2-year period 1988–90: The mean for the historically ineffective schools was 3.35, while for the historically effective schools it was 3.15. Two other trends in SES characteristic of the set of schools should be noted from 1983–85 to 1988–90: Overall, mothers' educational level increased, and the percentage of nonwhite students in the sample increased. Both trends reflect statewide changes in the student population.

Criterion-Referenced Test Results

The state changed the CRT it administered from the time of LSES–III to LSES–IV. Thus, we have no data in LSES–IV on the tests that were used in the initial selection procedure. The scores in Table 5.12 are on a different scale from those presented in Tables 5.1 and 5.2. The new state CRT (the LEAP test) was designed to test a broader range of curriculum objectives than those tested in the original BST. Consequently, the scores in Table 5.12 are lower than those reported in Tables 5.1 and 5.2. The cutoff score for passing the CRT was 47 for language arts and 53 for mathematics in 1989–90.

Of the eight pairs, five produced results consistent with their original classification. For Pairs 1, 3, 5, 6, and 8, the historically effective school outscored the historically ineffective school on the new CRT. Of the three pairs in which there were reversals, two pairs (Pairs 2 and 7) had experienced significant SES changes since LSES–III. In both cases, the higher scores by the historically ineffective school were at least partially due to SES changes.

For Pair 4, however, the reversal was not due to SES changes because the schools stayed well matched. These CRT changes reflect changes in teacher behaviors noted in Tables 5.9 and 5.10 for Pair 4. There was a large increase in both student and teacher performance at

TABLE 5.12. Criterion-Referenced Test Data (LEAP) for LSES-IV Schools, 1988–90

Outlier		1988–89 Scores		1989-90 Scores		Composite Across Years and Tests
Num.	Status	Language Arts	Math	Language Arts	Math	
1	Negative	57.7	64.7	56.6	64.1	60.8
	Positive	58.2	68.6	62.0	69.2	64.5
2	Negative	64.0	67.5	61.2	64.6	64.3
	Positive	55.0	64.6	61.0	71.0	62.9
3	Negative	57.9	65.3	62.9	69.1	63.8
	Positive	58.5	68.4	61.8	67.5	64.1
4	Negative	54.7	64.2	56.9	64.2	60.0
	Positive	54.8	64.1	51.3	59.0	57.3
5	Negative	52.0	63.4	54.5	64.2	58.5
	Positive	57.9	73.9	58.7	71.1	65.4
6	Negative	54.9	60.0	54.7	61.6	57.8
	Positive	62.9	72.3	60.4	70.4	66.5
7	Negative	59.3	69.9	64.9	73.8	67.0
	Positive	53.1	70.2	58.6	64.2	61.5
8	Negative	54.1	62.0	59.9	67.2	60.8
	Positive	56.1	63.2	60.2	64.1	60.9
OUTLIER MEANS						
	Negative	56.8	64.6	59.0	66.1	61.6
	Positive	57.1	68.2	59.3	67.1	62.9

the historically ineffective Pair 4 school. Details about these changes will be given in Chapter 8.

As noted in Table 5.12, the historically effective schools collectively outscored the historically ineffective schools on CRTs in 1988–90. While these data provide some evidence for the stability of school effectiveness processes over time, there is also evidence for school change in Pairs 2, 4, and 7.

Norm-Referenced Test Results

The same NRT was administered in the fall and spring semesters of 1989–90. As noted in Table 5.13, the historically ineffective schools slightly outscored the historically effective schools at both testings. This

TABLE 5.13. Norm-Referenced Test Data for LSES-IV, 1989–90

| Outlier | | Raw Scores | | Gain |
Num.	Status	Fall	Spring	Index (%)
1	Negative	21.6	27.3	26.6
	Positive	26.5	32.0	33.4
2	Negative	27.7	31.6	25.4
	Positive	23.9	29.2	27.5
3	Negative	26.5	32.1	34.3
	Positive	25.2	29.5	24.2
4	Negative	18.6	25.9	30.0
	Positive	21.4	25.2	17.3
5	Negative	20.7	26.4	25.6
	Positive	21.7	27.9	29.1
6	Negative	22.4	24.9	11.9
	Positive	17.6	25.2	29.8
7	Negative	28.5	34.2	51.7
	Positive	22.2	28.7	31.3
8	Negative	27.9	30.2	15.3
	Positive	26.0	30.6	27.1
OUTLIER MEANS				
	Negative	24.2	29.1	27.6
	Positive	23.1	28.5	27.5
OUTLIER MEANS WITHOUT PAIRS 2 & 7				
	Negative	23.0	27.8	24.0
	Positive	23.1	28.4	26.8

Note. The norm-referenced test data are from the research version of the 3R's *Test, Level Nine* (Riverside, 1983). There were a total of 43 items on the text. The gain index is computed by dividing the gain score from fall to spring by the number of items missed in the fall testing.

was partially due to the historically ineffective schools having higher overall SES ratings than the historically effective schools. As indicated in Table 5.11, this was particularly the case for Pairs 2 and 7. If these pairs were eliminated from the analysis, then the historically effective schools slightly outscored the historically ineffective schools during both fall and spring semesters.

One way to control for differences in SES ratings between schools is to perform regression analyses in which achievement scores are predicted by those variables. Table 5.14 presents the predicted scores and residual scores for two such analyses in which spring NRT data were predicted from mothers' education, student ethnicity, and fall NRT data. One regression analysis included Pair 6, which had unstable mothers' education data, while the other analysis excluded it.

In both analyses the historically ineffective schools were predicted to outscore the historically effective schools because as a group by LSES–

TABLE 5.14. Results from Regression Analyses Predicting NRT Results, Spring 1990

Outlier		All Schools			Minus Pair 6		
No. Status		Predicted	Residual	Diff. in Resid.	Predicted	Residual	Diff. in Resid
1 Negative		27.2	0.1		27.6	-0.3	
Positive		30.1	1.9	1.8	30.5	1.5	1.8
2 Negative		31.2	0.4		31.9	− 0.3	
Positive		28.6	0.6	0.2	29.0	0.2	0.5
3 Negative		31.5	0.6		31.4	0.7	
Positive		30.5	− 1.0	− 1.6	30.5	− 1.0	− 1.7
4 Negative		25.1	0.8		25.0	0.9	
Positive		26.7	− 1.5	− 2.3	26.9	− 1.7	− 2.6
5 Negative		26.5	− 0.1		26.6	− 0.2	
Positive		27.0	0.9	1.0	27.2	0.7	0.9
6 Negative		27.2	− 2.3		NA	NA	
Positive		24.5	0.7	3.0	NA	NA	NA
7 Negative		33.0	1.2		33.0	1.2	
Positive		28.5	0.2	− 1.0	28.2	0.5	− 0.7
8 Negative		31.8	− 1.6		31.8	− 1.6	
Positive		31.5	− 0.9	0.7	31.2	− 0.6	1.0
Outlier Means							
Negative		29.2	− 0.9		29.6	0.4	
Positive		28.4	0.9	NA	29.1	− 0.4	NA

Note: The spring predicted scores and residual scores were derived from a regression analysis using mothers' education, ethnicity, and fall NRT scores. The difference in residuals were calculated by subtracting the negative outliers' scores from the positive outliers' scores. A positive difference indicates that the positive outlier had a more positive residual than the negative outlier.

IV they had on average slightly higher SES scores. When Pair 6 is left in the regression analysis, the historically effective schools had a collective positive residual (0.9), indicating that they scored above expectation. When Pair 6 is excluded, the residual scores for the two sets of schools are close to zero (0.4 versus −0.4).

The most important comparisons in Table 5.14 are between schools in pairs. The residual difference score indicates the difference between the historically effective and ineffective schools in terms of how they scored compared with how they were expected to score. A positive difference indicates that the historically effective school was doing better relative to expectation than the historically ineffective school. Five historically effective schools were scoring better than their historically ineffective match (Pairs 1, 2, 5, 6, and 8). For three other pairs (Pairs 3, 4, and 7), there was a reversal—that is, the historically ineffective school did better on the NRT than its historically effective match.

Hierarchical Dimensions of School Effectiveness

A new instrument, the 12 HD, was completed by all observers in LSES–IV. It consisted of observers' ratings of school-, classroom-, and student-level dimensions, which had been found in LSES–III to be relevant to discriminating between higher- and lower-achieving schools (Stringfield & Teddlie, 1991a). Observers' ratings on the scale are shown in Table 5.15.

Altogether, the historically effective schools slightly outscored the historically ineffective schools on the 12 HD. If Pair 6 is eliminated from the analysis, as it has been in earlier comparisons, the overall difference between historically effective and ineffective schools increases.

The most important comparisons are between pairs of schools, since the rest of this chapter and the next three chapters focus on evidence for stability and change in these matched pairs. These data argue for some stability and some fairly dramatic changes, as can be seen in Table 5.15. Pairs 1, 3, and 8 are stable outliers on this indicator. Data from Pairs 2 and 4 indicate reversals, with the historically ineffective school outscoring the historically effective school. Pairs 5 and 7 have scores so close that no difference is apparent.

The changes in Pairs 2 and 4 have already been discussed: The historically ineffective school in Pair 2 improved due to changes in student body and school philosophy, while the historically ineffective school in Pair 4 improved dramatically due to a new principal. Data from the 12 HDs will be discussed in a later section of this chapter, which will compare all pairs of schools across all indicators.

**TABLE 5.15. School Scores on Hierarchical Dimensions
of School Effectiveness, LSES-IV**

Number	Outlier Status	School	Teacher	Student	Total Score
1	Negative	15.5	5.9	3.4	24.8
	Positive	47.1	16.4	10.2	73.7
2	Negative	39.6	11.5	8.3	59.4
	Positive	31.1	10.8	7.6	49.5
3	Negative	22.9	8.9	7.1	38.9
	Positive	39.1	10.6	11.9	61.6
4	Negative	37.8	10.5	8.3	56.6
	Positive	27.4	7.9	5.8	41.1
5	Negative	50.1	14.3	10.4	74.8
	Positive	46.8	13.8	11.2	71.8
6	Negative	31.0	7.5	7.7	46.2
	Positive	18.9	7.7	5.0	31.6
7	Negative	26.4	9.1	7.1	42.6
	Positive	29.8	9.8	5.2	44.8
8	Negative	19.5	7.5	6.6	33.6
	Positive	23.2	8.6	7.0	38.8

Note: A total of 91 points was possible on this scale (56 on school dimensions, 21 on teacher dimensions, and 14 on student dimensions). There were a total of 13 indicators with a range from 1 (very ineffective) to 7 (very effective) for each item. Eight different observers were involved in the compilation of these ratings. Individual observers' scores were standardized to the overall group mean for all items.

Changes in School Personnel

While changes in student body SES have had effects on the schools, changes in personnel have also had an impact. As noted in Table 15.16, half of the principals and 49% of the teaching faculty changed between LSES–III and LSES–IV. These changes could have propelled the schools toward greater or lesser effectiveness.

Of the four principalship changes in historically ineffective schools, two changes (Pairs 2 and 4) had a direct positive impact on the school, while the other two changes (Pairs 1 and 6) had negligible effects. Of the four principalship changes in historically effective schools, two were

TABLE 5.16. Changes in School Personnel from LSES-III to LSES-IV

Outlier		Principal	Teaching Faculty	3rd-Grade Teachers
Num.	Status	Change	Retained (%)	Retained (%)
1	Negative	Yes	50	0
	Positive	No	72	100
2	Negative	Yes	42	50
	Positive	No	50	100
3	Negative	No	55	50
	Positive	Yes	57	75
4	Negative	Yes	52	0
	Positive	No	70	50
5	Negative	No	41	67
	Positive	No	50	100
6	Negative	Yes	52	33
	Positive	Yes	43	100
7	Negative	No	81	100
	Positive	Yes	47	100
8	Negative	No	40	33
	Positive	Yes	28	33
OUTLIER MEANS				
	Negative	50	50	41
	Positive	50	53	77

Note: Regular teachers include all teachers in grades K–6. No special education, Chapter One, or other ancillary teachers are included in this count. The total percentage retained for positive and negative outliers is weighted by the number of observations in each school. Percentage of the thrid-grade teachers retained refers to those still teaching at that grade level.

associated with declining performance (Pairs 3 and 7), although the decline at Pair 7 may have been more a function of changes in the student body.

Interestingly, about 77% of the third-grade teachers in historically effective schools remained at their schools, while only 41% of third-grade teachers remained at historically ineffective schools. Since a large percentage of the classroom observations were at the third-grade level, this may partially explain the persistence of positive teaching effects in historically effective schools, as illustrated in Table 5.9.

Also, if Pair 7 (where the historically ineffective school had high retention) were eliminated from the analysis, the historically effective faculties would have a 54% retention rate, as compared with only 48% for the historically ineffective schools. It should be noted that an overall teacher retention rate of slightly over 50% after a 6-year period is similar to that reported in many other studies (see Willett & Singer, 1991).

The highest retention rate for overall teaching faculty was in the Pair 7 historically ineffective school. As noted earlier, several positive events occurred during the period between LSES–III and –IV at this school, resulting in increased student performance and better morale among the faculty. While the principal stayed the same, he had hired a curriculum coordinator who made several positive changes. This school is a good example of leadership emerging from sources other than the principal—in this case, from the interaction of a new curriculum coordinator and a stable faculty.

The second most stable faculty was the Pair 1 historically effective school. This faculty was probably the most cohesive in the entire study, as will be illustrated in Chapter 7. The principal at this school allowed her teachers much control in the organizational decision-making process. Thus, leadership at the school was jointly shared by faculty and principal.

At the other end of the spectrum, there was great turnover at both Pair 8 schools. At the historically effective school, the former principal died, triggering a large staff turnover. The school was struggling to maintain its effectiveness status. At the Pair 8 historically ineffective school, the school moved to a modern new facility and 60% of the faculty changed. The new facility and faculty did not result in positive school changes—the school was still as chaotic in LSES–IV as it had been in LSES–III.

At the historically ineffective Pair 4 school, a dynamic new principal had completely changed the third-grade teachers through transfers and retirements. The new third-grade teacher group displayed better teaching behaviors, as illustrated in Tables 5.9 and 5.10, resulting in positive changes in student achievement.

One final interesting trend in the data from Table 5.16 concerns faculty retention when the principalship changes. For faculties in which the principal changed from LSES–III to –IV, only 47% of the teaching faculty stayed. In schools where the principalship stayed the same, over 56% of the faculty remained.

Student Absenteeism over Time

Several authors have argued that school effects outcomes should not be limited to achievement on CRTs and NRTs. Student attendance is often mentioned as another plausible outcome measure. Data on student attendance from both LSES–III and –IV are presented in Table 5.17.

Correlations between student absences and scores on NRTs and CRTs from both LSES–III and –IV were positive, but rather small. The correlation between student absences and the indicated scores is as follows:

1. NRT scores from LSES–III: .13
2. CRT language arts scores from LSES–III: .28
3. NRT scores from LSES–IV: .21
4. CRT language arts scores from LSES–IV: .08

A problem with using student absences meaned at the school level as a school effects outcome is lack of variance. As indicated in Table 5.17, the range of scores for absences in LSES–III was only 2.6% (94.3%

TABLE 5.17. Percentage and Change in Student Attendance, LSES-III and LSES-IV

	Outlier	Percentage of Students in Attendance		Change in Student
Num.	Status	LSES–III	LSES–IV	Attendance
1	Negative	96.5	96.0	− 0.5
	Positive	94.8	96.4	+ 1.6
2	Negative	96.8	97.7	+ 0.9
	Positive	94.8	96.5	+ 1.7
3	Negative	96.0	95.8	− 0.2
	Positive	96.0	96.7	+ 0.7
4	Negative	96.1	98.0	+ 1.9
	Positive	96.6	96.5	− 0.1
5	Negative	96.8	96.7	− 0.1
	Positive	96.4	98.4	+ 2.0
6	Negative	94.3	92.1	− 2.2
	Positive	NA	94.0	NA
7	Negative	96.9	95.9	− 1.0
	Positive	95.3	96.4	+ 1.1
8	Negative	95.0	94.8	− 0.2
	Positive	94.4	95.8	+ 1.4

Note. Percentage of students in attendance is average daily attendance divided by average daily membership.

to 96.9%), while in LSES–IV it was 4.4% (from 94.0% to 98.4%). A better longitudinal measure of student absences may be change over time, in this case operationally defined as the difference between student absences in 1989–90 as opposed to 1984–85.

One interesting aspect of this difference index is that it is a good indicator of change in overall school effectiveness status. The change in student absences over time coincided with the overall school effectiveness typology described in Table 5.18 in 67% of the cases (10 out of 15 schools for which data were available).

A PAIRWISE COMPARISON OF SCHOOLS AT LSES–IV

All LSES–IV data are summarized in Table 5.18 in order to determine where school stability and change occurred. Comparisons in this table are between schools in a pair, since the schools were initially matched that way. The data present evidence for both stability and change over time.

1. Two pairs were stable matches over time (Pairs 1 and 8).
2. Pair 6 had never had a truly effective school, and both schools appeared to be stable ineffective schools over time.
3. Pair 5 changed slightly as the historically effective school maintained its status and the historically ineffective school improved.
4. Pair 2 was no longer well matched on SES, and both schools seemed to be relatively effective with their diverse student bodies.
5. Three pairs changed considerably, with the historically effective school declining and the historically ineffective school improving (Pairs 3, 4, and 7).

It was difficult to place schools in effectiveness categories by using multiple indicators. Our results agree with those of Mortimore and colleagues (1988a), who found inconsistencies across multiple indicators of school effectiveness.

Evidence for Stability over Time

The two stable effective/ineffective matches, the stable ineffective pair, and the pair that changed slightly (Pair 5) will be discussed in this section. The Pair 1 schools were probably the most stable over time in the study. The historically effective school outscored its matched school

TABLE 5.18. Pairwise Comparison of Historically Effective (HES)
and Ineffective (HIS) Schools at LSES-IV

School Pairs	Classification Across Time	Socioeconomic Status of Students	Stability of Faculty	Criterion-Referenced Tests
1	HIS = stable HES = stable	Still well matched	HES more stable than HIS	HES much better than HIS
2	HIS = improving HES = stable	HIS has higher SES than HES	HES more stable than HIS	HIS slightly better overall, but HES much better in one subject area
3	HIS = improving HES = declining	Still well matched, but HES has more foreign students	HES changed principal; staff stability the same	Very close scores
4	HIS = improving HES = declining	Still well matched	HIS changed principal and much of faculty; HES stayed stable	HIS better than HES
5	HIS = improving HES = stable	Still well matched	Both equally stable	HES much better than HIS
6	HIS = stable HES = stable ineffective	Appears well matched, but data problems at HES	Both changed principals and much of staff	HES better than HIS
7	HIS = improving HES = declining	HIS has much higher SES than HES	HIS much more stable; HES changed principal and faculty	HIS much better than HES
8	HIS = stable HES = stable	Still well matched	HES changed principal and much of staff; HIS more stable	Very close scores, with HES scoring better on more subtests
Source	All tables	Table 5.11	Table 5.16	Table 5.12

Norm-Referenced Tests	Change in Student Attendance	High-Inference Teaching Behavior	Time-on-Task	Hierarchical Dimensions of Schooling
HES much better than HIS	HES = improved HIS = declined	HES better than HIS	HES much better than HIS	HES much better than HIS
HIS better on raw scores; HES better on residual scores	Both improved	HES better than HIS	Very close scores, with HES declining slightly from LSES-III	HES better than HIS
HIS better than HES	HES = improved HIS = declined	HES better than HIS	Very close scores; both improved from LSES-III	HES better than HIS
HIS better than HES	HES = declined HIS = improved	HIS greatly improved and better than HES	HIS better than HES	HIS better than HES
HES better than HIS	HES = improved HIS = declined	HES slightly better than HIS	HIS better than HES	Very close scores
Very close scores, especially at spring testing	HES = not available HIS = declined	HIS better than HES	Very close scores	HIS better than HES, but both scores low
HIS much better than HES	HES = improved HIS = declined	Very close scores	HES slightly better than HIS	Very close scores
Very close raw scores; HES much better on gain and residual scores	HES = improved HIS = declined	HES better than HIS	HES slightly better than HIS	HES better than HIS, but both scores low
Tabs. 5.13 & 14	Table 5.17	Table 5.9	Table 5.10	Table 5.15

on every dimension in Table 5.18. This is especially noteworthy inasmuch as the two schools were well matched on SES characteristics and were quite close geographically. The historically effective school staff was one of the most stable in the study and was given much autonomy in running classes and the school. Despite serving a student body that was becoming less affluent, the staff's teaching behaviors and the resultant test scores stayed high over time. The historically ineffective school had low scores on teacher behavior and student achievement in LSES-IV despite a change in principalship and school policies. Chapter 7 contains case studies of these two schools.

The Pair 8 schools were also a stable pair, with the historically effective school outscoring the historically ineffective school on all dimensions. The difference was larger on process variables (VTBI, time-on-task, 12 HD) and less pronounced on product variables (CRT, NRT). There were considerable changes at both these rural schools: The historically effective school's principal died, and there was a large staff turnover; the ineffective school moved to a new site and also had considerable staff turnover. The persistence of teaching differences at these schools despite staff turnover indicates the long-lasting effects of teacher socialization (see Chapter 11).

The Pair 6 schools also showed stability, although those schools have been designated a pair of matched ineffective schools. The school designated as historically effective was a false positive (Stringfield & Teddlie, 1990), probably due to testing irregularities on the CRTs. Both schools serve students from the inner-city core of a metropolitan area. They had the lowest measures of all the 16 schools on both the high-inference and low-inference teaching indicators in LSES-IV. These two schools also scored the lowest of all the schools on the spring NRT. The environments of both schools were described as chaotic by observers. Even though both schools experienced principalship changes, neither of the new principals was able to change the schools.

The schools in Pair 5 were a well-matched, rural set with fairly stable faculties. The historically effective school clearly outdistanced its matched school on student achievement, especially on the CRTs. The process data in the classrooms were more mixed, with the historically effective school doing better on high-inference measures and the historically ineffective school better on low-inference measures. The principal at the historically ineffective school, who had just arrived at the time of LSES-III 5 years earlier, instituted some school-level changes that resulted in improvement, especially in time-on-task. Also, the only third-grade teacher at the historically effective school was on sick leave during much of LSES-IV, and her class was taught by a substitute, thus decreasing time-on-task. Chapter 6 contains case studies of this pair of schools.

Evidence for Change over Time

Of the four pairs that demonstrated less stability (Pairs 2, 3, 4, and 7), there was evidence of student, faculty, and leadership change. For Pairs 2 and 7, there was change in student SES accompanied by staff adaptation. For Pairs 3 and 4, the most obvious change involved school leadership.

The schools in Pair 2 seemed to be serving different student bodies at LSES–IV. Both were extended-day schools and drew their students from wide geographic areas: The historically ineffective school served the children of commuters to a downtown government/business complex, while the historically effective school was in a cluster of schools grouped together for integration purposes. The combined VTBI scores for these two schools were higher than those for any other pair, thus indicating that excellent teaching was occurring. For the historically effective school, this was at least partially due to stability of the staff, which had the same principal and 50% of its faculty. For the historically ineffective school, a new principal adapted the school's philosophy to more adequately serve the children of downtown commuters. This school's academic program was probably the most broad-based in the study, and this translated into higher achievement.

For Pair 3, the two schools stayed relatively well matched on SES variables, although the historically effective school was serving a larger foreign student population. While the historically effective school had previously revelled in its ability to integrate such students into the mainstream, observers heard many faculty complaints during LSES–IV about having to serve such a diverse clientele. The current principal had just taken over in the spring semester of LSES–III, following a dynamic principal who had been largely responsible for the school's success. Although a hardworking, competent individual, the current principal lacked the vision and leadership ability of the previous principal. Hence, the historically effective school deteriorated on several dimensions from LSES–III to –IV. The historically ineffective school, on the other hand, improved slightly over time on indices such as time-on-task. These changes seemed to be characteristic of what has been called "technological improvements" (Stringfield & Teddlie, 1990) that might improve test scores, but would not dramatically change the social psychological climate in the school or classroom.

For Pair 4, there were dramatic positive changes at the historically ineffective school, plus some deterioration at the historically effective school. Neither of these changes could be attributed to changes in the student bodies, which stayed stable over time. A new principal at the historically ineffective school made a series of changes at that school, including enforcing the school schedule, appointing teacher leaders at each grade level, developing a codified set of school rules and procedures, and departmentalizing instruction at each grade level. All these changes resulted in better classroom teaching and student achievement during LSES-IV. The historically effective school, on the other hand, appeared to be a victim of entropy, to use a term employed in the TSEL (Slater & Teddlie, in press).

According to this principle, it is easier for a successful school to deteriorate than to improve or stay the same, and it takes some effort for an effective school to stay that way. Observers of the historically effective Pair 4 school described a school that was "stuck" (Rosenholtz, 1989), one that was content with the status quo and not changing. For instance, the principal was not knowledgeable about the specific teaching weaknesses of his faculty and therefore allowed them to persist. More detail on these two schools will be found in Chapter 8.

There were also changes at the Pair 7 schools, and SES fluctuations appeared to account for some of them. In LSES-III, it was apparent that the historically effective school was attracting a lower-SES clientele due to an industrial plant closure. As a result, the principal and much of her staff left. The new principal was working diligently with the faculty during LSES-IV, as indicated by high time-on-task scores, but the achievement deterioration over time was still apparent.

At the historically ineffective school, several positive changes occurred, as described above. The new building, more active PTA, and new curriculum coordinator all contributed to positive change. The school leadership was composed of the curriculum coordinator and the staff, which had an 81% retention rate. The historically ineffective school was a "moving" school (Rosenholtz, 1989) with definite academic goals that led to higher achievement.

SUMMARY OF RESULTS

There are several salient findings across this 8-year study of school effects at eight matched pairs of schools.

1. There was considerable evidence for the persistence of school effects during LSES-III, which was conducted in the year following the 2-year period when pilot data were gathered. Thus, schools appeared to be consistently categorized in terms of their effectiveness across an initial 3-year period.
2. Teaching behaviors at the schools during LSES-III were consistent

with school effects; that is, there was evidence of more effective teaching at more effective schools, and less effective teaching at less effective schools. This was more apparent on high-inference indicators of teaching effectiveness than on low-inference measurements.

3. Results from NRTs were somewhat, but not totally, consistent with those from CRTs at the time of LSES–III. Due to significant positive demographic changes in the historically ineffective schools, regression analyses were run that resulted in residual scores more consistent with initial classification data than were the NRT raw scores.

4. Testing irregularities at one school resulted in a false positive. For this case, we concluded that we had a matched pair of ineffective schools.

5. There was evidence for the persistence of teaching effects at the time of LSES–IV on high-inference indicators. This was due, at least partially, to the 77% teacher retention rate at the third-grade level of effective schools.

6. There was evidence for the persistence of school effects through LSES–IV at four pairs of schools: three pairs consisting of effective and ineffective schools and one consisting of a matched pair of ineffective schools. At one pair, the historically ineffective school was slightly improved.

7. There was evidence for considerable change at the other matched pairs of schools. At these four historically ineffective schools, there was evidence of naturally occurring school improvement. At three of the historically effective schools, there was evidence of deterioration, although changes at one of those three schools seemed linked directly to SES changes.

8. It is important to note that in every LSES–III and –IV case in which significant achievement changes occurred, there was also a change in either contextual variables or clear changes in school processes.

9. Three of the five schools that were improving during LSES–IV (historically ineffective schools in Pairs 2, 3, and 5) had been identified as experiencing naturally occurring school improvement at the time of LSES–III (Stringfield & Teddlie, 1990).

10. A typology of schools in four categories emerged from these analyses over time. Four schools were stable more effective (Pairs 1, 2, 5, and 8 historically effective schools), while four were stable less effective (Pairs 1, 6, and 8 historically ineffective schools, plus the misclassified Pair 6 effective school, which was actually an ineffective school). Five schools were improving (Pairs 2, 3, 4, 5, and 7 historically ineffective schools), while three were declining (Pairs 3, 4, and

7 historically effective schools). This typology will be used in Chapter 9, in which the principals' roles in the stable and changing schools is discussed. Overall average scores on the 12 HD instrument confirm the typology, with stable more effective schools scoring highest (58.5), improving next best (54.5), declining next best (49.2), and stable less effective schools worst (43.1).

LSES-III and -IV employed the case history approach and looked at both effective and ineffective schools over time. The overall results regarding stability were mixed. Over the short term (3 years, 1982–85), there were stable school effects. Over a longer term (8 years, 1982–90), half of the schools retained their effectiveness status, while half changed.

The importance of the roles of principals, teachers, and students over time is well illustrated in this chapter. Half of the schools changed principals, and in many cases (e.g., Pair 4 historically ineffective school) this resulted in dramatic changes in teacher behavior and student achievement. There was also considerable faculty change, with only 52% of the teachers still at their original schools at the time of LSES-IV.

The importance of the student body is also borne out in this study. Lower-SES students are often not as academically ready as higher-SES students. Therefore, at some schools (e.g., Pair 7 historically effective school), a decline in the SES level of the student body may have contributed to a deterioration in school effectiveness indices. It is at this point that effective principals and staff (e.g., Pair 1 historically effective school) adjust their approach to maintain school excellence.

Chapters 6–8 present extended case histories of some of the schools studied in LSES-III and -IV. These case histories serve as a counterpoint to the extensive quantitative data presented in this chapter. Many authors (e.g., Patton, 1990) have called for triangulation of information sources, or the reconciliation of qualitative and quantitative data. In a discussion of observers' abilities to predict schools' outlier status based on LSES-III information, we (Stringfield & Teddlie, 1989, 1991a) concluded that qualitative observations confirmed results of outlier status based on regression analyses. Chapters 6–8 present qualitative data, based on observations and interviews, that confirm many of the quantitative results presented in this chapter.

6 A Longitudinal Study of a Pair of Rural Schools

In this chapter, case studies are presented on a pair of rural schools at two points in time (1984–85, 1989–90). Chapters 7 and 8 present case studies on a pair of suburban and a pair of urban schools, respectively, for the same time period. Each case study will be broken down by years and subdivided into four areas—school context and indicators of effectiveness, principal, teachers, and life in the school. Each chapter will close with a comparison of the two schools over time.[1] In reviewing the case studies of rural, suburban, and urban schools, the reader is urged to draw comparisons among schools from different urbanicity and SES contexts (Teddlie & Stringfield, 1992; see also Lightfoot, 1983, for portraits of urban, suburban, and elite schools).

There are few areas in which Alan DeYoung's (1987) observation that "the history of American education has been primarily an urban history" (p. 123) is more clearly relevant than in school effects research. Of the major correlational school effects studies conducted in English-speaking countries, two were conducted by the ILEA (Rutter et al., 1979; Mortimore et al., 1988a). A third, conducted in Michigan, offered separate samples and analyses for urban schools, but none for rural schools (Brookover et al., 1979). Also, the best-documented school improvement studies—Milwaukee's Project RISE (McCormack-Larkin & Kritek, 1982), New York City's C-SIP (McCarthy, Canner, & Pershing, 1983), and the San Diego County School Effectiveness Project (Chrispeels & Pollack, 1989)—have all taken place in urban contexts.

Perhaps the paucity of rural school effects studies explains why surveys of rural educators have repeatedly identified rural school effects at or near the top of rural educational research needs (e.g., Nachtigal, 1982; Hubel & Baker, 1986). Systematic studies of rural school effects (i.e., studies that nest classroom observations within a school effects

---

1. The schools in the case studies are referred to by pseudonyms. In order to further protect identities of individuals at these schools, some information about their personal characteristics (such as sex, age, and ethnicity) has been changed.

framework) would be even more expensive and time-consuming than their urban counterparts. It is not surprising that studies that meld systematic school-, classroom-, and student-level data gathering and analysis in rural contexts have materialized slowly.

The pair of rural schools described in this chapter (Pair 5 in the preceding chapter) is located in one of Louisiana's most economically disadvantaged districts. The first school, Theodore Roosevelt Elementary, served a predominantly minority, highly economically disadvantaged community. Roosevelt's history was one of poor academic achievement. Over the years of LSES, Roosevelt's students made significant academic advances. Those changes began during LSES–III and were fully visible in LSES–IV. Unlike Roosevelt, the second of the pair of schools, Harry Truman Elementary, entered LSES–III with a several-year history of relatively high performance on state achievement tests. Truman continued that record through LSES–IV, scoring well on both the state tests and the LSES-administered tests.

THEODORE ROOSEVELT ELEMENTARY SCHOOL, 1984–85

School Context and Indicators of Effectiveness

Roosevelt stood on a gentle rise at the edge of a small town. Outside the front door was a flagpole and beyond that a fallow field. A large playground, most notable for its lack of play equipment, was behind the school building. Beyond a fence at the back of the play area stood the regional fire departments' training facility. The school building was a low-budget, 1950s single-story structure. In the rear, and off to one side, stood "temporary" buildings, which appeared to be more than 10 years old. The school served about 400 K–6 students, and its classrooms were small, crowded, and dark. Roosevelt bore the stark look of a dirt-poor southern elementary school and is described in the tables in Chapter 5 as "Negative 5."

Table 5.1 indicates that for the 2 years preceding LSES–III, the school had scored below prediction on the state BST. On the NRT, Roosevelt third graders scored among the lowest (see Table 5.8).

Principal

In 1984, Theodore Roosevelt Elementary had a new principal. Mr. Green was a soft-spoken man with a reputation for toughness. For several years he had been assistant principal at a local secondary school.

When the superintendency became available, several influential community members asked him to apply. A man in his thirties, he decided instead to take the Roosevelt principalship.

Roosevelt had no library but did receive an allotment of elementary school library books each year. Mr. Green described coming to Roosevelt his first day and finding the teachers' lounge virtually inaccessible due to boxes of books. He learned that the former principal had simply stored all incoming library books in the teachers' lounge, doing nothing to distribute them. Mr. Green's first action as principal was to distribute hundreds of library books to classrooms. A small library was created in each classroom; teachers were encouraged to trade books; students were encouraged to read widely. The literal and symbolic meanings of that first step were not lost on the teachers: A new day had dawned; academics, especially reading, were to be stressed.

A new discipline policy was implemented at Roosevelt. Laissez-faire was no more. The bell meant that all students should be working in their classrooms. The principal instructed the faculty to push forward academically. If a student did not achieve, he or she was called in for a talk with the principal. Students who made the principal's newly installed honor roll found their names printed on a bulletin board outside the school office and listed in the local newspaper.

Teachers

Two separate research teams observed the implementation of the new principal's policies in the fall and spring and agreed with the majority of the teachers that the changes were improvements. Several teachers reported that for the first time in years their classes were going to complete their grade-level texts by the end of the school year.

The 1984–85 second- and third-grade teachers presented both areas of commonality and great diversity. The areas in which observers noted the greatest commonality across classrooms concerned discipline and time-on-task. Teachers reported that both areas were subjects of major emphasis by the principal.

The Roosevelt students displayed nearly model deportment. As can be seen in Table 5.5, teachers spent minimal time concerned with discipline. Several teachers reported that discipline had been a major problem in years past and that the reason for the change was the new policies and actions. The principal had made clear to teachers and students that "the teacher's job is to teach, and the student's job is to learn." Any student who interfered with these jobs was sent to the office. A student sent to the principal's office for disciplinary reasons could expect an opportunity to tell his or her side of the story, and a quick determination of responsibility. Assuming that the principal ruled in favor of the teacher, as was typically the case, the student could expect a stern lecture, clear and firm punishment, and if it was a repeated offense, a call to the student's parents. Parents were almost universally supportive of the school, and students often seemed more concerned about what would happen when they got home than with the principal's punishment. The result of this discipline policy was a remarkable lack of need to use it.

This simple technique would probably not have worked in several of the urban schools in the LSES. Table 5.5 indicates that the three schools with the least classroom time spent on discipline were all rural (Positive 5 and 8 and Negative 5). In urban areas parents are not likely to be uniformly supportive of their school's principal. But in this rural community, such shared support was a given, and the new Roosevelt principal quickly demonstrated skill at using that advantage.

The second common factor—and change from previous years—was also related to the principal's notion of "teachers' and students' work." The principal toured the school regularly, and when he visited a class he expected to see students at work. There were three immediate effects of this expectation. First, as can be seen in Table 5.5, LSES measures of students' time-on-task at Roosevelt were among the highest in the study. A second impact, reported by several teachers, was that most classes were on pace to finish their texts by the end of the year. This surprised teachers, many of whom had apparently never finished, for example, their math texts during the 9-month school year.

A third, less fortunate, outcome was the generation of huge numbers of ditto sheets. All teachers knew what to do: start class on time and keep the students at work. Many did not yet know how to simultaneously maintain discipline and facilitate the development of "higher order" skills. During LSES–IV, almost all of Roosevelt's students were engaged in great numbers of skill drills. In one class an observer counted eight ditto sheets passed out in a 2-hour period.

The newness of the changes can be seen clearly in Table 5.5. The excellent scores in discipline and time-on-task stand in sharp contrast with the teachers' much less impressive ratings in the areas of presentation of new content and teacher expectations. Teachers and students were working harder, but they were not yet skilled at "working smarter."

A second explanation for the relatively low ratings in presentation and expectations concerned the great variance among teachers in styles and techniques. Some teachers attempted to obtain high rates of student time-on-task without having to become active participants in the process. For such an effort to succeed, the teacher must provide an unending flow of "tasks" on which students can expend time. These became the greatest ditto-sheet-pusher teachers in the study. Other teachers increased their lecture rates or student reading assignments. The results, presented in Table 5.5, are large standard deviations on both presentation and expectations.

Life in the School

Most observers did not enjoy visiting Roosevelt during the 1984–85 school year. The principal's discipline code seemed very strict. The atmosphere was often oppressive, there wasn't a lot of exciting or innovative instruction to be seen, and the awkwardness of half-made change was all around. A few teachers talked about how much better things had been before (though others described the previous situation as near anarchy).

Students seemed to be adapting more rapidly. They came to school on time and in general worked hard in class. But there was not a lot of joy in the students, or the faculty, or, in fact, the principal.

The observers' sense was of a school that had made substantial progress, yet had a distance to go. Children were being put through their paces more than challenged. Similar to Lightfoot's (1983) description of George Washington Carver High School, the quantitative and qualitative data from Roosevelt documented a tightly run, improved school, but one without a vision for instructional excellence.

THEODORE ROOSEVELT ELEMENTARY SCHOOL, 1989–90

School Context and Indicators of Effectiveness

Revisiting Roosevelt proved a rewarding yet confusing task. The confusion derived from the fact that very little of the physical environment had changed. Smoke damage from a fire in the school kitchen resulted in a pleasant new coat of paint for the cafeteria and office, but otherwise the physical plant, and the arrangement of most adults within it, was identical. The same flagpole stood unadorned in the front yard, and the playground remained dusty. There was still no library. School lunches remained excellent. The Chapter 1 and special education programs were housed in the same "temporary" buildings. The same principal continued to work earnestly with his faculty and students. Two of the three third-grade teachers taught in the same rooms. Yet Roosevelt was a different place.

In 1990, the teachers *assumed* that virtually all students would finish their texts. Several complained that the district curriculum coordinators sometimes "hold the teachers back" from moving as rapidly as they felt some students were capable of progressing. Teachers asked students more questions; fewer ditto sheets were seen. In many classes, time was set aside for sustained silent reading. During schoolwide reading days, students, parents, and community members read books together.

Table 5.11 indicates that Roosevelt continued to serve one of the least educationally advantaged communities in the study. Roosevelt also provided services to one of the most predominantly African-American student bodies in LSES–IV. However, as Table 5.14 indicates, by the 1989–90 school year, Roosevelt third graders were scoring very near their predicted achievement levels on the LSES-administered achievement test. This indicates that while Roosevelt was not becoming a "positive outlier," it was no longer a "negative outlier."

Principal

The principal at Roosevelt, Mr. Green, seemed to be one of the more stable features in the LSES. He remained cordial, intelligent, and energetic. If a student discipline matter came to his office, teachers, students, and parents could still count on his rock-solid firmness. He continued to demand seeing students and teachers "doing their jobs." He continued to believe in his school and in its central role in improving young people's lives.

However, many aspects of Mr. Green's job had changed. Half of the Roosevelt teachers in 1985 had retired or otherwise left the school (see Table 5.16). These included several of the least energetic and imaginative teachers, more than one of whom Mr. Green had encouraged to retire early. He had worked a variety of informal networks to find competent, energetic replacements. One result was that Mr. Green felt less need to closely monitor his staff.

Second, the district had made several curriculum changes. The two clearest effects were a lock-step movement through the curriculum and a recreational reading period. The result of the first was a uniformity of progress among teachers and students, geared toward mastery of "basic skills." The second resulted in something not seen 5 years earlier: students reading for the joy of it. Mr. Green endorsed both changes and did not report noting any conflict between them.

Third, the district's Chapter 1 office had instituted a series of reading and math tests. The math tests were administered six times a year. All Chapter 1 students took these tests, and remediation was retargeted quarterly. Most of the remediation took place in the classrooms, but a small computer laboratory was also available.

Reading and math test results were sent to both the teachers and the principal. The district office mandated that the principals initial each class-sheet. In Mr. Green's case, that requirement was unnecessary. He carefully monitored all outcome data. As in LSES-III, Mr. Green examined every child's report card.

Working in a district with modest resources, Roosevelt's classes had labored for years without many of the basic support resources that are usually taken for granted, such as encyclopedias. Not having a central library, the Roosevelt school had no single location at which students could do "research." Mr. Green responded to this by organizing a series of community fund-raising events. Over the 5 years between LSES-III and -IV, this resulted in every classroom having an encyclopedia set. The primary classes each had a set of Childcraft books. At Roosevelt, this was a major achievement.

Finally, in conjunction with the teachers, Mr. Green had decided that a tracking program would best meet student needs. In Grades 2–6, Roosevelt was operating on a departmental basis. Each grade had a reading teacher, a teacher who focused on math/spelling, and a third focusing on science/social studies.

Teachers

The first- and second-grade teachers presented a mixed picture. Two of the first-grade teachers were new to the field and were having problems that are not unusual to new teachers. During LSES observations we visited two first-grade lessons that ended before the allotted time was over. The lessons had gone well, but the inexperienced teachers did not have backup activities scheduled. While neither situation resulted from teacher sloth, both resulted in wasted time.

The second-grade teachers included one excellent teacher and two who were more typical. The excellent teacher used dolls, puppets, and a variety of books to interest students. She encouraged discussion and supplementary reading.

Two of the three third-grade teachers had worked at the school 5 years earlier. One was a first-year teacher in 1984–85. A member of the LSES team who observed her in 1985 noted that she was an energetic but not highly skilled novice. Five years later that teacher had become seasoned. Her classes were marked by high rates of questioning, lessons structured around questions, and thematic development of instructional units. Within the instructional system of the school, this teacher taught reading to all third graders. Her energetic presentations, combined with her openness to students' ideas and perceptions, made her reading hours pleasurable for both her students and the observers.

The second third-grade teacher was one of the school's senior teachers. She was late middle-aged and considerably overweight, and had limited energy. Her strength was in her clarity of presentation. She was widely traveled and skilled at relating personal experience to the topic of the lesson. Given that she taught social studies and science to all third graders, her discussions of her travels and her open curiosity regarding science worked to her students' advantage. The LSES team member who had observed this teacher 5 years earlier reported stability in her instructional style and energy level. The same observer noted that this teacher may have presented a positive example of a phenomenon he generally viewed negatively: primary grade departmentalization. In this case however, the restricted number of presentations appeared to allow the teacher to display her skills without overly burdening the students with the limitations of her energy for preparation and presentation of diverse content.

The third teacher taught math to all third graders. This was her first year in the public school system. She had taught in a private school for nearly 20 years, where she worked under two principals whom she viewed as possessing only marginal skills. She was a hardworking instructor, who seemed to fit into Roosevelt's departmentalized structure easily. Her classes moved forward smoothly, and students appeared to enjoy the challenges she posed.

As a group, the three third-grade teachers brought considerable strengths to their tasks. They treated their students with personal and intellectual respect. All three consistently assumed that children were independent thinkers whose primary tasks involved the construction of knowledge. All three acted with an awareness of the value of hard work. Their students were "on task" a relatively high percentage of the time.

The Roosevelt third-grade reading teacher was one of the few teachers in the study to experiment with "whole language" instruction. Five years before, the entire school had seemed driven to achieve order; during LSES-IV, teachers were able to assume order and devote energy to exploring new areas.

The upper grades contained several of the most senior, least instructionally focused teachers. Observers sat through several upper-grade lessons in which it appeared that the teachers were not prepared. Instruction was, at best, highly traditional. Teachers read directly from teachers' editions of texts, and students seemed aware that they were not being intellectually challenged. There were exceptions, but in general the earlier grades appeared to be the strength of the school.

Table 5.10 indicates that in spite of the often weak upper-grade classes, Roosevelt was obtaining rates of interactive teaching and total student time-on-task that were above average for the study.

Life in the School

The school had not solved all its problems. A small number of the faculty, including two of the most senior members, continued not to prepare for classes or to actively instruct; local youngsters continued to vandalize the outdoor basketball courts; and both teachers and students might have benefited from a revitalization of the curriculum if the district had allowed it. However, the battle for a fundamental academic mission at Roosevelt had been won.

HARRY TRUMAN ELEMENTARY SCHOOL, 1984–85

School Context and Indicators of Effectiveness

The road to Truman was not easily navigated. Leaving the small airport at the nearest small city, a prospective visitor followed an interstate highway for about 2 miles, a four-lane road for a mile, a two-lane, farm-to-market road for less than 2 miles, and a smaller farm-to-market road for 12 miles. The visitor then turned right at an unmarked intersection, turned left after 3 miles onto a smaller road, turned right after another 2 miles, and only then found himself or herself at the Truman community. Historically a small commercial area for local and tenant farmers, in the agribusiness age Truman consisted of a school, a few houses, a branch library, and a convenience store. A traveler who found Truman could not miss the elementary school. The large sign out front read, "Truman High School."

Truman was a 12-year school until the 1960s. It included a junior high, complete with football teams until 1986. The female football coach, who had an excellent win–loss record, was something of a local legend.

Truman's physical plant was old but comfortable. Designed to provide the full 12 years of education, the school included a dated but adequate library, a small gymnasium, and ample outdoor sports fields.

The main building was a one-story structure. Each classroom's 10-foot ceiling was met on the outside wall by tall inviting windows that ended only 3 feet from the floor. The old sashes were well counterbalanced and opened easily. The result was rooms that were well lit and cheerful despite not having been painted in years. The grounds were neatly maintained. During the 1984–85 year, the school had one teacher at each grade, K–8, plus special education and Chapter 1 services.

Truman is described in the tables in Chapter 5 as "Positive 5." Table 5.1 indicates that Truman had scored well above prediction on the state BST for each of the 2 years preceding the study. Table 5.2 indicates that Truman scored above its matched school in both math and language arts on the BST during the year of LSES–III. In Table 5.8, Truman's students demonstrated achievement levels on the NRT that, corrected for SES, were among the highest in the study.

Perhaps as important, Table 5.5 indicates that Truman classroom instruction was notable for the rarity of discipline problems and the uniform height of teacher expectations. Table 5.6 indicates that during LSES–III Truman students averaged over 85% academic time-on-task (interactive plus noninteractive time-on-task). This was the highest on-task rate in the study.

Principal

The principal, Mr. Smith, was a genial, late middle-aged educator, who had been raised in rural schools in a neighboring state. Unlike many male elementary principals of his generation, this principal's original college education had been in elementary education. He had taken five courses in teaching reading.

Mr. Smith was not a man who attempted to dominate conversations. Interviews with him were easy in the sense that conversations flowed naturally. However, obtaining detailed information required time and regular probes. In his quiet way, he expressed a long-standing commitment to public education ideals. It slowly became clear that the principal was knowledgeable about his community, school, students, *and* quality teaching. His geniality and seeming acceptance of a diversity of teaching styles had a firm bottom line. "I will not," Mr. Smith informed an LSES team member, "allow anyone to hurt one of our students."

In practice that meant teachers were required to perform their tasks in such ways that students demonstrated clear gains on both local and nationally normed tests. It also meant that when the principal walked down the school's halls, or visited classrooms, he expected to see teachers and students at work. Neither rule was written, but both were well understood.

If a teacher was having trouble with classroom discipline, or with teaching a particular reading concept, the principal would allow the teacher time to work out the problem without interference. If the problem was not resolved, he would quietly intervene. Intervention consisted of discussions, modeling by the principal and other staff, bringing in district curricular specialists, and, on rare occasions, the removal of a staff member. Mr. Smith always spoke softly, but neither teachers nor parents doubted his firm commitment to every young child's education.

Because he had been at Truman for over a decade, Mr. Smith had hired almost every teacher there. He knew their backgrounds and could discuss the particulars of each one's teaching style. Although slow to criticize any staff member, he could detail the strengths and instructional limitations of all teachers. The LSES team spent 3 days conducting classroom observations on each of four occasions at Truman. No data were gathered that stood at dramatic variance with Mr. Smith's informal assessments of teachers' strengths and limitations.

Teachers

The most striking features of the teaching at Truman concerned consistency, pacing, resources, and grouping. Each grade had one teacher, and each teacher taught one group. Teaching was uniformly "traditional" in the sense that students read, listened, responded, and completed individual assignments. Whole-group lecture and drill, followed by individual seatwork, was the rule at Truman. Observers saw no team research projects and no cooperative learning efforts. At the same time, the lack of differentiated grouping, combined with the unwavering expectation that all Truman's students would achieve at least the basic skills, resulted in all students getting the same quality instruction.

Throughout LSES-III and -IV, observers noted the role of Chapter 1 instruction in facilitating this one-lesson-for-all format. With a high percentage of students eligible for Chapter 1 services, the school had one full-time Chapter 1 teacher and several aides. During both years, this configuration allowed the school to target supplementary, small group, aide-led instruction to the students who were not "getting it." The Chapter 1 instruction was typically provided on an "in-class" basis, with the aide working with a small group on reading at the back of the class while the rest of the students worked on supplementary activities, or in a separate Chapter 1 classroom located in a portable building. Chapter 1 at Truman operated almost seamlessly with regular instruction. This coordination appeared to be the result of efforts by the principal and teachers to make the program sensible and valuable for the students.

Resources were notable by their absence. The district was among the poorest in one of the nation's least affluent states. Although the size of the library was adequate, the holdings appeared to include more publications from the 1930s through the 1950s than from the 1970s and 1980s. Newer book stamps indicated that the books had been purchased with federal funds. We saw very few paperback trade books and no whole class sets of novels. Without federal Chapter 1 and 2 funds, this school's set of instructional resources would have been extremely modest.

Except for fifth grade, instructional pacing could be described as "measured." No class ground to a halt, but no class moved at a rapid pace. A typical classroom scene would begin with a teacher introducing a lesson. This might take 2 minutes and would often include asking the students questions in an effort to raise interest. Then the teacher would hand out relevant books or workbooks, which would take 2 to 5 minutes. Students were to remain silent as books were distributed and, to the surprise of the observers, they usually complied. The students and teacher might work through a few items in the book together, then the students read or answered problems silently. After most students had finished the silent work, the teacher would call on a few students. If the lesson was in arithmetic, students might come to the board. Often, only one student at a time would be called forward, so that working a half-dozen problems might take 10 minutes.

The exception was the fifth-grade class. This teacher, a late middle-aged African-American female, established a lively pace, asked many questions, and constantly challenged her class to think across subject areas, moments, and phases in history, and between academics and their everyday lives. Her lessons moved forward rapidly without leaving any students behind.

The third-grade teacher, Mrs. Jones, was also a late middle-aged African-American female. She was more "traditional" in her teaching style, relying on teachers' versions of texts to guide her introductions, assignments, and questioning patterns. Regarding discipline, she was firm without being harsh. As an instructor, Mrs. Jones was deliberate, clear, and measured. Her classes began on time and she had clear control of her charges and of the academic material. Her questioning of students was typically at a factual level, and she made very few attempts to have students integrate material across content areas or between their daily lives and their texts. However, she kept the class on task and moving forward, and she did ask a lot of factual questions. As was typical at Truman, no student was left out of her questioning. A considerable strength of Mrs. Jones was her unquestionable love for her students. She knew the community well and had taught many of her students' parents. Parents and children alike had no doubt that this woman cared for them. In a community that probably values caring and respect more than "book learning," this teacher was well regarded.

Across Truman's classes, academics began promptly, and students tended to remain engaged throughout their tasks. The level of discipline problems was the lowest in the entire study. Table 5.6 indicates that at Truman all teachers actively taught. During the 1984–85 observations, levels of time-on-task (86%) and teachers' interactive teaching (63%) were among the highest and most uniform in the study. This level of schoolwide academic consistency was one of the school's strengths. The materials were old, teachers appeared unaware of many of the previous decade's advances in curricula and instruction advances, but in every class teachers began class on time, conducted lessons with a sense of purpose and a determination that all children could and would learn, and tolerated no significant interruptions. The result was a school at which the academic "ceiling" was not high. Observers saw no "innovations" and few student projects that demanded teamwork or extended use of the library. However, the academic "floor" was probably the highest in the study. No student was allowed to fall behind or not participate in class. No needy student was denied Chapter 1 or special education services.

It was a simple, commonsense system. Serving a 97% minority, 90 + % free- or reduced-price-lunch population, Truman produced BST achievement test scores among the highest in the district and the study, extremely high student and teacher attendance rates, and a generally pleasant ambience.

Life in the School

The Truman students came from the surrounding agricultural community. Their parents worked in the town, which was less than 20 miles away, and in the small convenience stores, or were on welfare. (The principal observed that although the school encouraged parents to come and have lunch with their children, most parents could not because the school did not accept food stamps.) The majority of the students' grandparents had been sharecroppers, but modern agricultural equipment had virtually eliminated the need for unskilled labor in the cotton and rice fields. Many families remained because this was where they were from and what they knew, rather than because they retained hope for finding employment in Truman.

The most striking feature of the students was their desire to be seen as "good children." To a much greater extent than their urban and suburban counterparts, Truman's students would say "yes ma'am" and "no ma'am" or "I'm sorry, Sir" or "Thank you." They would say these things in response to almost anything. Having "good manners" seemed to be extremely important to these children, especially those in the primary grades.

Observers often described the instructional pace as slow, yet students would sit compliantly. Several observers stated that urban students would have forced fundamentally different management and instructional techniques upon the teachers, but at Truman a slow pace was rarely challenged.

The instructional advantage of such a circumstance was that teachers were allowed the freedom to focus on academics. Particularly in the primary grades, there was little need to focus on management and discipline issues at Truman. It is possible that this state of affairs, combined with the rural isolation, created a disadvantage. For teachers who were accepting of traditional rural instruction, Truman's students offered little resistance and little reason to change.

Beyond the classrooms, Truman's most notable features were orderliness and warmth. The principal knew all the students by name and expressed a genuine caring for each student's well-being. The janitor and the lunchroom staff demonstrated a strong sense of obligation to protect and raise "good children."

The principal knew most parents and all of the community leaders and did not hesitate to call a family in to solve a child's problems. The school played a central role in community life, and the children felt safe and at home in the school.

The paint on the walls was old, but had no graffiti. The windows were drafty, but they were large and lent an air of connectedness between the classrooms and the community. The students were economically poor, but at school they felt that they belonged. Truman was a part of who they were.

HARRY TRUMAN ELEMENTARY SCHOOL, 1989–90

School Context and Indicators of Effectiveness

In the 5 intervening years, the trek required to reach Truman had not shortened. Having had no industry, the Truman community had lost none, but neither had any new industry moved into the community or the county. Agriculture continued to dominate the surrounding countryside, but that economy remained highly mechanized. The school had not received a new coat of paint, and the walls, still graffiti free and clean, now had a dingy look. As Table 5.11 indicates, the families served by Truman Elementary remained over 95% African-American. The principal stated that a total of two students in the school did not receive free or reduced-price lunch.

Tables 5.12–5.14 indicate that Truman's students were continuing to do well on both the CRT and NRT. This third-grade achievement was being maintained in circumstances that were in many ways suboptimal. As a result of district consolidation efforts, the school had lost its seventh and eighth grades and its football team. As can be seen in Table 5.16, the school retained its principal and 50% of its faculty over the 5 years since LSES-III. A new special education teacher had proven inadequate for the task, and was quietly counseled out of education. New fourth- and sixth-grade teachers were still learning their craft, but showing promise.

Principal

Mr. Smith remained the Truman principal. Given retirements and other faculty moves, he had now hired all but two of the teachers. His easygoing but firm philosophy of administration remained unchanged, as did his school's standing on the state-mandated CRTs. Mr. Smith saw the loss of the seventh and eighth grades, and in particular the loss of the football team, as the only significant change in Truman over the 5 years.

Teachers

The kindergarten teacher had been at Truman for 25 years and was in her final year before retirement. The observers often noted that she worked as if she had one foot out the door.

The first-grade teacher, an African-American female, had been the second-grade teacher 5 years earlier. When the former first-grade teacher temporarily moved from the building, she had asked to be transferred to first grade. She was an energetic teacher, and highly interactive. Her students enjoyed responding to her energy and her questions.

The second-grade teacher, a middle-aged white male, had been the first-grade teacher 5 years earlier. A year before LSES–IV he had decided to leave teaching and left Truman. Within a few weeks, and before a permanent replacement had been identified, he concluded he had made a mistake, and asked for his old job back. Having already promised the first grade to the woman who had previously taught second grade, the principal offered the second grade to the male, and he quickly accepted. He described himself as having "very nearly made the biggest mistake of my life." This gentleman had unusually effective, nonpunitive control over his students. Without ever raising his voice or criticizing, he was repeatedly able to direct and focus students' attention on the academics of the day. His instruction was not lively; rather, it was methodical. Yet he brought topics and materials from the world outside the classroom to his students, and they clearly responded with interest and respect. The second-grade teacher had his students keep journals, and all students spent at least 15 minutes each day reading from a library book of their choosing. Classes began and ended at the scheduled times. Students' average time-on-task during academic periods was very high in second grade.

The third grade situation at Truman was anomalous during the LSES–IV observations. The week before fall observations began, the African-American female who had been the Truman third-grade teacher for more than 15 years had been struck by a car and had broken bones in one leg and wrist. She had entered an extensive, several-month-long rehabilitation program, and was not teaching during the fall observations. She was replaced initially by a substitute teacher and later by a retired teacher. It spoke volumes about Truman's isolation and the community's education level that no qualified, preretirement substitute teacher could be found. Still, the retired teacher was a good sport and a clearly giving person. Her instructional pace was slow, even by Truman's standards, and she relied on ditto sheets and the teacher's editions of texts more than any other teacher at the school. The principal intervened by bringing the skilled, energetic Chapter 1 teacher into this classroom during reading and math periods. The result was minimal loss of core academic time.

The fourth-grade teacher, while technically a "new" teacher, was a woman in her forties who had been an aide at Truman during LSES–III. She was a no-nonsense person who came to class prepared and enjoyed challenging her students to think through questions. In the judgment of the observers, her primary limitation was that she was never seen "walking the second mile" in her preparations or during active teaching times. She would repeatedly end her formal presentations and simply tell her class to read the following several pages silently.

The fifth-grade teacher, who had been the strongest teacher in 1985, remained an energized, thoughtful, and demanding professional. As an introduction to one assignment, she distributed mixed fruit to her students. Each student was to feel, smell, and then taste a fruit. They were then to write about the messages coming into their minds through their senses. Every student responded energetically.

The new sixth-grade teacher had just graduated from college. Teaching a cohort that the principal had regarded as having been "a handful" throughout their elementary years, she was severely challenged. Discipline was such a problem that it interfered with her often clever instructional plans. During the fall semester, the principal had provided assistance and had also brought in district personnel to help. He regarded the teacher as having potential, but by Christmas it was clear that his sixth graders were falling behind in reading. His solution had two parts. The first was to have the fifth-grade teacher provide reading instruction to both fifth and sixth grade and have the sixth-grade teacher teach math to both groups. Second, he continued to seek curricular and instructional support for the teacher.

These simple interventions provided the rambunctious sixth graders with reading instruction from a person they already knew to be excellent and firm. The students quickly began catching up. It also provided the first-year teacher with a new experience in one subject in a new class. At year-end it was not clear to the principal, or to the teacher, whether she should remain in education. It was clear to both that she had been offered an opportunity to develop professional skills in a way that minimized costs to students. For the 1990–91 school year, she chose to teach first grade, a decision that necessitated her moving to another school in the district that had a first-grade opening. The principal's switching of fifth- and sixth-grade teachers for English and math probably saved the students, and the young teacher, from a difficult situation.

During the 1989–90 school year, as 5 years earlier, the research team was struck by the nearly seamless use of Chapter 1 services. Aides came into classes, helped teachers or worked with small groups of students, and quietly moved to the next class. A pull-out computer lab was well organized and efficiently paced. Teachers knew when it was time for a small group to leave and when to expect them back.

Throughout this rural, poor district, Chapter 1 teachers administered the district and state tests. Although the tests were scored at the central office, a system of courier and electronic mail resulted in teachers being able to see scores on the quarterly district CRTs the morning after giving the tests. Another advantage of this testing program was that each student's need for Chapter 1 was assessed quarterly, and the system appeared to move children out of "Chapter" as quickly as practical.

Life in the School

As had been the case 5 years earlier, Truman was a comfortable, safe, warm place for children. The continuity of the principal, the relative stability of the teaching staff, and the considerable stability of the community gave a timeless air to revisiting Truman.

In both the third and sixth grades, students were at risk of falling behind. In both cases the principal quickly and quietly addressed the potential problem. The school, with its sign still reading "Truman High School," remained an academically solid elementary school on both district and LSES-administered tests.

A quantitative summary of LSES–IV observations can be seen in Tables 5.9, 5.10, and 5.15. Students remained on task a majority of the time, and their assigned tasks allowed opportunities for them to make academic sense of their schooling. Teachers pushed forward on the district curriculum, displaying an "average" level of interactive teaching. The principal and faculty created an atmosphere that was at once academically focused and friendly. Academic time was well protected. The principal was seen regularly around school and remained highly conscious of the strengths and weaknesses of his program. He continued to hire, develop, and, as necessary, remove staff from his school. The adequate library, which received the services of a professional librarian half a day each week, was used moderately, if not creatively. The school made modest efforts to recognize or reward students' progress. The school's greatest weakness, which local educators may have viewed as a strength, was an absence of efforts to bring ideas and curricula into the school.

COMPARISONS BETWEEN ROOSEVELT AND TRUMAN OVER TIME

The two schools provide several points for comparison and contrast within a rural district. The two schools were in the same very economically disadvantaged district. Both schools received little fiscal support from their district beyond salaries and basic building maintenance. Together with other LSES sites, they can also inform discussions concerning contrasts among urban, suburban, and rural school effects.

During LSES-III and -IV, both schools had stable, capable, caring leaders. In the case of Truman, this stability facilitated the school's remaining effective. The principal recruited intensely, evaluated teachers honestly, targeted staff development to weaker teachers, and removed less-skilled teachers. The Roosevelt principal followed the same prescription. Both men were interested in the individual needs and achievements of their students. Both monitored teachers and students closely.

Both schools received the support of their parent groups. The two principals were figures of no small standing in the communities. Both went about the business of trying to improve their schools in a plain-spoken, commonsense fashion.

In spite of principals' efforts, both schools had a few teachers who appeared to take little interest in instruction beyond reading to students from the teacher's editions of texts and making assignments. In both schools, these were the most senior staff members. Both principals were aware of the problems and judged that encouraging the individuals to take early retirement was the best solution. A paradox was that by 1990 both schools were pleasant places in which to teach. A senior staff member who was "just holding on" could continue at either school for years. In an urban setting, the same teacher might see the environment as being too threatening, the students as too disrespectful, or the new educational fad as requiring too much energy. In an urban setting, the "holding-on" teacher might already have retired. In these two schools, the situation was calm, the students were well mannered, the principals readily addressed discipline problems, and there were not a lot of new fads or district office mandates. So both principals faced personnel problems that required quiet diplomacy and that were not always successfully addressed.

At the same time, both schools were blessed with many teachers who were of a type that has nearly vanished in urban schools. These rural schools each had several female teachers who went into teaching in part because they saw no other viable career options in their settings. In urban America, they might be bankers or lawyers, but in these rural settings, they remained excellent teachers.

On the negative side of the equation, there was not a great deal of innovative instruction going on at either school. The district had instituted a basic skills-based curriculum in the mid-1980s and did not provide training or staff-development opportunities to teachers in any new areas of curriculum and instruction. Observers saw no cooperative learning lessons and (with the exception of Roosevelt's one third-grade teacher) very little "whole language instruction." It is possible that the local educators viewed this lack of newness favorably. They were being spared the worst aspects of educational faddism. But it is equally possible that this isolation was denying both adults and students opportunities to learn and grow.

The major historical difference between the two rural schools concerned relative achievement. At Truman, the student achievement rates would have made them a "positive outlier" for at least 2 years prior to LSES–III, and in all probability throughout the 1980s. Stable leadership, many stable teachers, and a solid relationship with the community continued to produce positive results.

At Roosevelt, the principal who arrived in fall 1984 inherited a myriad of problems. He faced many of them directly and brought immediate changes to his school. The first effects of his presence had a negative tone: Discipline was tight, and teachers focused on getting students to work more than think. But over the years between LSES–III and –IV, some teachers explored methods of keeping students on task *and* thinking. The result was a set of classrooms that were often much more pleasant to visit and appeared to provide greater intellectual stimulation.

One final trend demonstrated in this rural pair was replicated in other rural pairs during LSES–III and –IV. In rural districts, changes were brought to ineffective schools. The changes did not always succeed, but in every case something was tried. At Roosevelt the arrival of a new principal brought more order and higher achievement. At other rural negative outliers, a variety of interventions were attempted, ranging from new principals to new buildings. We have speculated elsewhere (Stringfield & Teddlie, 1991b) that perhaps small rural districts are more attentive to their school's needs.

In the urban and suburban pairs of LSES schools, we saw some schools that remained ineffective throughout the study. Distressingly, in some of those schools there was no evidence of a systematic effort to improve the schools based on their particular needs. Rural communities, however, appeared to define a level below which schools were not allowed to fall. While the "ceiling" of services available in rural areas may not be as high as in some suburban/urban environments, the floor does not appear to be as low.

A final aspect of the rural cases has to do with the qualities affecting school effects in rural schools. The literature on "school restructuring," the "effective schools movement," and other essentially urban phenomena are often couched in terms of "bold initiatives," "new programs," and attention-grabbing "hooks" and "sound bites." In LSES urban/suburban schools, principals and teachers often talked about Madeline Hunter (in 1984–85), "whole language" (in 1989–90), and "assertive discipline" (throughout). Those discussions were virtually absent in most rural LSES schools.

Rather, principals either thought or did not think about curriculum and instruction. They spent more (or less) time recruiting, developing, nurturing, and removing teachers from their schools. They either spent time in classrooms learning how their teachers were teaching and how their students were learning, or they didn't. School days were or were not structured to maximize instructionally available time.

Teachers worked together or were isolated. The ground-level curriculum was driven by the district, or the text series, or available ditto sheets, or the creativity of an individual. Teachers actively taught or passively distributed worksheets.

Academics made sense to students in some schools; in others, the students did not appear to consider the possibility that academics might ever make sense. But in none of the rural schools were the choices and actions accompanied by a program, a label, or fanfare.

Our rural school observers were repeatedly struck by the non-flashy, catch-phrase-free, atheoretical nature of rural schooling. Rather, adults and children appeared to be going about the logical activities of schooling in more or less active and more or less commonsense fashions. The typical rural school had a more reflective, more even-paced approach.

This fundamental conservatism buffered the rural schools from many of the worst aspects of educational fads. Our only reservation was that it appeared to simultaneously block out some of the more thoughtful movements in education. Rural schools appear to offer many opportunities for students to experience more extended study of the natural sciences, reading of whole books, cooperative learning, and other, less faddish changes. Yet we saw almost none of these in the rural sites.

7 A Longitudinal Study of a Pair of Suburban Schools

In this chapter, case studies will be presented on a pair of suburban schools based on information from LSES-III and -IV. These schools are referred to as Pair 1 schools in Chapter 5. While well matched on context variables, these two schools were very differing in terms of effectiveness. The final section of the chapter summarizes the differences between the schools that persisted over time.

CALVIN COOLIDGE ELEMENTARY SCHOOL, 1984–85

School Context and Indicators of Effectiveness

Calvin Coolidge Elementary School was located in a residential section of what the U.S. Bureau of the Census (1988) refers to as a metropolitan statistical area—an urbanized "nucleus" and the surrounding counties (parishes) that are socially and economically integrated with the core area. Though originally settled by middle-class employees of a nearby industrial plant, the neighborhood had grown increasingly poor. Despite changing demographics, however, the area had kept its suburban, tranquil feel: a patchwork of tidy streets and modest houses with neatly trimmed lawns.

The school, which had been built in the early 1970s, was well maintained, housing about 400 students in Grades K–5. It sat on more than 10 neatly mowed acres, but had little playground equipment. The building consisted of two long hallways converging on a central recreation/assembly area, with each classroom accessible from either a hallway or outside. Contiguous classrooms were partitioned by portable walls, allowing the free exchange of students and staff when the walls were folded back. The cafeteria was at one end of the building, while the office, library, and teachers' lounge were clustered at the other.

The hallways were clean, with photographs and displays breaking

112

up the expanse of walls. On first impression, Coolidge projected a positive image—that of a modern suburban school.

The student body was racially mixed, with an approximately equal number of African–Americans and whites. The faculty was primarily white, while the principal was African-American.

While one's first impression of the school was positive, Chapter 5 data tell a different story. Calvin Coolidge Elementary is designated as "Negative 1." Table 5.1 shows that the school scored well below its predicted CRT scores during 1982–83 and 1983–84. This trend continued into 1984–85, when the school scored below its positive match on both the CRT language arts and mathematics tests, as indicated in Table 5.2.

As for teaching behaviors, data indicate that Coolidge classrooms were marked by below-average instruction. The matched positive outlier outdistanced Coolidge on all effective teaching dimensions, and Coolidge scored the worst of all schools on classroom discipline (see Table 5.5). The total time-on-task was only 50.7% (see Table 5.6). This, again, was the lowest score in the study.

The SES characteristics of the students were constant over the 1982–85 school years, although there was a gradual drop in percentage of white students (see Table 5.7). On the NRT, Coolidge scored well below its positive matched school and below its predicted score (see Table 5.8).

Principal

Ms. Sanders was a school system veteran who had taught for a number of years and had at one time received the district's Teacher of the Year award. She could be described as an up-and-coming principal in the system—an individual with a proven track record and good central office connections. Ms. Sanders projected a professional appearance, always well-dressed and articulate. Adept at public relations, she was often off-campus, visiting the central office or attending various meetings around town. The school had a number of adopters, or corporate sponsors.

Ms. Sanders greeted the observers warmly and assured us that "we have nothing to hide. All our teachers are great." She was frequently visible in the hallways, but was very seldom observed in the classrooms. Her hallway interactions with students appeared friendly, but her faculty relationships were more difficult to assess. One observer got the impression that the faculty didn't have much respect for Ms. Sanders. Another felt that Ms. Sanders lacked confidence and felt uncomfortable mentoring teachers. Despite these disquieting perceptions, there was a facade of competence at Calvin Coolidge that was projected and tenuously maintained by the principal.

Teachers

The facade began to crumble when observers started interacting with faculty. The teachers were both unfriendly and suspicious in their dealings with the observers, tending to ask hostile questions about the study's purpose. On one occasion, the counselor asked the study's purpose and was told that it dealt with school effects. She belligerently replied, "Well, why are you doing this research? Why don't you just ask teachers? They'll tell you why schools work and why they don't."

The incident occurred in the teachers' lounge within earshot of other staff members. The lounge itself was described by several observers as a closed and unfriendly place where teachers could "get away from their students."

The two third-grade teachers were observed in some depth. The observers were struck by the confusion and lack of discipline that categorized their classrooms, especially given the principal's glowing preview. One observer noted, "Classrooms, especially in third grade, were unmitigated disasters."

One third-grade teacher, Ms. Peters, wore very casual dress, usually consisting of a T-shirt over stretch pants and open leather sandals. One observer described her as the most "disruptive element in the classroom." Unable to focus on her lessons, she repeatedly interrupted herself to ask observers, "Am I doing this right?"

The team was very concerned by this teacher's apparent insensitivity to the feelings of students and parents. Her classroom behavior seemed to revolve more around her own needs than those of her students, as demonstrated by one disturbing incident. Ms. Peters had asked a mother to come to class to discuss her son's disciplinary problems. The mother complied, taking time off from work to consult with the teacher. Rather than taking the woman aside to talk, the teacher recounted her difficulties in disciplining the child in front of the entire class and the observers. The mother appeared extremely embarrassed and left shortly thereafter without resolving the problem.

Ms. Peters took long lunch breaks, leaving before and coming back after the other third-grade teacher, and wasted valuable classroom time attempting to line up her students on the way to and from lunch. What instruction she did deliver was peppered by her own frequent lapses into childhood reminiscences, most of which were only tangentially related to the lesson at hand. As a result, the recorded time-on-task in her classroom was very low.

While Ms. Peters's classes were characterized by odd anecdotes, she had an energetic presence. Such was not the case across the hall in Ms. Appleton's class. Ms. Appleton and Ms. Peters were both in their mid-thirties and had begun teaching about the same time. Ms. Appleton, however, projected a phlegmatic and dour countenance. During our visits she rarely left her desk; instead, she barked commands in a monotone, often stumbling over names. Transition times were excruciatingly long; nearly 35 minutes could be consumed simply collecting money.

The school climate questionnaire was administered to all teachers. One item asked faculty to indicate where they expected to be in their texts 3 weeks later. Ms. Peters wrote, "I plan only 2 weeks in advance, sir," while Ms. Appleton indicated she was uncertain where she would be. These responses were indicative of the overall academic chaos and lack of instructional coordination typical of Coolidge.

Life in the School

As the observers made their classroom rounds, one question recurred with frequency: "How can Ms. Sanders tell us that she has good teachers? Is she totally unaware that so little learning is going on?" The answer seemed rooted in the widespread confusion and lack of focus that characterized Coolidge.

The "Save the Statue" campaign underway during our spring visit typified the confusion endemic at the school. Though the campaign, whose purpose was to raise funds to refurbish the Statue of Liberty, had potential educational linkages, its administration was disjointed and disorganized. The practical effect was a day-long interruption, starting in the morning with money collection, followed by numerous intercom announcements about the project, and punctuated by special events.

The campaign aptly symbolized the waste of academic time at the school. Though the posted class schedule called for lessons to start at 8:15, it was not unusual for teachers to still be collecting money at 8:45. Recesses started early and ended late. A cacophony of sound filled most classrooms during academic time, leading one observer to note that the students were quieter in the cafeteria than in their classrooms. While the principal attributed the disruptions to the Save the Statue campaign, the observers saw this as an excuse. "If it weren't the campaign, it would be something else."

The image cast by Coolidge Elementary in 1984–85 was unfocused. The facade of competence so studiously maintained by the principal masked chaos underneath. What was going wrong?

CALVIN COOLIDGE ELEMENTARY SCHOOL, 1989–90

School Context and Indicators of Effectiveness

The neighborhood surrounding Coolidge Elementary had continued its economic downturn over the intervening 5 years. The percentage of lower-SES families had grown—a trend that was reflected in the student body makeup. Approximately 80% of the students were African-American (see Table 5.11), as opposed to 59% 5 years before. About 70% of all students participated in the free or reduced-price lunch programs.

The school looked better than it had previously, thanks to the new principal, Mr. Lambert, who set a priority on keeping the school attractive. At his direction, the hallways were repainted and the walls hung with current faculty/student photos. He was adept at window dressing, taking to the intercom one day to announce: "Listen up teachers. Parents are coming next week. Be sure that lots of student work is on display." By the end of the next day, the walls were laden with student artwork and writing samples. One first-time observer was so impressed with the facility's external appearance that she remarked, "This must be an effective school."

Appearances aside, the facility had its shortcomings, most notably the portable classroom dividers. The school had recently been restructured by the central office as a means of increasing site-based management. The restructure called for the departmentalization of instruction, which meant that students were required to switch classes often. Because some same-grade classrooms were contiguous, the divider walls were constantly being opened and closed as students shuffled back and forth. Teacher conversations even further decreased valuable class time as the faculty tried to keep track of the students and their assignments. Comments such as, "Did you give the homework assignment?" or "Would you watch my classroom for a moment?" were heard often.

Data on student performance and classroom teaching behavior were as dismal as they had been previously, in spite of a change in principal and a 50% turnover in instructional staff (see Table 5.16). As indicated in Tables 5.9 and 5.10, teachers again scored well below the positive matched school on all effective instruction dimensions. While interactive and total time-on-task had improved from 5 years before, these indices were still well below those attained by the positive school in Pair 1.

Coolidge also scored below its matched pair on the CRTs and NRTs (see Tables 5.12–5.14). The NRT scores were slightly higher than those attained earlier, but these gains had not affected Coolidge's relative status. Calvin Coolidge also scored well below its matched positive outlier on all hierarchical dimensions of school effectiveness, as indicated in Table 5.15. Coolidge's scores on these indicators were among the study's lowest.

Principal

Mr. Lambert had been principal for 2 years, having replaced Ms. Sanders, who was promoted to the central office. Mr. Lambert resembled his predecessor in their shared flair for public relations. The combination auditorium/recreation room now boasted a banner emblazoned with the names of eight school sponsors.

Mr. Lambert had an assertive style of interacting with teachers, parents, and students, as contrasted with his predecessor's more easygoing style. A former teacher who considered himself a reading specialist, Mr. Lambert did not hesitate to offer teachers what he considered to be constructive criticism, and was observed leading a demonstration in one teacher's class. His attitude was counterproductive, however, for he seemed to be telling the teacher, "I am a reading specialist, and I am going to show you how to teach reading." The teacher did not appreciate the principal's apparent attitude of superiority.

The janitor had worked for both principals. He contrasted them as follows: "Ms. Sanders was really laid back. On the other hand, Mr. Lambert wants everything yesterday. If he asks you to do something, he says 'You should have thought about that before I told you.'"

As with Ms. Sanders, Mr. Lambert portrayed the school in a positive light. However, he was more openly critical of some teachers. After observing for several days, one team member said she was initially impressed with Mr. Lambert's energy level, but eventually came to see his leadership as negative. The turning point, she said, was Mr. Lambert's differential treatment of teachers. Though he liked to think of himself as a peer of the teachers (having once commented, "I guess you might say that I am a leader of leaders—a jack of all trades—the head flunky"), this was not the way he related with every teacher.

The observer related an incident in which Mr. Lambert needed a table and chairs to set up a kindergarten classroom. He approached an experienced teacher and said, "Listen, if you can find an additional table and chairs, I would like them." He then approached an inexperienced teacher and told her, "I need a table and chairs now. Send them to me as soon as possible."

Certain teachers were his obvious favorites. One language development teacher was a clear favorite and was consulted on a variety of issues. The principal had even given this teacher the authority to conduct an important parental survey on the restructuring project.

There was a group of teachers with whom the principal seldom interacted. Mr. Lambert confided that these teachers were intimidated by him and did not want him to observe their classes. When he made school rounds, he peeked in these rooms, but did not enter. An observer suggested that "mutual intimidation" was going on since the principal apparently stayed out of the classrooms by mutual consent.

The observers saw other incidents of abrasive behavior between principal and staff. His relationship with the counselor was particularly negative. Mr. Lambert, who apparently felt that the counselor wasted time and should instruct more, strode into the woman's office one day and announced, "Listen, you are not here to fix your nails. You're going to teach 30 minutes a day, and you're going to counsel students and form groups." The counselor became very upset and took off the costume she had made for a special activity. The principal later commented, "I know she is upset, but I don't care."

On another occasion, Mr. Lambert angrily canceled a faculty meeting because some teachers had scheduled medical appointments at that time. He told the observer, "The evil side of me came out. I tore into them and told them I didn't appreciate their scheduling appointments on faculty meeting days—that we would have meetings when everyone could attend, regardless of other meetings." The teachers hadn't talked to him since then, he confided, adding that he "didn't care."

Teachers

The faculty and staff at Coolidge seemed splintered into cliques apparently shaped by relations with and allegiances to the principal. Some teachers resented the principal's attitude of superiority with regard to his teaching expertise, while others seemed to respect and get along with him. So many faculty members were preoccupied with their own relationships that the school's overall atmosphere seemed much more staff- than student-oriented. Though good teaching could be found in some classrooms, the overall level of instruction at Coolidge in 1989–90 was as low as it had been previously.

The trend was apparent at the third grade, where Ms. Peters and

Ms. Appleton had been replaced by two equally unimpressive teachers. One, Ms. Harrell, was nearing retirement and preferred to sit in one spot from which she would address the class in tones laced with criticism and sarcasm. Her behavior contributed to a negative climate.

It appeared that Ms. Harrell had been a good teacher at some point but had long since "burned out." She indicated that she would retire the next year and planned to move her son from Coolidge because she didn't want the child's education "wasted in a school like this." She projected a sense of academic futility—a belief that nothing could be done to improve Coolidge and that she had wasted much of her own career at the school.

The other third-grade teacher, a young woman named Ms. Bain, was making a better effort. She was one of Mr. Lambert's favorites and was good at math instruction. However, her reading lessons were fragmented—20 minutes of reading, then recess, then 20 minutes of reading. Taking transition time into account, the result was only 10–12 minutes of actual reading instruction a day. When asked why she had scheduled the lesson around recess, Ms. Bain replied, "Our enhancement is math, so something else has to give. In our school, it's reading."

At other grades, highly skilled and much less competent teachers taught side-by-side. Two kindergarten teachers taught in contiguous rooms. One, an experienced instructor in her forties, was energetic and adept at coordinating several classroom activities simultaneously. Her colleague, a woman in her early twenties, struggled simply to maintain classroom control. Several students were off task during entire periods, including one child who behaved disrespectfully toward her. The observer wondered, "Why didn't the other instructor help her young colleague cope with simple managerial issues?"

The quality of instruction was also uneven at other grades. One male teacher ran his fifth-grade class like a boot camp, crisply addressing his students as "Mr.," "Miss," and "Sir." One observer sat through an entire recess before realizing the class was not in session. The teacher, a stern disciplinarian, had kept 90% of the students in for various reasons.

Ms. Peters, the former third-grade teacher now assigned to second grade, continued her often inappropriate behavior. She once interrupted her students' seatwork for an impromptu lecture on the importance of respecting the school and its principal, and even solicited random student testimonials. At another point, she excused her class to go to the restroom, then became so engrossed in a one-sided conversation with an observer that she didn't realize the children had finished using the restroom and were trying to get back into the classroom.

The observers found themselves asking, "Where is the principal, and how can he allow this to continue?'' Whatever good instruction was occurring seemed a function of individual teachers' native ability and determination. The range of teaching behaviors was broad, and the principal was either unwilling or incapable of helping those at the lower end of the scale.

Life in the School

The atmosphere of disjointedness and inappropriateness at Coolidge Elementary was best exemplified by the curious status of the janitor, who had assumed duties and responsibilities far beyond those of custodial staff. The janitor could be seen in the office four or five times a day, answering the telephone and calling parents to pick up sick children. Once he asked the secretary to teach him to use the computer so he could access student files. When one substitute secretary asked him what he did, he said, ''Well, my title is janitor, but I am better known as assistant principal, assistant secretary, assistant counselor, and, at times, disciplinarian. In fact, I disciplined a child today.'' The principal not only tolerated but seemed to encourage this unusual role.

The observers found Coolidge's academic life little changed from the chaos they had encountered 5 years earlier. The new principal was more assertive than his predecessor, but his authoritarian style had done more to alienate teachers than improve them. Although Mr. Lambert wanted to develop a positive learning environment, he placed little emphasis on making the school more child-centered. Rarely did the observers hear the principal or faculty discuss decisions in terms of what option best served students.

One of the more pervasive characteristics at Coolidge was the waste of ''school time'' as opposed to ''class time.'' School time is spent under the control of administrative policy and encompasses the processes whereby classroom time is organized and protected. The administration tolerated such inefficiencies as scheduling reading periods before and after recess at a loss of time-on-task. Excessive time was also lost shuttling students in and out of class for special activities.

The principal's frequent use of the intercom cut further into class time. When the school pictures came in, the principal used the intercom in the middle of a class to ask each teacher to send a student to the office. Mr. Lambert also used the intercom to castigate teachers in front of students and colleagues. He once used the intercom to criticize individual teachers for allowing their students to run during a fire drill. On another occasion, he used it to berate a beginning teacher for requesting too many manila folders. All the teacher could manage in reply was an embarrassed, ''Yes, Sir.''

Despite the principal's heavy-handed attempts at management, discipline was largely lacking during recess. An observer watched a teacher yell at a blind student as he clung to the playground fence at the end of recess. The teacher later brought the boy to the office for discipline. Because the principal had no paddle card (the parental consent form for corporal punishment) for the child, he ordered him to stand with arms extended for more than 30 minutes. When the child's arms began to hurt, he started to cry, prompting the principal to say, "Shut your mouth. I'm trying to telephone someone. I don't want you whining in the background." A group of students surrounded the child, giggling and taunting him. This incident so upset a substitute secretary that she threatened to call the school board.

If this incident reflected the institutionalized lack of caring at Coolidge, the chaos that accompanied the loading of school buses mirrored the school's lack of organization. Though classes were released to the loading area one-by-one, students were allowed to run in front of cars and buses as they arrived, making the children targets for accidents. One bus driver said that he wished the principal would control the situation.

Mr. Lambert's lack of perception and disregard for the feelings of others were underscored at an awards ceremony. A number of perfect attendance awards were presented, but only a few academic awards. Only about 15 parents attended, yet this didn't prevent the principal from launching into an attack on the faithful few, declaring, "We have several students getting awards, but these attendance awards don't mean anything. We need students to get academic awards. We want you to also know that your children are disrespectful. They don't learn this at school—they learn it at home."

JOHN F. KENNEDY ELEMENTARY SCHOOL, 1984–85

School Context and Indicators of Effectiveness

John F. Kennedy Elementary School was located in the same residential area as Coolidge. The two schools were situated only a mile apart and serviced students from the same area. In 1984–85, the student body was evenly split along racial lines, mirroring the student body composition at Coolidge.

The physical plant at John F. Kennedy was older than that at Coolidge, dating to the late 1950s. The building was well maintained, however, and was freshly painted at the time of the fall 1984 visit. Its layout was typical of elementary schools of that era—two classroom wings joined by a breezeway, with the administrative offices, counselor's office, and teachers' lounge clustered alongside the school foyer. Three temporary buildings housed special programs. The school was located on a very large lot, covering several acres.

Visitors entering the school immediately encountered a bank of African violets—35–40 plants lovingly kept by the principal. During our visits, these plants came to symbolize the homelike atmosphere that characterized the school.

The walls of the school were laden with displays ranging from samples of student work, to bulletin boards associated with the school's positive reinforcement program, to classroom honor rolls. Many displays were intended to integrate student art with the school's basic skills program.

The Kennedy lounge was markedly different from that at Coolidge. The teachers were much more cordial and seemed genuinely interested in the study. The principal was a visible presence in the lounge, and the faculty seemed at ease with her, often joking about school events. The bulletin board in the adjoining workroom was professionally oriented, carrying announcements of in-services and committee activities.

The school had many resources, including a social worker, a school psychologist, a safety program, and several special education programs (Compensatory Education, Chapter 1). A resource room boasting a one-to-three teacher/student ratio was available, as was a half-time gifted and talented teacher.

The students seemed genuinely enthusiastic about learning. While the children came from modest SES backgrounds, it was obvious to one observer that their appearance "had been checked over before they left home." The team's impression was of a caring environment for children, both at home and at school. Kennedy appeared to be a modest income, suburban school that was working.

The data in Chapter 5 confirm these impressions for both student achievement and teaching behaviors. As indicated in Table 5.1, students at Kennedy (denoted as "Positive 1") scored well above Coolidge students and their own predicted scores on the CRT. This trend continued into 1984–85 (see Table 5.2).

The Kennedy teachers scored excellently on all dimensions of classroom instruction, as indicated in Tables 5.5 and 5.6. These scores were well above those for Coolidge and were among the best in the study. Total time-on-task was 72% in school year 1984–85.

The SES characteristics at Kennedy stayed fairly constant over the 3-year period 1982–85, although there was a drop in the percentage of white students (see Table 5.7). On the NRT, Kennedy students outscored

Coolidge students at both the fall and spring testings (see Table 5.8). They also scored above their predicted score on the NRT for both testing periods.

Principal

The principal, Ms. Davis—a very gracious woman in her late forties—had headed Kennedy for the past 8 years, taking the same kind of personal interest in her school that she took in her African violets. This was Ms. Davis's first principalship, and it was apparent from conversations with her that it would be her last. She had no desire to go up the career ladder to the central office.

Kennedy was reputed to be a good school, and the faculty was marked by great stability. The school had been headed by only three principals in its entire history. During LSES-III, the school had no beginning teachers.

The more the observers got to know Ms. Davis, the more she reminded them of the stereotypical "Iron Magnolia," a southern woman with a gracious demeanor who could become hard as flint when defending something important to her. Though she maintained a controlled environment at the school, she also allowed the faculty considerable autonomy on instructional issues. This autonomy was partially due to the experience level of her teachers and to their lengthy tenure at the school. For instance, all three third-grade teachers had been at the school before Ms. Davis came.

Since the school was a middle class suburban school, it is useful to think of Ms. Davis as an exemplar of the effective middle class principal described in Chapter 3—a manager of her faculty who facilitates what they need to create an appropriate classroom environment. Because most of her faculty were mature teachers, there was little need for her to champion the assertive instructional leader role. Her role was more subtle, to nurture the already positive learning climate and to protect the school from negative influences within the community or school system.

That is not to say that Ms. Davis was not a dynamic leader. In fact, one of our observers noted that "Ms. Davis drives the whole learning process at the school. She is the guiding force in the positiveness that characterizes Kennedy." There were a number of innovations at the school that were clearly the principal's. Approaching the school, one could see a large sign heralding the "Employee of the Week," a program Ms. Davis had initiated to integrate school support personnel with the faculty.

She was curious about the observers' time-on-task instrument, stating that she was thinking of using such an instrument herself. During the 1984–85 visit, she was quite visible in the halls and was often seen in the classrooms. Ms. Davis and the counselor had initiated a positive reinforcement campaign for school discipline. Every time a child did something good, he or she received a sticker. The students knew the rules and followed them closely.

Teachers

In our 1984–85 visit, no teacher had been at the school less than 3 years, and most had taught there longer than 10 years. This led to a very cohesive faculty, which worked well together and seemed to genuinely like one another. We saw none of the bickering that characterized relationships at Coolidge.

The teachers' work day seemed long, since there was only one recess at 10 A.M. This was the major opportunity for the faculty to interact as one large group. While there was some initial standoffish behavior at the observers' presence, the faculty quickly warmed up and accepted us into their group.

There seemed to be an especially strong camaraderie among the third-grade teachers, who had been working together a long time. They occupied three classrooms at the end of one of the buildings and worked with considerable independence. Ms. Davis respected them as teachers and interacted with them primarily in terms of facilitating their needs.

The senior third-grade teacher, Ms. Cooper, had been at Kennedy over 15 years and was characterized by one observer as "the best teacher I have seen in the study." During transitions between classes, she would start the new lesson before the last child sat down. One transition between a large group lecture and a small group discussion took less than 15 seconds. During one observation period, she moved the class through a lesson solely by asking questions. She would wait long enough for each child to respond, then gradually work the answer around to make it correct before moving on to the next point. Ms. Cooper had perfected the Socratic method for 8-year-olds.

Mr. Runnels was the second third-grade teacher. His forte was science, and he kept his class involved in hands-on activities. He often took students outside to look at trees and animals. Upon returning to the class, he would have them describe what they had seen. Blessed with a wry wit, Mr. Runnels was the prankster of the group.

The least experienced of the three teachers was Ms. Brewton, although she had over 10 years of experience. Her area of expertise was social studies, and she drew on numerous classroom materials to help the students. All three teachers seemed to respect one another and worked together well.

The teaching at Kennedy was generally excellent, as indicated by high time-on-task. There were two weak teachers (one each at the second- and fifth-grade levels). Ms. Davis was aware of their problems and had taken steps to help them. She noted, however, that it was difficult to change veteran teachers and generally assigned peers who taught at the same grade level to help in the specific areas of weakness.

Life in the School

The order at Kennedy was excellent from the time that buses entered the grounds until dismissal. The bus routine was the most orderly of the 16 schools we visited. Students were greeted by teachers in the morning and rapidly transported to classes. When classes adjourned in the afternoon, the children left without incident—with no running or shoving. This order was in direct contrast to the chaos at Coolidge.

Discipline was not a problem at Kennedy. The principal made it a point to be in the hallways during each transition time. One observer noted that a line of students quietly talking immediately stopped when the principal left her office some 45 feet away.

That is not to say that the atmosphere was oppressive at Kennedy. On the contrary, one observer noted that she "was immediately impressed by the students' enthusiasm for learning." Ms. Davis and her staff had accomplished the difficult task of teaching children the minimal required rules without dampening their enthusiasm. Ms. Davis remarked to one observer, "I've found that often more learning is occurring in rooms where some noise is tolerated. If kids are excited about learning, they'll want to make a little noise."

Observers commented on how little time was lost during the day. Part of this was a function of the principal's scheduling, which guarded school time. Only one 15-minute recess was scheduled. Teachers accompanied their students to lunch and began class immediately after returning from the lunchroom. The basic classes, reading and math, were scheduled in uninterrupted blocks, so as to maximize time spent on lessons.

The third-grade teachers each taught only one math group in their own classroom. This made whole-group instruction possible, enabling the teacher to cover more material. The teachers indicated that there was little variance in students' math knowledge at the third grade, thus allowing this homogeneous grouping.

There was more variance in reading, but the three teachers had developed a system for handling this. They changed the structure of their classrooms according to the reading level of the students. This cross-grouping arrangement resulted in a small number of reading levels. Groups included students from all three classrooms. At the time of the early spring 1985 visit, the teachers had two groups reading the second third-grade level book, one group reading the first third-grade level book, and one group reading the second-grade level book. Four groups across three teachers allowed the teachers to often teach an entire class on one level, thus increasing quantity of material covered.

JOHN F. KENNEDY ELEMENTARY SCHOOL, 1989–90

School Context and Indicators of Effectiveness

Kennedy had undergone the same kind of student SES changes that occurred at Coolidge during the time since our previous visit. In 1989–90 the student body was about 20% white, and the overall SES of the students' parents had declined. While a few veteran teachers were concerned about these changes, overall instruction and discipline were very similar to what we saw in 1984–85.

The secretary, principal, and teachers were again very friendly and showed an interest in the observers' careers and families. One observer who spent several days at the school indicated that "the faculty here seemed genuinely interested in what was going on in my life."

Again, the teachers' lounge was hospitable, with such "homey" touches as snacks set out by cafeteria workers. The bus drivers came into the lounge about 20 minutes prior to dismissal to drink coffee and chat. The congenial atmosphere stood in stark contrast to Coolidge, where bus drivers never entered the building unless they needed to talk with the principal about problems. The conversation in the lounge was often student-centered, and the interactions among faculty often concerned academic problems that certain students were having and strategies that could be employed to help the children.

A restructuring program had been imposed by the district at Kennedy since our last visit. It emphasized environmental science and mandated the formation of a school redesign committee consisting of faculty and parents. The PTA was actively involved in various fund raisers.

Data on student achievement and teacher effectiveness are very similar to what was found 5 years earlier. This is especially interesting given the student body changes reported in Table 5.11. In spite of those changes, Kennedy was maintaining a high effectiveness level. Kennedy's scores on the measures of teaching effectiveness were, again, much higher than Coolidge's, and were among the best recorded in 1989–90 (see Tables 5.9 and 5.10). The rate of interactive time-on-task in LSES-IV was 56% and total time-on-task was 71%.

Similarly, the Kennedy scores on the CRT, found in Table 5.12, were well above Coolidge's on all tests across the 2-year (1988–90) period. These trends were also found on the NRT, where Kennedy students scored above Coolidge students and well above their predicted scores (see Tables 5.13 and 5.14). Kennedy scores on the hierarchical dimensions of school effectiveness (see Table 5.15) were much higher than Coolidge's and were among the best in the study. As indicated in Table 5.16, the faculty exhibited great stability with 72% of the 1984–85 instructional personnel still on staff in 1989–90.

Principal

Ms. Davis was still principal at Kennedy, and her presence contributed greatly to the sense of continuity at the school in spite of the change in student body. Continuity was a defining quality at Kennedy, while Coolidge seemed in a protracted state of flux. Ms. Davis was much the same as before, projecting a soft exterior, yet defending her school against any threats. She saw the district restructuring project as another bureaucratic infringement, yet she made the necessary changes to keep the school in compliance with guidelines.

As the good manager described in Chapter 3, Ms. Davis was very organized. She took work home every night, much of which was associated with the restructuring project. She said she didn't have "time at school necessary to do the paperwork." While Ms. Davis worked approximately 3 hours at home each night, the principal at Coolidge rarely took paperwork home.

Ms. Davis was particularly concerned about parental reactions to a survey about restructuring. She took the survey home and worked on it several hours, having it coded and organized the way she wanted. She pored over the parental comments to understand the effect that restructuring was having on the school's image in the community. At Coolidge, the principal turned the survey over to a teacher to conduct.

The discipline at Kennedy was still excellent, though Ms. Davis seldom used the paddle "because then she had nothing left to back up her control." Her preferred strategy in dealing with students who misbehaved was to kneel down to the student's eye level, put both arms on his or her shoulders, and describe the potential consequences of the child's actions. She would then give a "Do you see that paddle?" speech or place the child in an office corner.

After a student had two paddlings, she and the counselor would call in the school psychologist to discuss behavior modification for the student, again emphasizing positive rather than negative reinforcement. The administration at Kennedy recognized the need for external professional help with certain students and weren't embarrassed to use it.

Ms. Davis still served as a facilitator where instructional matters were concerned, consulting with her faculty and allowing them to take the lead in developing strategies. We never heard her tell any teacher that "this is the way to do it." When Ms. Davis did identify a problem with a teacher, she would call the teacher to her office and say, "I believe I'm seeing such-and-such a behavior in your class. Is this what I'm seeing?" She indicated that most teachers would immediately acknowledge the problem and together they would develop an improvement strategy.

Teachers

The Kennedy teachers constituted a very cohesive faculty, with an average tenure of 17.5 years. The teachers believed that Kennedy had been and would continue to be one of the best schools in the district in which to teach. One African-American teacher summarized this attitude as follows: "There's no bickering and talking about teachers here like there has been at some other schools I've taught. Ms. Davis wouldn't allow that kind of stuff to go on at Kennedy."

The counselor appeared to be the most in tune with Ms. Davis's goals. She served as the informal assistant principal and occupied an office next door to the principal's. This informal administrative structure was well accepted and quite appropriate, unlike the dysfunctional informal structure at Coolidge where the janitor assumed the role of second in command.

Ms. Davis didn't have an active program for faculty recruitment, since there had been so few staff changes during her tenure at Kennedy. When openings became available, she typically received several applications from teachers attracted by Kennedy's reputation. The principal went through the standard district process for hiring new teachers and considered herself to have been fortunate in making good hires.

Since our last visit, the librarian had transformed two contiguous rooms into a modern, computerized library. She had devoted her summer to this activity, indicating her commitment to Kennedy. A substitute teacher commented that this was the most attractive and best utilized library that she had seen in the district.

Life in the third grade remained stable, as the three teachers continued their careers at Kennedy. Among the three, they now had more than 60 years of teaching experience. Even though the SES of their students had declined, the scores on the NRT remained as high as they had been 5 years before.

The teachers had developed among themselves a method for minimizing classroom disruptions associated with the mandated departmentalization of the restructuring project. Instead of having students move from classroom to classroom as the subject areas changed, the teachers moved. This almost totally eliminated time lost in transitions from one class to another. This is an example of the instructional leadership of the Kennedy faculty, which had been nurtured by the autonomy that Ms. Davis allowed. It also illustrates the child-centered orientation, as opposed to an adult-centered mentality, which would have called for having the teachers stay in their own classrooms.

Two beginning teachers seemed to fit in well at Kennedy. Ms. Davis indicated that she liked getting new teachers "because she could mold them easier than veteran ones." She did note that one of the new teachers had discipline problems because her college internship experience had been with a "very relaxed" mentor. Ms. Davis said the young teacher had potential, but that the students needed more structure. After talking with the beginning teacher, she assigned an older teacher with excellent managerial skills to work with her.

Life in the School

There was a great emphasis at Kennedy Elementary on protecting classroom time. An example of this guarding of academic time concerned the use of the intercom. The only times one heard the intercom were at the beginning of the school day and 10 minutes before the end of the school day. Very little time was lost at Kennedy in going to recess or lunch. Observers estimated that Kennedy lost about one-half the time that Coolidge lost in transitions.

Ms. Davis felt that the strongest aspect of Kennedy was its academic program, and she resisted as much as possible any external restriction on it. While she accommodated the district-imposed environmental science enhancement, she made the minimum changes required in her curriculum. At Kennedy, there was a strong sense of school control over academic matters. On the other hand, the Coolidge principal warmly embraced the restructuring project, partially because the academic program there lacked internal direction.

The only aspect of the restructuring project that Ms. Davis truly endorsed was the school restructure team, composed of parents, teachers, and administrators. She said she had tried to initiate such a group for years, and she was glad that the group was functioning. She used the group to get things done around the school, such as moving an air conditioning unit, rather than getting it involved in academic matters.

Ms. Davis's interactions with students were very positive. Observers indicated in their field notes that students would come to the principal's door, which was always open, to say hello. She had a student council, and the officers helped her get the school newsletter out and run the candy sale at lunch. Students believed they were an important part of life at Kennedy.

Faculty cohesiveness was indicated by two incidents that occurred during LSES-IV. Our research included gathering pilot test data on a controversial, statewide teacher evaluation instrument. The only teachers to be evaluated on this instrument were the three third-grade teachers, who to that point had been very cooperative. These teachers decided that they did not want to participate in what they called "a dog and pony show" and asked the principal to excuse them from this aspect of the study.

Ms. Davis called us and apologized for the teachers' stance, but backed them up saying it was within their rights to refuse to participate. This was the only time in the 10-year history of LSES that anyone had refused to cooperate in any aspect of the study! While not collecting that particular data was a minor irritation, we were impressed with the staff solidarity and with the value that Ms. Davis placed on her teachers' opinions.

An even more dramatic demonstration of the faculty's cohesiveness occurred late in the spring. A district restructuring audit team came to the school, conducted a very brief classroom tour, and wrote a negative report on the school. The team was particularly critical of the school's academic program, which was the school's strongest suit according to Ms. Davis.

The faculty was initially upset by the report, but their disappointment quickly turned to anger and then concerted action. A special faculty committee was selected and composed a strong rebuttal to the audit team's report. The principal called the LSES director asking for a support letter. She sent a faculty member to help the researcher compose the letter and then sent another staff member to pick it up. The faculty put together an impressive packet of materials describing the school's programs and criticizing point by point the audit report, noting the "unconventional manner in which the audit team had conducted its business." The incident clearly demonstrated the faculty's pride in Kennedy Elementary.

COMPARISONS BETWEEN COOLIDGE AND KENNEDY OVER TIME

Coolidge and Kennedy Elementary Schools are the clearest examples in LSES of a pair of matched schools that maintained their relative status over time. These suburban schools experienced similar shifts in student characteristics, yet one maintained a highly effective delivery of educational services while the other continued to languish.

It was instructive to observe the leadership roles played by the principals in suburban schools serving working class, lower middle-SES students. The principal at Kennedy exemplified the positive managerial style associated with effective middle-SES schools that was described in Chapter 3. She saw herself as a manager of a strong instructional staff, an individual who shared academic leadership with her faculty and shielded them from outside distractions.

The two leaders at Coolidge never played this role. The first was unengaged with the faculty and didn't seem to recognize the school's academic problems; the second tried to emulate the strong, assertive leadership style so successful in lower-SES schools, yet his harshly critical and uneven treatment of the faculty and students undermined his success.

Major differences between the two schools in terms of school climate, teacher behavior, and student characteristics are summarized in Table 7.1. Since many of these differences have been presented in previous portions of this chapter, only highlights will be discussed in the remainder of the chapter.

The differences in leadership by the principal (Point 1, Table 7.1) have just been discussed, but these differences are further related to Points 2–6. The informal organizational structure at Kennedy involved shared leadership at the top between the principal and counselor, with a great deal of faculty input. For example, the teachers at the third-grade level felt free to organize their exchange of classes as they saw fit. The principal endorsed this and spent her time making sure the teachers did not suffer excessive external interference.

The principal and counselor at Kennedy worked together in determining overall school policy, including two positive reinforcement programs. When the principal was not at the school, it was apparent that

TABLE 7.1. Contrasts Between Kennedy and Coolidge Elementary Schools

John F. Kennedy Elementary	Calvin Coolidge Elementary
Principal	
1. Stable, appropriate leadership	1. Unstable, generally inappropriate leadership
2. Appropriate, informal organizational structure	2. Inappropriate, informal organizational structure
3. Shared academic leadership with faculty	3. Nonshared academic leadership
4. Resistant to external change	4. Accepting of external change
5. Close relationship among administrators	5. Strained relationship among administrators
6. Good use of academic support staff	6. Unimaginative use of academic support staff
Faculty	
7. Faculty is warm, friendly	7. Faculty is cold, guarded
8. Strong faculty cohesiveness	8. Lack of faculty cohesiveness
9. No obvious personality conflicts among faculty	9. Open bickering among faculty
10. Integration of support staff into faculty	10. Inappropriate and uneven integration of support staff into faculty
11. Cooperative efforts to enhance teaching	11. Top-down effects to enhance teaching
12. High faculty stability	12. Moderate to low faculty stability
13. High time-on-task and positive classroom climate	13. Low time-on-task and evidence of negative classroom climate
14. Fairly uniform teaching behaviors across classes	14. Large variances in teaching behaviors across classes
15. Assistance freely given new faculty members	15. Little assistance given new faculty members
Students	
16. Excellent discipline and understanding of rules	16. Poor discipline and understanding of rules
17. Students involved in running of school	17. Little or no student involvement in running of school
18. Little use of corporal punishment	18. Excessive use of corporal punishment
19. Student-oriented climate	19. Adult-oriented climate
20. Consistently high student achievement	20. Consistently low student achievement

the counselor was the senior responsible person. The principal and counselor made good use of their academic support staff, such as the school psychologist, to deal with especially difficult student problems.

At Coolidge, on the other hand, the informal organizational structure was very inappropriate, with a janitor taking over administrative responsibilities. This was partially due to the fact that the principal had not established a functional leadership team with the counselor or with a significant portion of the faculty. He had a negative relationship with the counselor, and he seemed to trust only certain teachers. The principal at Coolidge had tried to implement an assertive, centralized leadership style, but it had proven dysfunctional.

Given the lack of a consistent academic vision at Coolidge, the principal had readily accepted a district-imposed enhancement program. This emphasis resulted in several schoolwide scheduling problems, including a totally inappropriate reading block sandwiched around recess and lunch. Precious academic time was lost in accommodating to the district imperative.

Points 7–15 relate to faculty matters at both school and classroom levels. The Kennedy faculty was marked by great stability and cohesiveness. This faculty was proud of its academic programs, for which it felt a great deal of ownership, and was resistant to imposed change or district criticism that it did not believe was justified. This independent faculty epitomizes that described in effective middle-SES schools in Chapter 3. It should be remembered that this faculty served a more middle-SES clientele when it was developed several years earlier.

The Kennedy faculty was also involved in cooperative efforts to help one another and to successfully induct new members. While there hadn't been many new faculty members, the new staff members in LSES-IV were receiving appropriate grade-level mentoring. This mentoring resulted in highly uniform teaching behaviors across classes in the school.

At Coolidge, on the other hand, there was open bickering among faculty members, and the staff seemed divided among those loyal to or critical of the principal. While the principal tried to improve classroom-level performance through demonstrations, his attitude "turned off" teachers. There was moderately high staff turnover and great variance among classrooms in time-on-task and instructional quality. Variance in teaching behavior at ineffective schools is described in Chapter 10.

Points 16–20 concern differences at the student level. Kennedy students were directly involved in school-level activities such as fund raisers and hallway monitoring. There were many faculty comments about doing "what is good for the students." The faculty continued to communicate high expectations to students despite changing demographics. As a result of these and other faculty behaviors, the students continued to outperform students at Coolidge and to perform better than predicted based on their SES backgrounds.

Discipline was extremely weak at Coolidge at both the classroom and school levels, as exemplified by the chaotic loading of buses. This occurred in spite of the use of corporal punishment at the school level and sarcasm at the classroom level. Most decisions at this persistently ineffective school had to do with what was good for the adults, or a subgroup of the adults, rather than for the children.

8 A Longitudinal Study of a Pair of Urban Schools

In this chapter, case studies will be presented on a pair of urban schools based on information attained in 1984–85 and 1989–90. The chapter has the same structure as that found in Chapters 6 and 7. In this chapter, however, the conclusion will emphasize how the negative outlier had improved over time.

There are significant differences between these urban schools and the rural and suburban schools previously described. For instance, students at urban schools come from poorer SES backgrounds than those from suburban schools (refer to Tables 5.7 and 5.11, where Pair 1 are the suburban schools and Pair 4 are the urban schools). The descriptions of the schools and surrounding communities are also quite different for the urban pair as opposed to the rural. The urbanicity context variable played an important role in the strategies for success employed by these schools.

HERBERT HOOVER ELEMENTARY SCHOOL, 1984–85

School Context and Indicators of Effectiveness

Herbert Hoover Elementary School was an urban school in a metropolitan statistical area serving a community that was almost exclusively poor and African-American. While a middle class African-American subdivision was located very close to the school, no more than a handful of the children who lived there attended Hoover. Instead, the school pulled nearly all its students from two public housing projects located nearby.

Nearly 500 students in Grades 1–4 attended Hoover. The cramped classrooms housed an average of 30–35 students. Though each classroom appeared to have its own aide, they were often observed in the rear of the rooms, working with one student rather than assisting the teacher in whole group activities.

135

The building, which dated to the early 1950s, consisted of one long double row of classrooms divided by a central hallway. Two temporary buildings provided additional classroom space. Though the facility had seen its share of wear, it was very clean and fairly well maintained, as was the sparsely equipped playground. The classrooms were relatively big and well lit, with large windows facing onto either the street or playground.

The students at Hoover (designated as "Negative 4") scored far below those at their matched school on both CRTs and NRTs (see Tables 5.1, 5.2, and 5.8). In fact, they scored near the bottom of all 16 schools on these indicators. Hoover and its matched school also differed on indicators of classroom management and climate, with Hoover scoring much lower (refer to Tables 5.5 and 5.6). The total time-on-task of Hoover was only 52%, which was the second lowest of all schools in the study.

Though the data indicated that Hoover was falling well below expectations even for a low-SES, inner-city school, the staff not only seemed unaware that there was a problem, but actually said they felt the school was doing quite well. This misperception seemed due in part to Hoover's principal, Mr. Watson.

Principal

Mr. Watson had worked at Hoover for a number of years and was one of the "Grand Old Men" of the district's African-American school establishment. Mr. Watson had recently been asked to become the African-American candidate for superintendent, but had turned down the opportunity because "Hoover is my life."

Though Mr. Watson may have been a solid leader when he was younger, he was now nearing retirement and was seen by several observers as "asleep at the wheel" insofar as instructional leadership was concerned. He was, however, very cordial and warmly welcomed us during our initial visit, inviting us to become part of the "Hoover family."

When asked to comment about the school and his role, Mr. Watson spent most of his time describing the "extras" he had been able to get because of his central office connections. To hear him describe Hoover, it seemed as if the school were doubling as a social services agency. The principal arranged for dentists and doctors to come to the school to check the children's teeth, eyesight, and general health. Mr. Watson also spent considerable energy trying to develop an active PTA, going so far as to send school buses to housing projects to pick up parents. All in all, he apparently relished his self-defined role as "Granddaddy for the school."

It was clear that Mr. Watson saw his role primarily as the procurer of materials, supplies, and other extras for Hoover. In that sense, he was actually playing the manager role (Hall et al., 1984) described in Chapter 3 as characteristic of effective principals in middle-SES schools.

This school needed a principal who was more heavily involved in instruction, especially since the school lacked an academic focus. Our major impression of Mr. Watson was that he was not really "connected" to staff at the school. The principal was so preoccupied with "doing for" the school by bringing resources to it that his presence was seldom felt, and he seemed unaware of what was actually going on there.

Teachers

The observers were uniformly unimpressed with the teaching at Hoover in 1984–85, as indicated by the low scores the teachers received on measures of effectiveness. The school was experiencing three problems relative to teaching.

1. Because the principal was uninvolved in instruction, the teachers had to define their own goals and methods, which resulted in great variance across classrooms.
2. Much time was lost in transitions between classes as well as before and after lunch or recess.
3. The classrooms were overcrowded, which contributed to the chaos that characterized the classes.

The teachers' laissez-faire attitude toward their class schedules was consistent with a sense of complacency among Hoover faculty. Many believed they were doing a good job, and Mr. Watson's benign oversight did little to enlighten them otherwise. Because he rarely visited the classrooms and thus avoided the chaos there, the illusion of well-being persisted.

Despite this illusion, several teachers were harshly critical of students. One teacher openly referred to her students as "trash." We discounted racism as a source of animosity because both the teacher and the students were African-American. We concluded that the antagonism sprang more from the students' SES than from their skin color. Teacher expectations for student achievement were low, as exemplified by the slow pace at which students were taken through texts.

The three Hoover third-grade teachers were defensive about having their students tested by the LSES team. The lead teacher for the third grade, Ms. Holt, was a particular favorite of the principal; like many of her colleagues, she had been working for Mr. Watson for years and was treated with deference. Though Ms. Holt had the best discipline of all the third-grade teachers, her class of 35 students left her little time for interactive teaching. She made extensive use of ditto copies, as did several other faculty members. Another teacher told an observer that Ms. Holt "was not actually grading students' papers—she was making up the grades." While this comment may or may not have been true, it demonstrates the hostility aimed at a teacher who was perceived as one of Mr. Watson's favorites.

Ms. Anderson was the weakest of the three teachers. Her poor performance may have been partially due to what appeared to be severe emotional problems. One observer noted that she "appeared to be having a nervous breakdown" and hardly interacted with her students. She gave the class as many as 10 ditto sheets a day and sometimes neglected even to give them directions. The other two third-grade teachers were never seen helping Ms. Anderson. The principal was either unaware of the situation or simply chose to ignore it.

The final third-grade teacher, Ms. Austin, was the best of the three in instructing students, but acted very defensively toward us. She saw the research team as evaluators, though we described the research to her at some length. During one period, Ms. Austin led her class through a lesson on state symbols. Though most of the children answered her questions correctly, she gave them little or no positive reinforcement. As she proceeded, students began turning to the observer in an attempt to win approval. In this and other instances, we sensed that the students were desperately seeking attention.

Ms. Austin was poorly equipped in basic classroom management. She once justified at length not having separate reading groups. At almost all LSES schools, children were channeled into separate reading groups at the third grade, a level in which individual differences in reading are apparent. Ms. Austin indicated such groupings were impossible "because there is no way you could control the rest of the class while you work with one group." She did not consider using her aide more efficiently in class control.

Ms. Austin was not alone in underutilizing her aide. Each teacher had an aide, probably because the classes were so large. The aides appeared unsupervised and seldom seemed engaged productively in the classroom. One observer noted, "The aides were strictly there for the money. They simply went through the motions, shuffling papers as the teachers tried to teach. They were often in the lounge, smoking and watching the soaps."

The television was a focal point in the teachers' lounge. It played continuously, and teachers congregated around it during breaks. The principal was never seen in the lounge, which we came to view as the teachers' "hiding spot."

The observers detected an undercurrent of racial tension between the aides (who were virtually all African-American) and some of the white teachers. This was especially true in kindergarten, where a clique of African-American aides ignored the white teachers. Again, Mr. Watson was either unaware of this potentially explosive situation or simply chose to ignore it.

Life in the School

The Hoover students were from poor homes and came to school looking like "they hadn't been checked out by someone at home." From observing these children, it was apparent why Mr. Watson wanted the school to provide basic social services. The school, however, also needed to provide a positive educational experience, a service that was not evident. We were distressed that students received so little attention from teachers. One observer noted, "Students craved attention. They would come to us on the playground, take our hands, and stroke them against their faces."

Part of the problem was institutional—the student/teacher ratios were too high. Overcrowding had turned Hoover into a ditto factory, with classes taught through workbooks and with minimal interaction between teachers and students. Instead of making imaginative use of their aides, the teachers had them reviewing dittos with students.

The lack of grouping in math or reading turned instruction into a whole class experience. When poorly prepared, heterogeneous classes of 35 students go through a lesson together, there is no time for individual instruction and little time for student questions. Consequently, the classes were generally boring; several observers noticed children sleeping.

Students also tended to "act out" and to talk incessantly while the teacher tried to conduct lessons. One observer noted that "there were always three to four students segregated from the rest of the class for misbehaving." Though the segregation of students made the classroom more manageable, it also meant that these students missed much of the whole class instruction.

The most dramatic loss of time, however, occurred during breaks.

This loss of school time was attributable to Mr. Watson's failure to enforce the stated school schedule. The teachers were observed leaving the school at lunch to go shopping at a nearby mall, even though the break was not long enough to accommodate such excursions. Teachers covered for one another, with the result that classes received minimal monitoring.

A good example of this loss of school time occurred during the spring visit. The weather had been rainy for days, and even though the sun had finally broken through, the secretary decided (in Mr. Watson's absence) it was too wet for the children to have outside recess. The students had their 30-minute recess, which as usual dragged on an additional 15 minutes. Mr. Watson then arrived and signaled an outside recess. The students had been cooped up inside too long, he declared: They needed to go outside! Though his perception was accurate, the effect was to give the students a 75-minute recess.

All the third-grade classes were practicing skills that their counterparts at other LSES schools already had mastered. One third-grade teacher was leading a lesson in "the value of a group of coins," while her peers at other schools were presenting multiplication and division tables. The school's emphasis on basic skills and the severe loss of class time had a cumulative effect, placing the students far behind those at Hoover's matched school.

Extracurricular activities at Hoover, many of which dealt with African-American history or pride, were not coordinated with classroom activities. While these programs were aimed at instilling pride and hope in the students, the school was not giving them the education that would help them rise above their disadvantages. It was as if the Hoover staff believed children could swallow a "motivation pill" that would imbue them with attitudes more conducive to learning. Meanwhile, the faculty was killing time, waiting for student attitudes to change, before they would begin serious instruction.

HERBERT HOOVER ELEMENTARY SCHOOL, 1989–90

School Context and Indicators of Effectiveness

Hoover's physical plant and student characteristics had changed little since 1984–85. The student body was 100% African-American and drawn from nearby public housing projects (see Table 5.11). The building was still well maintained and bore a fresh coat of paint. The playground itself was a little better equipped thanks to a local chapter of the Jaycees, who had adopted the school.

The school itself had been restructured and now consisted of Grades K–6. Rezoning had turned Hoover into more of a neighborhood school; most students now walked to and from home. The rezoning had also drastically reduced the average classroom size to the low 20s from 30 or more per class 5 years earlier.

The new principal, Mr. Jameson, also an African-American, who had come to the school 3 years earlier, contended that rezoning had destroyed the school's PTA. Most students who now attended Hoover came from single-parent households, he said, adding that many parents had very negative attitudes toward schooling.

In addition to the new principal, there had been a 48% turnover in the instructional staff (see Table 5.16). These changes in instructional staff were accompanied by much more effective teaching in the classrooms (see Tables 5.9 and 5.10). Hoover teachers in 1989–90 actually outscored their positive matched school on all dimensions of effective teaching.

The changes in instructional effectiveness were reflected in student achievement, as can be seen in Tables 5.12–5.14. Hoover actually outscored its positive matched school on the 1989–90 CRTs and the spring 1990 NRT. These data indicate that Hoover students were scoring above expectation on the NRT. Hoover also outscored its matched school on the hierarchical dimensions of school effectiveness (refer to Table 5.15).

Principal

Herbert Hoover was a radically different school than it had been 5 years earlier. Observers were immediately aware of a greater adherence to the school schedule and of better teacher performance.

Though the previous principal (Mr. Watson) had seemed oblivious to Hoover's problems, Mr. Jameson recited an insightful litany of the difficulties he had met when he first came to Hoover. Most of the problems he cited were mirrored by the research team's findings: poor adherence to an ill-defined school schedule, excessive use of the lounge, low time-on-task, low student achievement, and underlying racial tension among faculty members.

While Mr. Jameson respected Mr. Watson's reputation within the community, he was critical of the state in which he found Hoover. Originally a sabbatical replacement, Mr. Jameson decided to straighten the school out as much as possible before his appointment was up. When Mr. Watson decided not to return, Mr. Jameson took the helm permanently. Mr. Jameson considered his predecessor too accepting of bad teachers, saying that Mr. Watson had accepted more than his share during the annual "dance of the lemons" (Bridges, 1986). Mr. Jameson developed a reputation for toughness; four teachers and the secretary retired soon after he came. He had ample opportunity to rebuild the faculty, because nine teachers resigned over the next 3 years.

Mr. Jameson had institutionalized many changes since taking over Hoover. He made it clear that he had received no forewarning from the central office of the school's problems, nor had he been asked to "straighten out the school." His work at Hoover was an excellent example of "naturally occurring school improvement" (Stringfield & Teddlie, 1990).

Mr. Jameson described himself in terms reminiscent of a "maverick orientation" (Levine & Lezotte, 1990). The principal not only was willing to "take on" faculty members or central office staff, but was also ready to bend rules when he perceived external regulations as dysfunctional. As he noted, "I'm not political enough for some board members and district office staff. I'm someone who won't be controlled, and as a result I've been bounced around several schools. But I know what I want at Hoover, and we're getting there."

In order to achieve these goals, Mr. Jameson circulated memos during his second semester, notifying the staff of changes in schedule and procedures. He enforced these amended rules the very next semester. He showed an observer his first memo, which began, "I find it imperative that the lunch schedule for faculty, aides, and tutors be restated or brought to your attention." When some teachers continued to dawdle, he confronted them and forced them out of the lunchroom.

Even as Mr. Jameson cracked down on his faculty, he tried to buffer the teachers from external pressures—a technique described as characteristic of effective principals in lower-SES schools (Hallinger & Murphy, 1986; Teddlie et al., 1989). He controlled all parental access to classrooms, requiring that parents first meet with him and be given a hall pass.

Despite his efforts on their behalf, Mr. Jameson realized that his faculty had some serious attitude problems. He thus began a campaign to weed out disgruntled teachers by documenting undesirable behaviors. He also began performance files on each teacher, which had never been done before. The practical effect of this pressure was the aforementioned resignations.

One particularly rebellious clique of teacher aides at the kindergarten level had succeeded in demoralizing and forcing out a number of teachers. Mr. Jameson broke up this clique by reassigning some of them to different grades and then enacting rules designed to keep them physically segregated.

The most institutional of Mr. Jameson's innovations was the promulgation of an administrative handbook; bound with a red cover, it soon became known as "the redbook." The "redbook" had a three-ring binder allowing the insertion of new material. The handbook covered all aspects of school life. For example, the section on operation/administration included descriptions of the district philosophy, the superintendent's goals and objectives, the philosophy at Hoover, Mr. Jameson's goals and objectives, and the goals and objectives voiced by individual teachers. Each teacher was allowed some autonomy in goal-setting within the overall framework.

Discipline had improved greatly since our last visit, again due to Mr. Jameson's innovations. While the district had a three-step disciplinary process culminating in suspension, Mr. Jameson installed a five-step process at Hoover designed to keep children in school as long as possible. After a student had been given corporal punishment, the parent/guardian was summoned for a conference. This parent conference, instituted by Jameson without the district's sanction, often led to resolution of the problem. Mr. Jameson's approach was working at Hoover, and students were now seldom suspended.

Mr. Jameson was enthusiastic about a new statewide teacher evaluation system that was being piloted. Though he had been aware of general problems with instructional delivery, he confessed to having had difficulty pinpointing his teachers' specific problems. With the new evaluation system, Mr. Jameson determined that his teachers were weak in questioning skills. He consequently researched how best to question students and how to use wait time properly, and was preparing a faculty in-service on what he had learned. His response to the faculty's weaknesses is an excellent example of the type of instructional leadership behavior associated with effective lower-SES schools, which often have a younger and less well-prepared faculty.

Teachers

The teacher resignations made recruitment and socialization of new teachers a major part of Mr. Jameson's job. The task was not easy given the school's reputation and the fact that it served a community in decline. Jameson recruited by word-of-mouth and by carefully perusing the files of prospective teachers at the central office. To avoid "lemons," he called at least one previous employer prior to making a job offer.

In interviews with prospective teachers, Mr. Jameson looked for an enthusiastic personality coupled with a willingness to work within guidelines. New teachers were immediately introduced to the omnipresent "redbook" and given a 1-day, individualized in-service program personally conducted by Jameson. He also assigned a teacher to mentor the newcomer—typically, an experienced teacher working at the same grade level.

When Mr. Jameson took over as principal, he held separate faculty meetings by grade level and subject area. These meetings enabled him to identify teachers who were more participatory and who might make good lead teachers at the various grade levels. The designation of lead teachers was an important part of the school's reorganization, since those individuals handled all routine communications between principal and staff.

None of the three third-grade teachers from LSES–III were still at the school. Of their replacements, two were experienced teachers whom Mr. Jameson had recruited from other schools, and one was a beginning teacher. The most experienced teacher, Ms. Dawson, had been recruited by Mr. Jameson and was designated lead teacher for the grade. Though her style of interacting with students was old-fashioned, she had a high energy level that invigorated the classroom. Ms. Dawson was a resource person not only for her grade level, but for math instruction schoolwide. The beginning teacher, Ms. Warren, was often seen consulting with her.

The other experienced teacher, Ms. Bell, was the third-grade reading instructor. She had some unusual teaching techniques. One team member observed Ms. Bell leading something akin to a "Simon says, what am I?" lesson in which students pulled items out of a bag and described them, thus illustrating adjective use. As the observer noted, this task "was a stretch for many students, who found it difficult to describe their belongings precisely. They got much better as the lesson progressed."

The novice third-grade teacher, Ms. Warren, was nervous and tentative. Her transitions took too long and sometimes her answers to questions were wrong. On the other hand, she had good rapport with students and often injected humor into lessons. With Ms. Dawson's technical assistance, she had the potential to become a good instructor.

Life in the School

Mr. Jameson had made many changes at the school level: enforcing the school schedule by monitoring it himself, making the lounge off limits except during designated times, removing the television and phone from the lounge, instituting consistent rules and policies through the "redbook," and protecting teacher time by restricting parental access to classrooms and by shifting most classroom paperwork to the office. He had worked diligently with the special education teacher to devise a school schedule that maximized classroom time. Hence, the tremendous amount of time wasted in transition in 1984–85 was a thing of the past.

Classroom time was also better spent. Though the reduction in average class size contributed to the increase in efficiency, part of the improvement was attributable to initiatives taken by Mr. Jameson and his staff. For example, the advent of departmentalization had made ability grouping feasible, greatly contributing to classroom efficiency. Low time-on-task had been tolerated under the previous principal, who was oblivious to teachers' shortcomings. Mr. Jameson knew who his weaker teachers were and had initiated personalized in-services to correct each teacher's problems.

The principal was aware that greater teacher autonomy would be desirable and indicated that his philosophy was to "tighten up, then lighten up." It was evident that faculty members already were being given more authority for running their classes.

The student experience at Hoover was much more positive in 1989–90 than it had been 5 years earlier. The school was more student-oriented, and the children seemed less starved for attention. While life at the school was more structured, this was more reassuring to the children than the chaos that had previously existed.

Mr. Jameson not only indicated satisfaction with the changes that had been made, but also showed a clear appreciation of what remained to be done. According to him, the two problems still confronting Hoover were (1) the recruitment of qualified teachers, and (2) improvements in classroom management and instruction. We felt that teacher recruitment might be an ongoing problem, because it takes time for a school's reputation to change; nonetheless, we also felt that the increases in school achievement scores would help. We also felt that Mr. Jameson's sensitivity to instructional problems spoke well for continued instructional improvement at Hoover. If the principal kept pinpointing and addressing specific instructional problems, then incremental improvement should continue.

LYNDON B. JOHNSON ELEMENTARY SCHOOL, 1984–85

School Context and Indicators of Effectiveness

Lyndon B. Johnson Elementary School was located in the same metropolitan statistical area as Hoover Elementary. The site was a stone's throw from two large public housing projects whose residents were almost exclusively poor and African-American.

The facility, whose size and physical layout gave it the feel of a middle school, was a modern, two-story building with an office, library, lunchroom, and auditorium on the ground floor. Several temporary buildings at the rear of the main building provided additional classrooms. The buildings and grounds were well maintained, though the temporary buildings needed painting and suffered from the problems attendant to such structures.

The main building, which was roughly 25 years old, was attractive and spacious, with wide halls separating a double row of classrooms. The classrooms were comfortable—large, airy, and well lit by numerous windows. Motivational posters and bulletin boards were posted throughout the school, sporting such slogans as, "I know I'm somebody 'cause God didn't make no junk" and "The only thing more expensive than education is ignorance."

Johnson housed approximately 700 students. Its 38-member faculty was evenly split along racial lines and was so large that teachers could use the lounge only in shifts. It was difficult to gauge teacher morale based on observations in the lounge because the room was so crowded and the teachers so constrained by the short amount of time they could stay inside.

Johnson and Hoover Elementary Schools were located in one of the more politically oriented school districts in the state. It was not unusual for principals and teachers to have friendships with central office staff and board members and to use their personal relationships to the school's advantage. Johnson's principal, Mr. Thompson, was typical of the group, in that he was well connected politically to the central office.

Johnson (described as "Positive 4") served the same clientele as Hoover: low-SES African-American students coming primarily from housing projects (refer to Table 5.7). The data from LSES–III indicated that Johnson easily outscored Hoover on both the CRT and NRT (see Tables 5.1, 5.2, and 5.8). Johnson also scored higher than predicted on both tests. Data on indices of effective teaching (refer to Tables 5.5 and 5.6) confirm that there was much better teaching at Johnson than at Hoover during LSES–III. Johnson's total time-on-task was near 70% in that school year.

Principal

Mr. Thompson was a neighborhood product who had managed to rise above a bleak childhood in a nearby housing project. He had gone on to become a football hero at a local college and even played professional football briefly. Well known and well respected in the community, he was also politically ambitious.

Mr. Thompson had been teaching at the secondary level when a principalship became available at a local high school. Though it was assumed he would pursue the high school post, Thompson opted instead to become principal at the less prestigious elementary school, saying he wanted to work with younger children. He took over as principal in difficult circumstances, just before LSES-III. The former principal, an older white man who had run the school a number of years, had a reputation for being abusive and had been forced to resign following an incident in which he had beaten a student.

Though he had been at Johnson only a short time, the observers found Thompson on his way to establishing a "cult of personality." A dynamic individual, he had a definite message to relay: "I know who you are. I came from the ghetto like you, but I made it out. You can make it, too, if you try." In keeping with that message, he established a school culture characterized by discipline and the belief that any student could succeed.

Mr. Thompson had earned a reputation as a disciplinarian and was complimented by teachers for being "able to handle these kids." He confided to one observer, however, that he wasn't as harsh as some thought. "Sometimes students are sent to my office for discipline and arrive crying. When I ask them why they're crying, they say, 'Because you're going to spank me.' So I say 'What would you think if I told you I'm not going to spank you? We're going to talk instead.'" This approach relaxed the students and encouraged them to see the principal as a friend. Apparently, Mr. Thompson's disciplinary style was working at the school. He noted, for instance, that "I can be gone all day and as long as my car is here, the students think I'm here and behave. If the kids don't see my car, they're more disorderly."

Mr. Thompson was often visible on the playground, in the cafeteria, and in the hallways during our 1984–85 visits. His concern for the students' welfare was genuine. For example, he stopped an observer in the cafeteria to tell her that he was taking up a collection for a student who had been "walking on his socks," having worn holes in his shoes. Mr. Thompson had called the boy's mother and learned that the family was having a hard time. "Why didn't you call me?" he asked her, adding, "That's my job, too." He then collected a few dollars from each teacher—enough to buy the child a pair of sneakers and a haircut.

Teachers

The faculty did not seem very cohesive, perhaps because there were few opportunities for all teachers to socialize with one another. Racial differences also may have contributed to the faculty segmentation.

There seemed to be racial segregation by grade level; for example, all the third-grade teachers were African-American, while most kindergarten/ first-grade teachers were white. Inasmuch as Mr. Thompson arrived following the dismissal of an unpopular white principal, the faculty may have felt some residual uneasiness over his predecessor's firing.

Faculty recruitment was a problem at Johnson. A large percentage of the staff was untenured, implying that they had been employed only recently by the system. Mr. Thompson noted that it was difficult to recruit teachers because other districts paid higher salaries. In the circumstances, it appeared that if he were to improve instruction, Thompson would have to improve the skills of his present faculty rather than rely on new recruits.

There was great variance in teacher behavior throughout the school, including the third grade, where the abilities of the four teachers ranged from excellent to below average. Ms. Sims, the third-grade teacher with the best instructional skills, was around 40 years old and very professional in demeanor. Her classroom walls were peppered with displays and posters, which not only brightened the room but offered positive reinforcement. Her students quickly finished the NRT administered by the researchers and scored quite well.

Ms. Taylor, another third-grade teacher, had a class that also was very orderly and well-behaved. Ms. Taylor was generous in her praise and had organized her lessons into solid blocks of uninterrupted work time. Her students seemed self-directed, getting up to sharpen their pencils or performing other classroom management activities without asking permission or disturbing others.

The other third-grade teachers were less impressive. Ms. Lagrange, the most colorful of the group, was matriarchal in her interactions with students, often referring to them as "little boy" or "little girl." Though her speech was colorful, it was not always grammatical. Her incessant use of the word "what" ("We are going to . . . What? Open our books to page 38 and study . . . What? Spelling") appeared to be her sole method for keeping lessons moving. Our perceptions of Ms. Lagrange were mixed. On the one hand, she could be humorous, and she clearly had classroom control. On the other hand, she often repeated herself and apparently didn't prepare carefully for class. It was hard to see how her old-fashioned patterns of interacting with students fit the modern realities of urban teaching.

The last third-grade teacher, Ms. Holmes, was difficult to assess. One observer felt she "acted pretty mean toward the kids," and she was frequently overheard yelling. Her classroom was the most sparsely decorated of the four, which didn't seem to bother her. Her class was not well-behaved and appeared intimidated by her taciturn demeanor.

Given the variance in instructional quality at the third-grade level, there was an obvious need for instructional leadership. Though Mr. Thompson indicated that he planned to visit classrooms often, he did not strike the observers as likely to follow through. He was primarily interested in motivating and working directly with students. Since he was only in his second year at Johnson, it was difficult to ascertain what his academic leadership legacy would be.

In one area of instructional leadership, however, Mr. Thompson already had left his mark: the library. When Mr. Thompson took over at Johnson, the library was run down and many books were stored in boxes. He quickly "stole a librarian" and gave her free rein to do what she wanted. She turned the library into a showcase: two rooms for students, housing more than 12,000 books, with numerous displays and audiovisual equipment. One room, which was set up classroom-style, offered students a quiet retreat to watch videos or read. The Lyndon B. Johnson library was a facility of which any affluent suburban school could be proud.

Life at the School

Since becoming principal Mr. Thompson had taken a number of steps to improve the school climate. A believer in the power of symbols and positive reinforcement, he had posted slogans throughout the building. He also brought in African-American doctors and lawyers to serve as role models and launched various ongoing community relations activities, including the sale of school T-shirts.

While the emphasis at the school was on order and discipline, the principal tolerated and even encouraged some levity. The walls outside the lower primary classes were dotted with student drawings that depicted Mr. Thompson in all colors. He took great delight in pointing out these drawings to visitors, laughing heartily at the ones that portrayed him with blond hair.

On the other hand, Mr. Thompson was perceived as an individual "you don't cross"—who set certain standards of conduct and expected everyone to live by them. His compulsion to simultaneously control and motivate his students came out of his own struggle to escape poverty and his genuine desire that Johnson students do likewise. His tirade to one unruly fourth-grade class was particularly telling. He "read them the riot act," an observer recalled, telling them, "I made it out of the ghetto. I personally don't care if some of you don't, but there are kids here who want to succeed and I'm not going to let you mess up their chances."

Mr. Thompson's relationship with the faculty was difficult to assess. It was entirely in character for Mr. Thompson to mix discipline with motivation in dealing with students, yet he seemed less comfortable with mentoring teachers. We could not envision him evaluating a teacher's performance and prescribing a personalized improvement program. His reticence to provide instructional leadership perpetuated the range of teaching abilities that characterized the faculty.

As a result, the educational experiences of individual students were mixed. Students assigned to a kind, competent teacher such as Ms. Sims were likely to have positive experiences both in and out of class; their teacher's instructional talents would keep them engrossed in class and her superior classroom management would make it unlikely for them to be sent to the office. On the other hand, students assigned to an insensitive teacher with poor classroom management, such as Ms. Holmes, would be in double jeopardy. Bored and frustrated in class, such students might "act out"; the teacher, unable to handle the situation, typically responded by sending them to the office, where they would be seen as a discipline problem.

The school's learning environment also was colored by the fact that everyone was driven hard. Apart from the principal's own desire to push the students, a court order mandated extra instructional pressures on both students and staff. The court order not only imposed a basic skills emphasis but dictated how much time the staff would devote to those subjects beyond the state standards. The principal had devised a rigorous schedule committing the entire morning, with the exception of one 15-minute homeroom period and lunch, to reading and math.

A few teachers protested that the schedule was too strict for young children and that more flexibility should be allowed, but to no avail. These accumulated pressures may also have contributed to low faculty morale. Thus, the principal's frequent motivational speeches fell on deaf ears where some faculty members were concerned. For progress to be sustained and enhanced at Johnson, Mr. Thompson would have to improve faculty morale while upgrading the mediocre skills of some teachers.

LYNDON B. JOHNSON ELEMENTARY SCHOOL, 1989–90

School Context and Indicators of Effectiveness

Physically, Lyndon B. Johnson looked very much the same in 1989–90 as it had 5 years earlier. The student body numbered roughly 650 and, with the exception of fewer than five white students, was entirely

African-American. This was very similar to the makeup of the school in 1984–85 (see Table 5.11).

The size and layout of the facility worked against the staff's ability to create the sense of intimacy so tangible in many effective elementary schools. Nonetheless, the faculty and staff were working to create a pleasant environment for the children; most of the rooms were well decorated and there were numerous plants throughout the building. The custodial staff was doing a good job of keeping the main buildings neat and clean, though some windows were dirty and some areas needed repainting. The "temporary" buildings were showing the wear of 15–20 years of use. One observer called them "dysfunctional mobile homes"; several others noted that the buildings, though only a few yards from the main Johnson complex, seemed "disconnected from the academic life" of the school. The "t-buildings" seemed dirtier than the rest of the school, and the teachers assigned to them had more difficulty creating a positive learning environment.

Mr. Thompson characterized Johnson Elementary as a neighborhood school, and that appellation rang true. Most of the students walked to and from two nearby housing projects. The community ties were obvious in the way that parents walking students to school would exchange greetings with other parents, crossing guards, and school staff. The school had become the focal point of the two housing projects, whose residents constituted virtually the entire school community.

A new sign proudly announced an upcoming carnival staged by the Parent Teacher Organization (PTO), which was one of Mr. Thompson's pet projects and had more than 150 members. The sense of community was particularly evident on Fridays, when students and staff wore T-shirts or sweatshirts emblazoned with the school mascot. Money from the PTO fund raisers also flowed back into the community by way of assistance to needy students.

While Mr. Thompson clearly had been successful in establishing Johnson as a community school, data on student achievement and teaching behavior had deteriorated from 5 years earlier. The staff had remained relatively stable, with 70% of the teaching faculty retained from LSES-III (see Table 5.16).

On the teaching-effectiveness measures (see Tables 5.9 and 5.10), Johnson teachers in 1989–90 scored lower than those at Hoover. Even so, the rate of interactive time-on-task at Johnson had increased from LSES-III to -IV. Differences between Johnson and Hoover on the teaching dimensions in LSES-IV were largely due to improvement at Hoover. Johnson was also outscored by Hoover on the CRT and NRT in LSES-IV (see Tables 5.12–5.14). This was especially apparent on the CRT, where

Johnson students had poor performance in 1989–90 compared with earlier years. On the NRT, students at Johnson tested below their predicted
scores.

Principal

Mr. Thompson remained very much the central figure at Johnson
Elementary, though several observers felt that he was less enthusiastic
than he had been previously. His sense of commitment was still there—
he still talked about "making Johnson an integral part of the community," even though he had already succeeded on that count. He often
sounded more like a community activist than an instructional leader.
When asked what he would do to improve a school, his first suggestion
was to "get the parents together and tell them the goals and expectations you have. I would get parents to have meetings in their homes
about improving the school."

Mr. Thompson was proud of the political clout he wielded and
used the community newspaper "to get the word out" when problems
emerged. When he wanted to improve the library, he persuaded the
paper to run articles about fixing it up. He had planted a rose garden in
memory of students who died in a fire, and said the garden had since
become an important community symbol.

Mr. Thompson was much less clear about the organizational and
instructional changes that had been made at Johnson during his tenure.
Several procedural improvements had been made; according to many
faculty members, Mr. Thompson was more successful than his predecessor at acquiring materials and supplies. Mr. Thompson's curriculum
changes were primarily limited to keeping his staff in step with statewide guidelines. To ensure this, he required that they periodically sub-
mit their lesson plans to him. He claimed to spot check classrooms
regularly, but we seldom saw him do so. Though he had hired a curriculum coordinator, it was unclear if she had really made her presence felt.

As one observer put it, "Mr. Thompson wants to run a tight ship,
but he accepts a certain latitude among teachers. The idea of maintaining a 'technology of curriculum and instruction' is probably foreign
to him." The observation was correct, for indeed Mr. Thompson was
reluctant to put his stamp on the instructional process. He left teaching to teachers, while he "rallied the troops" through motivational
speeches and community projects.

Mr. Thompson's preference for quick-fix solutions over long-term
strategies was evident in his approach to recruitment. Johnson had experienced a recent spate of resignations as teachers retired or were lured

away by out-of-state districts paying higher salaries. In keeping with his philosophy of selecting experienced teachers, he hired five teachers out of retirement. Unfortunately, they could stay no longer than a year due to a special school board policy governing retiree employment. The principal also hired a 72-year-old on permanent appointment after she taught several semesters without pay. While this hiring philosophy addressed the school's immediate teacher shortage, it was no way to build a long-term instructional staff. Not only could most former retirees stay only a short time, it is uncertain how many would be receptive to new teaching techniques.

Another example of the principal's failure to affect instruction was his decision against adopting a voluntary departmentalization program. The Hoover principal had adopted this system because it gave him the flexibility to maximize his faculty's instructional strengths. Mr. Thompson stuck to the self-contained system except for sixth grade, which was semi-departmentalized. Had he gone to departmentalization, Mr. Thompson would have had to evaluate the instructional strengths of his teachers. Even if he had allowed self-selection, he would still have had to gather information to validate the self-selection. He did neither, opting instead for the status quo.

Furthermore, Mr. Thompson did little to improve even the status quo. The 1989–90 faculty demonstrated the same wide variance in skills that were observed in 1984–85. Such variance called for an active in-service program through which the skills of weaker teachers could be upgraded. When asked to discuss in-service opportunities at Johnson, Mr. Thompson merely indicated that the central office offered an in-service program and that he had designated teachers to coordinate faculty participation. No individualized in-service programs were available at Johnson, though the staff would have greatly benefited from them.

Teachers

The great variance in ability among teachers at Johnson was readily apparent from researchers' observations. One observer noted that some teachers "really seemed to like teaching and used a variety of explanations in class." In contrast to these teachers (who typically used manipulatives in math/science and had several class assigned projects), other teachers were described as "just there." Part of the variance reported in 1989–90 stemmed from the addition of seven new teachers. The in-service program for new teachers was minimal, thus failing to decrease the natural heterogeneity among the teachers. A one-day in-service by grade-level chairpersons on goals at Johnson was woefully inadequate.

One observer noted that Johnson had no single schoolwide climate, but rather "separate climates for each grade level." The various grade levels, which typically consisted of four classes, operated according to their own schedules, with considerable autonomy. The kindergarten and first-grade faculties used this autonomy to advantage, creating "closely knit families" of teachers who worked together to establish their own positive climates. At other grade levels (third grade, for example) a much less positive climate was engendered.

The experience level of the third-grade teachers may have contributed to their apparent inability to pull together and pursue common goals. The four teachers, all of whom had taught third grade more than 15 years, averaged 56 years in age. Two, Ms. Sims and Ms. Lagrange, had been at Johnson many years; the others, Ms. Evans and Ms. Jones, had moved to the third grade level since LSES–III. Given the teachers' experience level and the self-contained nature of the classes, there was less sharing of teaching strategies and philosophies than might have been the case with younger teachers operating with less autonomy.

Ms. Sims had been described as the best third-grade teacher in 1984–85. Five years later, her classroom was still pleasant and her time-on-task rating good, but she wasn't nearly as warm toward the students as before. Her classroom dialogue was peppered with admonitions to "be quiet and think. You see, you go to arguing and you don't know where you are. Be quiet now!" During one classroom period, she spent so much time writing on the blackboard that she had little time for interactive teaching.

Ms. Lagrange was as colorful and matriarchal as before. She was at times inappropriate and insensitive in her student interactions. During one reading period, she told a boy, "Now, Renaldo, I know you have a speech defect, but go ahead and read anyway." While more in-service was clearly needed at Johnson, the observers were uncertain whether such training would have any influence on Ms. Lagrange, given her age, her style, and her punitive approach toward students.

In contrast to Ms. Lagrange, one of the newer teachers, Ms. Evans, was described by one observer as "a bright, energetic woman who works hard at her students' math lessons, yet also laughs at herself and with her kids." Her classes were characterized by frequent student/teacher interaction and positive reinforcement.

We came away from LSES–IV with the impression that veteran Johnson teachers could teach very well when they wanted to, but frequently lacked motivation. One particular incident involving Ms. Evans lent credence to our theory. A statewide teacher evaluation system was being piloted at Johnson during our visits. Mr. Thompson apparently failed to inform his faculty that the LSES team was also coming. Ms. Evans, mistaking our observer for the evaluator, launched into a specially prepared lesson that the observer called one of the best she had ever seen. When Ms. Evans later discovered the observer's identity, she said, "Well, the evaluator will see my usual lesson when she comes, and if she doesn't like it, tough."

The last third-grade teacher, Ms. Jones, had been brought out of retirement after teaching several semesters without pay. Her room was sparsely decorated and she spent much time turned away from her class writing on the board. On the other hand, she was a firm believer in positive reinforcement, such as encouraging her students to applaud each other for giving correct answers.

The third-grade deficiencies were not shared schoolwide. Excellent teaching and camaraderie were the norm at some other grade levels, most notably kindergarten and first grade. These teachers often conferred about what skills to emphasize and seemed to invest an exceptional amount of effort in language development with the children. One teacher was a particular standout and was characterized by several observers as the best kindergarten teacher they had seen during the LSES. Her students' eyes were turned to her through extended discussions in which she led them through lessons with a series of questions.

The observers found Johnson to have as much variance in instructional quality in 1989–90 as it had 5 years earlier—a situation that Mr. Thompson was either oblivious to or incapable of changing.

Life in the School

Life in the school reflected the same uneven atmosphere that characterized classrooms. Transitions still went quickly with few incidents, largely because individual grades operated according to such varied schedules that large student groups were seldom in simultaneous motion. While this was a boon logistically, teachers used their autonomy to greater and lesser benefit where instruction was concerned.

Johnson Elementary was a focal point for the local African-American community and was the site of frequent events. Teacher appreciation day drew 90 mothers to the school to help teach lessons, underscoring the high level of parent participation. Though parental involvement was highly valued, teachers did not seem particularly student-oriented. One menacing index of this was the omnipresent paddle. Each teacher had a paddle and brandished it throughout the day. This emphasis on the use or threat of corporal punishment stood in stark contrast to the principal's previous posture of paddling as last resort.

Though Mr. Thompson stressed discipline when he took over, the LSES–III observers believed he would ease off once order was restored. Five years later, they found discipline more harsh than at the beginning of his tenure. Students were constantly ordered to be quiet in the class-room and hallways, and one observer overheard two teachers cursing students at the end of a recess period, screaming, "Get your —— in that door now!"

In contrast to this was the library experience at Johnson. Five years earlier, the library renovation had symbolized the school's rebirth under Mr. Thompson. The observation team felt that the library was the most attractive and best run they had seen during the LSES. Students were allowed constant access to the facility. In addition to their regularly scheduled library period, students were encouraged to work on re-search projects during their last class period and were frequently seen walking to and from the library to do so.

If Mr. Thompson had devoted as much attention to classroom in-struction as he had to the library, positive academic change could have been institutionalized. Instead, the school seemed a good example of what Rosenholtz (1989) has called a "stuck school"—one that is not moving and changing in a positive direction. Almost all of Mr. Thomp-son's initiatives at Johnson had been at the school level—improving the school climate, adding positive symbols, improving the library, involv-ing the community, bringing in motivational speakers, enhancing the facility, and so forth. Innovation had not occurred at the classroom; therefore, school progress had been institutionalized only to a certain point. Enthusiasm accompanying Mr. Thompson's arrival had waned with his failure to affect classroom learning.

Epilogue

The school plays an integral, positive role in the community, thanks in part to the "cult of personality" its principal has fostered. While student scores on standardized tests slipped between LSES–III and –IV, they still weren't so low as to trigger pressure to improve. When teach-ing weaknesses are pointed out, Mr. Thompson can pin the blame on recruiting problems caused by out-of-state principals "raiding" his fac-ulty. He needn't mention the lack of meaningful evaluations and in-service programs at his school.

One potentially positive change was made at Johnson: the hiring of a curriculum coordinator. Recognizing that instructional leadership was not his forte, the principal charged the coordinator with such duties as evaluating lesson plans, acquiring textbooks, and working with weaker teachers. Thus far, however, her presence has had little impact, and Mr. Thompson has sensed that some teachers resent the coordinator's role.

How could teaching be improved at Johnson? Since many of the weaker teachers are also the most experienced, it is likely that they will continue to resist change. If Mr. Thompson is to affect and institutionalize classroom change, he must either recruit young teachers who are willing to work with the curriculum coordinator, or get more directly involved in teacher improvement himself.

COMPARISONS BETWEEN HOOVER AND JOHNSON OVER TIME

Comparisons between Hoover and Johnson are dramatic: During LSES-III Johnson was superior to Hoover on all indices; at the time of LSES-IV Hoover surpassed Johnson on virtually every indicator of teacher/school effectiveness. Since the schools served the same student bodies during both phases of the study, the changes were attributable to school leadership and faculty.

As described by the TSEL in Chapter 4, entropy occurs at effective schools when successful processes fall apart due to a failure to keep them moving. In the case of Johnson, this was a function of several factors.

1. Too much energy was expended on external community-oriented processes.
2. There was no meaningful monitoring and evaluation of classrooms by the school leadership.
3. There was no individualized in-service program to remediate weaknesses of faculty members.
4. The principal used inappropriate hiring strategies, opting for older teachers instead of younger ones, who could devote more years of service to the school.
5. The curriculum coordinator failed to assume the academic leadership role that the principal had abandoned.
6. Johnson was characterized by several distinct grade-level climates, rather than one overall school climate.

At Hoover Elementary a dynamic new principal was intuitively able to demonstrate the strong instructional leader role described by Edmonds

(1979a, 1979b) and Brookover and Lezotte (1979). As indicated in Chapter 3, this type of leadership role is appropriate for lower-SES schools with a young faculty, both of which characterized Hoover.

A summary of the changes at Hoover between LSES–III and –IV is found in Table 8.1. The new principal, Mr. Jameson, was site-oriented, staying at the school throughout the day and monitoring the facility and individual classrooms. He was highly aware of academic and social problems at the school, whereas his predecessor was oblivious to them. Mr. Jameson dramatically switched the school's goals toward academics, with a de-emphasis on social services.

Mr. Jameson actively sought to improve classroom instruction. Due to a 48% turnover of instructional faculty, he was able to hire teachers that fit his overall educational philosophy. Through extensive monitoring of their classrooms, the principal discovered overall faculty weaknesses and pinpointed specific in-services to address them.

The principal also made organizational changes at the school level that directly affected classroom-level processes: He departmentalized instruction and appointed grade-level teacher leaders. There was a sharing of responsibility at the grade level, with each member of the group involved in determining who taught specific subjects.

These changes directly filtered down to the student level. Better discipline and higher time-on-task were natural consequences of the organizational changes at the school level. Teachers developed more positive attitudes toward students' potential for learning. As student achievement scores increased, the level of expectations continued to rise.

The processes described above are a clear example of naturally occurring school improvement without district initiative or approval (Stringfield & Teddlie, 1990). In such efforts, the principal, or a group of teachers, develops a proactive strategy for improving a previously unsuccessful school. More detail on leadership behavior at effective or improving schools is found in Chapter 9.

CONTEXTUAL DIFFERENCES DUE TO URBANICITY

The issue of contextual differences in school effects can now be expanded to include urbanicity factors. As implied by the descriptions in this chapter and Chapters 6 and 7, there are differences in the routes to effectiveness depending on the urbanicity context of schools. Table 8.2 summarizes 16 characteristics of differentiation between urban, suburban, and rural elementary schools. These characteristics are grouped

TABLE 8.1. Comparisons between Herbert Hoover Elementary School at LSES-III and LSES-IV

LSES-III	LSES-IV
1. District-oriented principal	1. School site-oriented principal
2. Principal not an instructional leader	2. Principal an active instructional leader
3. Principal unaware of problems at school	3. Principal highly aware of problems at school
4. School served as social service agency	4. School's primary emphasis on academics
5. High emphasis on PTA involvement	5. Low emphasis on PTA involvement
6. Principal had favorites among faculty	6. Principal displayed no overt favoritism
7. Underutilization of teacher aides	7. Appropriate utilization of teacher aides
8. Poor articulation and understanding of goals	8. Goals clearly stated in the "redbook"
9. No buffer to community; parents had direct access to classrooms	9. Buffer to the community; controlled parental access to classrooms
10. Little or no assistance given to faculty by school leadership	10. Direct, individualized assistance provided to faculty
11. No use of computer for record keeping	11. Extensive use of computer for organizational efficiency
12. Nondepartmentalized instruction	12. Departmentalized instruction
13. No grade level leaders	13. Faculty leaders at each grade level
14. Generally negative attitude toward students; low expectations for performance	14. More positive attitudes toward students; higher expectations for performance
15. Poor adherence to school schedule	15. Strict adherence to school schedule
16. Inflexible, three-step suspension process	16. Flexible, five-step suspension process
17. Poor classroom- and school-level discipline	17. Excellent classroom- and school-level discipline
18. Low time-on-task	18. High time-on-task
19. High variance among teachers in terms of effectiveness	19. Reduced variance among teachers in terms of effectiveness
20. Low student achievement	20. Improved student achievement

TABLE 8.2. Contextual Differences in Elementary Schools Due to Urbanicity

Urban Elementary Schools	Suburban Elementary Schools	Rural Elementary Schools
Community and District Office		
Adequate resources, but often inefficient delivery system	Adequate resources and delivery system	Typically inadequate resources
Typically weak community involvement, requiring strong leadership to develop	Intermediate-level community involvement	Strong community involvement
Community from which students are drawn may change radically, or may stay very stable	Community from which students are drawn may change due to rezoning, restructuring, etc.	Stable community
School may buffer itself from negative community influences	Typically no buffer to community influences	No buffer to community influences
Leadership		
Strong instructional leadership required for success	Managerial style of leadership often successful	Personalized leadership style, intermediate between manager and initiator
Discipline typically a problem requiring principal intervention and monitoring	Discipline varies depending on community, faculty, and principal characteristics	Discipline generally good
Leadership has moderate ties to district office	Leadership has moderate ties to district office	Typically close ties to central office
More participation by faculty in roles such as grade-level lead teacher, due to larger school size	Moderate involvement by faculty in leadership roles such as assistant principal, counselor (acting as administrator), and grade-level lead teacher	Less participation by faculty in roles such as grade-level lead teacher, due to typically smaller school size

160

Urban Elementary Schools	Suburban Elementary Schools	Rural Elementary Schools
Faculty and Instructional Organization		
Most likely to be departmentalized	May be departmentalized	Less likely to be departmentalized, due to smaller number of teachers per grade
Faculty recruitment easy or hard depending on school's reputation; appropriate substitutes moderately easy to find	Faculty easier to recruit; appropriate substitutes typically easier to find	Faculty hard to recruit; qualified substitutes hard to find
Variable student expectations, with present expectations pushed first and future expectations later	Some focus on future expectations for students, as well as present expectations	Focus on present expectations
Large variance in faculty stability, with some schools having greater instability	Moderately stable faculties	Stable faculty
Curriculum and Professional Development		
Variable curricula, some emphasizing basic skills and other a broader curriculum	Typically broader curriculum beyond basic skills	Limited curriculum, usually emphasizing basic skills
Moderate to high technology in classrooms	Moderate to high technology in classrooms	Low to moderate technology in classrooms
Adequate opportunities for in-service	Adequate opportunities for in-service	Fewer opportunities for in-service
Curriculum innovation highly varied	Curriculum innovation at moderate to high level	Curriculum innovation at low to moderate level

within four general areas: community/district office, leadership, instructional organization, and curriculum/professional development. Lomotey and Swanson (1990) presented a similar typology of urban and rural school characteristics, including several comparisons that are noted here.

Under community/district office characteristics, for instance, urban elementary schools are likely to have adequate resources but inefficient delivery systems. Under these conditions urban principals may expend a disproportionate amount of time ensuring that their schools get a fair share of resources, as Mr. Thompson at Johnson Elementary School did. Successful urban elementary school principals may be considered "political" because their urbanicity context forces them to cajole adequate resources from "contacts" at the central office.

The role of the rural principal with regard to resource allocation is quite different. Since school district resources are often inadequate in rural schools, effective principals (such as Mr. Smith at Truman Elementary School in Chapter 6) gather resources through close contacts with the community and its business leaders. In small towns an effective principal can help the school to become the focal point of the community and garner additional resources along the way.

Resource allocation and delivery are usually not an issue at suburban schools, but many of the other characteristics in Table 8.2 are. We suggest that the reader consider the various characteristics listed in the table and think about how effective principals at schools differing by urbanicity might utilize different strategies to produce greater effectiveness.

PART III

Special Topics Addressed by the LSES

The chapters in this part present information from the LSES on three special topics: the principals' roles in stable and changing schools, the interaction of teacher and school effects, and teacher socialization in differentially effective schools. Major results from the study in these areas are summarized, including information on how those findings may inform school improvement projects.

9 Principals' Roles in Stable and Changing Schools

Robert K. Wimpelberg

"Context" emerged as a major analytical concept in educational research in the 1980s (Wimpelberg, Teddlie, & Stringfield, 1989). Taking account of context in studying school effectiveness and improvement leads to a conclusion that while principals' leadership remains important, there is no single set of "best managerial behaviors" associated with positive effects in school settings. There are patterns, however, among the activities undertaken by principals in more and less effective schools.

The first task of this chapter is to review the findings in the earlier phases of the LSES. In the data from LSES-III (1984–85), managerial images or metaphors proved to capture some of the differences among principals in the two groups of schools categorized as more or less effective. A second objective of this chapter is to discuss patterns apparent in the management of LSES schools during the 5 years of "naturally occurring change" between LSES-III and -IV.

PRINCIPALS' IMAGES OF THEIR WORK, 1984–85

The most general profile drawn of principals characterized their approaches to leadership according to organizational and managerial images (Wimpelberg, 1987a). Content analyses were conducted on interview transcripts of principals' reactions to five statements:

1. When people think about my school, it stands for something special.
2. I am able to monitor classroom instruction very closely.
3. The most important criterion I use for evaluating the effectiveness of my teachers is how well they teach reading and math.
4. I have a lot of latitude in deciding which teachers to hire and keep.
5. The factor that has the strongest effect on how much our students learn is their family background. (Wimpelberg, 1987a, p. 2)

School Mission

When it came to mission ("what my school stands for"), principals in more effective schools mentioned children more frequently than their counterparts in less effective schools did. They described their (more effective) schools as "a home, as opposed to jail, for poor kids," a "positive climate—without belittlement," "a place where kids are taken care of with self-respect," "a place for high expectations and positive discipline," and "enrichment" for children. By contrast, principals in less effective schools offered either value systems or social services they were providing in behalf of parents as the *raison d'être* for their schools. These principals noted the "Christian values" they provided or the dedication to teach the dictum that "good manners are never going out of style." One principal cited her school's before- and after-school care as its essential mission, and another principal complained that his school was used for health care services that parents should be providing.

Classroom Instruction and Hiring

All principals thought they were active "instructional leaders" because they made informal observations, circulated through the building regularly, and played a major role in hiring staff. However, the ways in which principals talked about monitoring instruction and hiring their teachers differentiated between those in more and less effective schools.

In less effective schools, principals kept a distance from classrooms. Two principals talked about using the district evaluation process as a way of knowing (at least annually) about instruction. One principal had teachers come to her office for conferences about instruction. Another said he monitored instruction through outcomes: by reading report cards and behavior reports. Another principal said she kept tabs on instruction indirectly, through a curriculum coordinator who had the day-to-day job of interacting with teachers in classrooms. In more effective schools principals talked about making teachers and children comfortable with outsiders (including themselves) who wanted to visit classrooms. One principal claimed to do frequent demonstration lessons for teachers, and another read teachers' daily lesson plans before taking her walks through the halls to monitor instruction. These principals, more than those in the matched schools, could give personalized accounts of their teachers' instruction.

On the question related to hiring, principals in less effective schools recounted district procedures that they followed—from announcing vacancies, to interviewing candidates sent to them from central personnel offices, to making a recommendation to that office for hiring. Only one principal in a less effective school reported otherwise. In his case, the district director of personnel operated as a "dictator," placing teachers in vacancies without any consultation. Among the effective schools, the initiatory quality of the principals' approach to hiring stands in real contrast. One principal said she virtually "lived" in the personnel office, investigating candidates' files to find a good match for a vacant teaching position. Two others talked about "using" or "playing" the district hiring system to get the teachers they needed, always arguing for special consideration because of a population of exceptionally poor, single-parent families in one case, and a need to stabilize the white proportion of an integrated school population in another. A fourth principal described the way the school and central office engaged in active consultation around vacancies, both trying to make the best match for the vacant teaching position.

Basic Skills

While all principals in LSES-III agreed that reading and math were important criteria in helping them judge their teachers' effectiveness, the principals in less effective schools qualified their responses differently from those in more effective schools. The net result was that principals in less effective schools described reading and math as "the most important among *equally* important" kinds of learning. Principals appended to their endorsements of "the basics," similarly strong preferences for "teaching children on their level," "everything in the state curriculum," "classroom control," and "teaching children respect." In contrast, principals in more effective schools considered reading and math to be tools for higher order learning. "They're fundamental, but there's much more," said one principal. Another clarified that "reading serves *learning*, and it's important only in that way." Others said they liked it when reading and math were taught in a problem-solving, inferential learning mode. A principal who promoted children's story "writing" and developmental reading from kindergarten onward said, "Our babies got to start *thinking*."

Children's Family Background

In less effective schools, principals thought that the home environment had a dominant, often insurmountable effect. "You try to put your values on these kids but they don't fit," said one principal. In a school with a mixture of home situations, a principal said that less afflu-ent families "lack concern," and claimed that the school had a hard time overcoming parental indifference. In more effective schools, principals accepted differences among parents and the support they brought to the school. Instead of complaining if parental involvement were low, they helped parents work on their use of discipline, communication of aspirations, and homework checking. One principal explained: "Many pitiful kids have done well because of teachers and coun-selors; family expectations are important but not as important as the school's."

Summary

Firestone and Wilson (1985) assert that administrators can be "linked" to instruction and school climate in bureaucratic and cultural ways. Principals in more effective schools managed with an "instru-mental" use of rules and regulations; they checked lesson plans *before circulating in the hallways*, and they took themselves to the personnel office and checked applicants' files to find the best teachers. We might consider these as "effective bureaucracies." In less effective schools, the principals played out the routines, filled teaching vacancies according to system guidelines, and walked the hallways for visibility but not with an ear for classroom activities. In these schools, bureaucratic linkages take the lifeless forms that give the word *bureaucratic* its bad connotation. The cultural connections that principals create also dif-fer between the two groups of schools. In the less effective schools, norms of distance and laissez-faire indifference prevail; in the more ef-fective schools, norms of inter*active* professional relationships are more common.

Bolman and Deal (1984, 1991) also have categories of bureaucratic ("structural") and cultural management in their schemata. In addition to these frames, a third one (the "political") helps differentiate the groups. Both sets of principals can be described in terms related to each of Bolman and Deal's frames, but each frame's nuances vary between groups. Principals in less effective schools were overly restrictive in their use of structure or procedures, were defensive in their approach to political interests, and generated dysfunctional cultural norms. In more effective schools, principals were more selective in their use of structural management, were motivated most by the developmental needs of children when they behaved politically, and set cultural values that focused clearly on children as clients of the school.

THE PRINCIPALS FIVE YEARS LATER

In 1989–90, principals in eight of the 16 schools were different from those in 1984–85. The distribution of new principals among schools historically categorized as more and less effective was even. Four of the new principals were in historically *less* effective schools, four in historically *more* effective schools. The new principals were evenly distributed between schools that were "stable" across the timespan from LSES–III to –IV and schools that had changed, either for the better or worse (see Chapter 5). Among the four principals in schools judged less effective in 1984–85, two had no noticeable effect, and two promoted positive change. Among the four new principals in more effective schools, two were in stable schools, and two were presiding over declining environments.

Several databases were presented and discussed in Chapter 5. Four summary categories were established to reflect the condition of the 16 schools after the 5-year interval between LSES–III and –IV: *stable more effective, stable less effective, declining,* and *improving.* The 16 schools are distributed among these categories as follows:

stable more effective: 4   improving: 5
stable less effective: 4   declining: 3

Questionnaire results from principals and teachers gave us three simple measures of principals' self-perceptions, behaviors, and attitudes that begin to differentiate the four groups. The first measure reflected the LSES–III analysis that drew from Bolman and Deal's (1984, 1991) concept of "managerial frames." LSES–IV principals were asked to characterize themselves on a semantic/descriptor form developed by Bolman and Deal called *Leadership Orientations* (Leadership Frameworks, 1988). The questionnaire distinguishes among attitudes and traits that fit Bolman and Deal's definitions of "structural," "humanistic," "political," or "symbolic" management/leadership. Principals also completed an extended questionnaire (the "Principal Questionnaire") that was repeated in LSES–IV after its use in LSES–III. Eight questions on this form were extracted for analyses because the questions related to the principal's assessment of school reputation, instructional quality, and student achievement. Also, some questions measured the principal's sense of efficacy in influencing teaching behaviors and student achievement. Summative averages of the eight questions, calculated for each group of schools, show some comparative differences. Finally, nine questions from the BTQ that related to the principal's knowledge of, interactions with, and support for new teachers were averaged cumulatively for each group. Again, differences emerge.

Management and Leadership: Principals' and Teachers' Impressions

Bolman and Deal's "Leadership Orientations" questionnaire (Leadership Frameworks, 1988) asks respondents to complete six statements.

My strongest skills are:
The best way to describe me is:
What has helped me the most to be successful is my ability to:
What people are most likely to notice about me is my:
My most important leadership trait is:
I am best described as:

Each stem is followed by four descriptors, fitting each of the four Bolman and Deal managerial frames. A respondent is asked to rate the descriptor most like him or her with a "4," the next most characteristic descriptor with a "3," and so on. Average scores across all six items can range from 1 to 4. Mean scores, averaged for all principals in each group, are presented in Table 9.1.

That all principals most frequently chose descriptors from the "human resource" frame comes as no surprise. Roussel (1988) found this to be true among a sample of principals statewide in Louisiana. Educators like to think of themselves as "good listeners" who have a "concern

TABLE 9.1. Principals' Managerial Frames

Management Frame	School Group			
	Stable–More Effective ($n = 4$)	Stable–Less Effective ($n = 4$)	Improving ($n = 5$)	Declining ($n = 3$)
Structural	2.3	2.4	2.9	2.6
Human Resource	3.7	3.2	3.2	3.2
Political	2.0	1.9	1.7	2.1
Symbolic	1.7	2.2	2.0	1.8

Results from the Leadership Orientations questionnaire (Leadership Frameworks, 1988) used by permission.

for people"—responses in the Leadership Orientations questionnaire that would lead to higher "human resource" scores. Highest in this category are the principals in *stable more effective* schools (mean of 3.7). The human resource average was the highest of the four managerial scores for all four groups. Generally speaking, the stable more effective schools were characterized by caring relationships between principal and teachers.

Principals with the highest mean "structural" score were in *improving* schools. These principals tended to see themselves as "analysts," "technical experts," and liking to "pay attention to detail." It is in these schools more than others that we see a systematic use of policies and planned activities intended to shape teacher and student behavior or academic performance.

Few principals saw themselves as political or symbolic managers; the ranges ran from 1.7 to 2.1 for political items and 1.7 to 2.2 for symbolic items. The principals in *improving* schools, however, tended to shy away from political descriptors more than the principals in the other groups. They tended not to describe themselves as "tough, skilled negotiators" with the "ability to succeed in the face of conflict and opposition." This outcome belies the assertiveness with which these principals commandeered resources for their schools, including "better" teachers, and the extent to which they influenced curricular and instructional decisions in their schools by using alliances among teachers with whom they felt most familiar and comfortable. Like other principals, those in *improving* schools may have avoided political descriptors on the questionnaire because "politics" is perceived as anathema to good educational practice.

The LSES "Principal Questionnaire" asked principals about their perceptions of matters like the reputation of their school, its achievement, the importance of academic subjects in the total curriculum, teachers' approaches to organizing instruction, and their self-perceived influence on teaching and learning. On summary averages of eight such items, the principals' groups divided into two categories. *Stable more effective* and *improving* school principals scored more positively; *stable less effective* and *declining* school principals scored less positively. Principals in the *stable more effective* and *improving* schools averaged 2.9 on these measures, on a scale of 5 (high) to 1 (low). Principals in the *stable less effective* and *declining* schools averaged 2.4 and 2.6, respectively, on the measures.

These results suggest a certain candor across groups; principals in stable less effective and declining schools reported that their schools' reputations and their students' achievement were not "among the best." They also thought that their schools' teaching of academic subjects and their teachers' use of individualization were less than optimal. As school "leaders," they tended to remove themselves from having a central role in affecting teaching methods and students' achievement. Principals in stable less effective and declining schools reported that their schools were having problems, but claimed that they had limited capacity or opportunity to make things better. In contrast, principals in stable more effective and improving schools were more sanguine about their schools' performance, and they ascribed more responsibility and influence to their own role in fostering better teaching and learning.

A third data source was the BTQ that asked novice teachers to describe their principals' levels of familiarity with their classrooms and instructional concerns, as well as the principals' efforts to support and assist them. Summary averages for nine items extracted from this questionnaire show some delineation among stable and changing schools. Principals in *stable more effective* and *improving* schools are rated the most positive (means of 5.0 and 4.4, respectively, on a scale that runs from 6 [highest] to 1 [lowest]). Principals in *stable less effective* schools had the lowest average score (4.0), and principals in *declining* schools fared as well as those in *improving* schools, with an average score of 4.6. The most notable outcome here is the low mean for principals in persistently less effective schools. Data on the nine BTQ items suggest that a lack of interaction between principals and new teachers, a shallow familiarity with new teachers' work and professional needs, and a paucity of supportive administrative help set this group off from the other three. To the extent that active socialization sponsored by the principal may be a necessary ingredient in positive school change, we have some clear evidence to explain the continued "stability" of less effective schools.

School Effectiveness Theory, School Stability, and Change

The TSEL posits that school effectiveness can be predicted by the "fit" among three sets of school elements: administrative appropriateness, teacher preparedness, and student readiness. Implied in this tiered approach to school effectiveness is the proposition that leadership appropriateness involves the principal's making judgments about the technical and motivational qualities of the teaching staff with a will to change instruction *or instructors* when children are not being well served. Administrative intervention may be indicated when "low readiness" children are not being offered clear, structured learning opportunities with ample repetition, practice, and reteaching. Also, children are not well served if they have a strong history of achievement but are subjected to overly structured, rigidly paced, and boringly slow instruction, and changes promoted by the principal would be in order. A similar approach to "appropriateness" and "fit" can be taken relative to extra-classroom life. Activities in the hallways, on the yard, at lunch and recess, and in meetings can be regulated with varying degrees of structure depending on the students' behavioral readiness. Too much procedural control is inappropriate when students perceive it as demeaningly distrustful and without cause. The psychological climate in a school (and one aspect of its effectiveness) will surely suffer. Likewise, a disregard for behavioral standards among students who are not ready to be self-regulating will also lead to school decline.

Administrative appropriateness is demonstrated in the *stable more effective* schools. In Kennedy Elementary (see Chapter 7), where norms of faculty cohesiveness and nascent student democracy were present in 1984–85 and persisted to 1989–90, the principal facilitated teachers' work with an informal touch, promoting the varieties of separate decisions that teachers made and reinforcing teachers' motivation to enact their ideas. Shifting the context to schools where teacher characteristics were different, two other principals (one at Truman Elementary, described in Chapter 6) had teachers who tended to work alone; they also had a continual pattern of teacher turnover that could have threatened the sustained achievement of students who, although from poor backgrounds, had performed well on the 1984–85 assessments. In these two schools, principals monitored instruction directly and frequently, and, when it weakened, took direct, decisive action, moving teachers among classrooms and instituting semi-departmentalization to take advantage of teachers' capabilities and reduce their difficulties. Among the *stable more effective* schools, appropriate leadership sustained schools in their effectiveness *relative to the characteristics of teachers in those schools*. In no case did the student body's collective "readiness" change, nor did the teaching staff's technical capabilities so accelerate that these schools became "unusually effective." They did, however, maintain their positive outlier status within their pairings.

Among *stable less effective* schools (such as Coolidge Elementary, described in Chapter 7), principals kept their distance from classrooms and developed few improvement plans. All these schools had student clienteles from low-SES backgrounds, urban and rural, and their teachers used instructional time poorly. Moreover, because the principals were unfamiliar with or unwilling to act on classroom conditions, leadership was *in*appropriate for these teachers. Such are the conditions for the TSEL stage labeled Type A (refer to Figure 4.1).

Administrative appropriateness in *declining* schools generates other scenarios. In two of the three schools (such as Adams Elementary, described in Chapter 10) in this category, a significant number of middle class students moved or were "districted" away from the schools during the middle 1980s. By 1989–90, a larger portion of the student body was achieving below grade level, compared with achievement in 1984–85. When we investigate the notion of "fit" between teacher characteristics and student readiness, we notice that one school declined because its new teachers didn't have the patience necessary for students who were distracted and needed well-structured pacing. In this school, new teachers tended to "cover material," wasting lots of time quelling interruptions that were, indirectly, the product of their own inept instruction. The principal delegated the task of helping struggling new teachers to the grade-level chairs without specific instructions or explicit expectations.

In another declining school (Johnson Elementary, described in Chapter 8), an energetic principal in LSES-III exhorted teachers with motivational slogans and a dedication to helping children from "the projects," just as he had been. By LSES-IV, the rhetoric was as loud but none of its energy was being transformed into instructional improvement. Teachers, who were relatively unskilled and intolerant, did whatever they pleased during class time, including paddling students as part of a physical approach to discipline that absorbed large parts of their time. The spirited, motivated environment that appeared to be paying off in 1984–85 had lost its punch, and the school was foundering. In both these schools, the principals' leadership modes were poorly matched to schools' teacher characteristics.

Leadership in *improving* schools has its own patterns. The principal at Hoover Elementary (see Chapter 8) helped his school by imposing behavioral structures on teachers' work, where laissez-faire permissiveness had prevailed. He individualized assistance for teachers, and established and maintained attention to the goal of helping each child succeed. This principal recruited new teachers who had a lively interest in teaching, and he eased out those "going through the motions." In another *improving* school (Fillmore, described in Chapter 10), the principal badgered teachers with testing procedures until they paid off; she also positioned and repositioned teachers at different grade levels and different subject emphases until the person's strengths found fertile ground or until the person's weaknesses had the least ill effect. In a third case, the principal was almost a bystander in a setting that inherited a curriculum coordinator who spent her days with teachers, helping them find materials and showing them new ways to reteach a lesson.

In another *improving* school, the student body changed and so did the teaching staff. In 1984–85 the school's clientele was a mixture of poor neighborhood children and children of professional families who were designated for this school because of its extended-care program. In 1984–85 the school focused its efforts on the out-of-school hours and special programs, meeting neither the needs of the more "at-risk" neighborhood children nor those of the academically "more ready" who commuted. In 1989–90, the school had a new principal who renegotiated the school's boundaries so that it would serve only professional families. She also brought several capable teachers with her. In all these stories of *improving* schools, we see evidence of leadership that "fit" the developmental needs of the teaching staff *given the pre-existing context of student readiness*.

LEADERSHIP AS A CULTURAL ORIENTATION

The analytical framework offered by the TSEL has an instrumental quality, suggesting that an organizational calculus is necessary to align principals, teachers, and students optimally. For this and other studies of the principal's role in creating or sustaining effective schooling, we also turned to Mitchell's (1990) cultural propositions about leadership. His cultural orientation, while not as extensive as to include teacher and student characteristics, helps us expand the TSEL notion of administrative appropriateness by introducing the prospect that principals may bring to their work varying kinds of *personal predispositions toward the nature of "best teaching" (and the "right" of teachers to define "best teaching")* that will further differentiate the ways they work with teachers. This section introduces the central elements in Mitchell's "cultural theory of the principalship" and applies it to the four groupings of schools that we have been using in our analyses.

Mitchell's Cultural Theory of the Principalship

In an integrative approach to thinking about principals' influence on schools, particularly through their effects on and interactions with teachers, Mitchell (1990) cross-references concepts originating in leadership theory and research. Mitchell borrows the dichotomies of "transaction" vs. "transformation" (Burns, 1978) and "task" versus "person" (Fiedler, 1967; Stogdill & Coons, 1957). He draws conceptual parallels between (1) transactional leadership and a leader's emphasis on task achievement, and (2) transformational leadership and a leader's emphasis on the persons doing an organization's work. These two fundamental orientations in the research literature—and important in the notion of administrative appropriateness in the TSEL—are further overlaid with other theoretical propositions that Mitchell argues also run parallel to the transaction/task and transformation/person dimensions.

To this fundamental duality Mitchell adds a cross-cutting set of "cultural orientations" that completes his cultural theory of the principalship. The two cultural orientations that cut across the transaction/task and transformation/person dimensions have to do with a leader's concept of work. The notion of culture concerns principals' orientations and the purposes they ascribe to schoolwork. Alternative "cultures" are not intended to be *Mitchell's* diagnostic categories for organizational contexts per se. They are alternative ways of typing *principals' cognitive predispositions* toward schools and the activities that take place in them. A leader might think of work as an impersonal set of standardized routines with a perspective reminiscent of the cultural orientation Weber (1946) calls *gesellschaft* and Mitchell calls a "settlement culture." Its counterpart is *gemeinschaft* ("frontier culture") where work activities are perceived as problem-solving opportunities, and adaption and analysis are ever present since change and uncertainty are accepted as conditions of work life. Figure 9.1 offers a simplified representation of Mitchell's theoretical proposition in a two-by-two grid of "principal orientation options." The intersections of the two leader orientations (transaction/task vs. transformation/person) and the two cultural orientations (settlement vs. frontier) produce the four principal orientation options of Supervisor, Administrator, Manager, and Leader.

Supervisor in a Settlement Culture. The principal as *supervisor* assumes that the school is a settlement culture where standard operating

FIGURE 9.1. Cultural Orientations Among Principals

	Transaction/ Task	Transformation/ Person
Settlement Cultures	SUPERVISOR	ADMINISTRATOR
Frontier Cultures	MANAGER	LEADER

Adapted with permission from Mitchell, 1990, p. 13.

procedures best govern workers' behaviors. The principal's own orientation to personal "theories" of leadership emphasizes task accomplishment and views the leader/worker contacts as "an exchange of valued things" (Burns, 1978, p. 19). The resources that leader and workers bring to bear on their interactions and the attitudes they have about their workplace negotiations are central to the transactional (hence, *supervisor*) orientation. Mitchell says that the principal-as-*supervisor* is diligent to see that teachers carry out well-structured lessons and teach with instructional techniques "known" to be effective. Such principals tend to reinforce loyalty to the curricular and behavioral programs adopted by the school or school district.

Administrator in a Settlement Culture. The principal as *administrator* sits at the intersection of the settlement culture and transformational/ person-oriented position. The *administrator* assumes that school activities can and must be coordinated through orderly and routinized procedures; unlike the *supervisor*, however, the *administrator* does not approach technical work of teachers with centrally prescribed performance rules. Instead, the *administrator* searches for structures that facilitate the independent efforts of teachers, who are expected to apply their professional training for maximized outcomes. Usually this approach involves the separation and coordination of distinctive staffs— a production staff (teachers) who work in a relatively detached manner using discretionary powers, and a support staff under the direct supervision of the *administrator*.

Manager in a Frontier Culture. The remaining two principal orientation options fall in the domain of the frontier culture. Like the *supervisor*, the *manager* devalues interpersonal relationships in favor of task performance. Unlike the *supervisor*, however, the *manager* does not see task execution as a matter of performing correct and prevalidated work behaviors. The *manager* stresses the continual diagnosis of problems for which the production staff is assumed (or trained) to have a repertoire of applicable techniques. Student learning styles, then, can be accepted in all their variations. The teacher's job, according to the *manager*, is to analyze the child's learning needs, plan an intervention, and match the most appropriate instructional techniques with the problem. The *manager* assumes that variations among children and learning environments require analysis and adaptation, and uses indices of student outcomes as the measure of success.

Leader in a Frontier Culture. The *leader* approaches teaching as a performing art, rather than prescribed behaviors (*supervisor*), delegated professional activity (*administrator*), or skilled craft (*manager*). Like the *manager*, the *leader* assumes that the organizational culture does not lend itself to standardizing work activities. Nevertheless, the *leader* does not conceptualize good teaching as diagnosis and planned intervention, as the *manager* would. Rather, the *leader* "depends on how well key staff adopt creative, high energy and deeply-engaged techniques like those characteristics of excellence in the performing arts" (Mitchell, 1990, p. 18). *Leaders* do not emphasize student outcomes so much as the robustness of school activities. When students are actively engaged, when teachers are continually adjusting and trying out instructional approaches, when excitement and energy are characteristic of the school environment, *leaders* have a sense that the organization and its workers are doing well.

Stability, Change, and the Cultural Orientations of Principals

Missing Leadership in Stable Less Effective and Declining Schools. Mitchell draws on the work of Burns (1978) in formulating his cultural theory of the principalship. An underlying principle in Burns's work is that *purpose* is critical. The reasons why a principal takes action or does not, or chooses to intervene rather than keep distant from teachers' work, have to do with "certain motives and purposes" that lead to the principal's use of resources to "arouse, engage and satisfy the motives of followers" (Burns, 1978, pp. 18,19). An important clarification here has to do with the scope of Burns's leadership theory; simply put, how much of the behavior of apparently ineffective, dysfunctional, or even destructive principals can be understood *within* the purposive approach that Burns lays out as he develops the two dimensions of transactional and transformational leadership. The view we will take here is that Burns's propositions imply that either transactional or transformational norms and behaviors can be developmentally positive. While there is surely a sense of value scaling that can be ascribed to them—in which we would advocate the conditions and political environment in which all principals could be *transformational* leaders—there is the prospect in Burns that even transactional leaders can preserve basically positive activities and climates for children. One question worth asking is whether the principals in stable less effective and declining schools fit into the Burns's leadership dichotomy and also into Mitchell's four-part model.

One issue raised by this question concerns the *audience* to whom a principal's purposive behaviors respond. Two declining schools (e.g., Johnson Elementary) and two stable less effective ones (e.g., Coolidge

Elementary) appeared to be suffering in 1989–90 with principals who "faced outward" and disregarded their teachers and students. One principal in a persistently less effective school sized up his problem as a matter of "public relations." "I have to change the school's reputation," he asserted, and his plans for hiring a new assistant principal when his student count would allow it included a primary charge to that person to "help with public relations." His price in landing a major company as a school "partner" was that it would "legitimize the school," "convey a new image to the community." Attending to public impressions and the external community is not a bad thing. What characterized this school is that concern with image dominated the principal's presentation of the school, and there was little developmental activity within the school to offset it.

In a similar situation in another school, a teacher described her principal as "caring more about getting the grass cut than whether children were learning." This principal was noticeably nervous when our observation teams were present, and frequently resisted or delayed our coming to the school. Both these principals who were concerned about external appearances also talked to their teachers in demanding, harsh tones. Observers noted that both tended to order teachers to come to the door for introductions when our researchers arrived. They habitually interrupted instruction, without apology or consideration. In the matter of *audience* these principals put a significant amount of energy into external relations, with little, if any, effort to develop teachers and instruction.

Another principal in a stable less effective school (Coolidge Elementary) who was also known as a good "public relations" person seemed to expend more time and energy outside his school than in it, and with debilitating effects. The principal challenged himself to amass a record number of business sponsors and to create positive images of the school for public consumption. Yet he was criticized by his faculty for the empty claims he made for the school. Two observers noted that in interviews he simultaneously (1) criticized teachers and students in sarcastic terms, and (2) made positive claims about the school's instructional program. In responding to a question about how one could make a bad school better, this principal said he would assume that the problem was a difficulty "in teaching material," which he would fix by close supervision of teachers. In isolation this statement might be reasonable; in the context of his treatment of teachers and in light of their comments, the response characterizes a principal who works diligently on external impressions and is harsh with faculty.

In fact, while he was especially conscious of the external audience, he had two different internal ones. He relied on some teachers to help with tasks and spent a moderate amount of time outside his office in their classes. Other teachers were disregarded altogether, including one who routinely humiliated students. At times, this principal acted a bit like Mitchell's *supervisor*, offering "correct" techniques for teaching math. He had no noticeable follow-through, however, that would express an interest in his teachers sustaining the "best methods" he was advocating. If it is a prerequisite of the *supervisor* orientation that prescriptive instructional methods not only be maintained as a work activity norm but also be reinforced in a systematic manner, the behavior of this principal would fall outside Mitchell's leadership grid.

In its purest expression, nonleadership took the form of neglect (benign or not) in two declining schools and one stable less effective school. One declining school (Adams Elementary) appeared to be coping, with decreasing success, with student population change and teacher turnover. The principal described her earlier years (in the mid-1980s) in the principalship as a period of reluctance, saying she wasn't sure she wanted to be a principal and hadn't learned how to act as one. Her calm, steady temper made her a likable person, but it was also the source of frustration among teachers who wanted her to exercise a stronger role as a disciplinarian. Learning symbols that had characterized the school under its previous leadership had fallen victim to neglect. Newer teachers—whom she acknowledged as having difficulties and whom our observers recorded as being harsh and inefficient—were dependent on the occasional attention of a grade-level lead teacher. This principal lacked even the energy that those described earlier directed toward outside audiences. She maintained an orderly environment with little press or activity that could exemplify any of the principal orientations in Mitchell's theory.

Another principal in a historically more effective school (Johnson Elementary)—who had infused a considerable degree of energy into his school in LSES-III, had raised the positive consciousness of the staff and children for African-American culture (through omnipresent slogans and pictures of African-American heros), and had talked eloquently about the importance of "getting our babies to think"—did little more than toot the same horn in the intervening 5 years until LSES-IV. Meanwhile, teachers were paddling children to keep them under control and were conducting lessons with unusually high rates of time-off-task. Even though the principal was constantly on the move throughout the building, there were no signs that he was at all bothered by excessive noise in classrooms, teachers' use of paddling, and a relentless reliance on seatwork as a mode of instruction. His neglect could be considered neither "leadership" nor a benign form of withdrawal.

Yet another principal in a stable less effective school, who had taken over her school between LSES-III and -IV, acted reserved and shy in interactions with our research team and with her teachers. Her teaching and administrative experience in secondary schools made the elementary level new to her, and she talked about expecting a secondary school assignment in time. She could talk with detailed understanding about many of her teachers, and she appeared to appreciate the special qualities of her stronger new teachers, yet we saw no overt efforts to develop her faculty either through promulgating standardized instruction or coordinated support (as the *supervisor* or *administrator* might undertake) or by encouraging sharing of craft and performance knowledge (characteristic of the *manager* or *leader*).

Principal Activity in Stable More Effective and Improving Schools. Four principals in schools that appeared to be noticeably more effective in 1989–90 than they were in 1984–85 can be called incipient *administrators*. One school (Hoover Elementary) had higher test scores that could be attributed directly to higher time-on-task and a more serious learning climate. This school moved from random, often chaotic activity under one principal to significantly tighter structure (and visibly improved teacher attitudes) under a new principal. The new principal talked about part of his task as taking the paperwork load off teachers and "creating a safe and orderly environment" for them and their students. Although "structure" more than "human relations" shapes the dominant images of this man's school (he requires teachers to refer to the "redbook," which is his internal policy manual), the intent to create a predictable and certain environment for teachers rather than a rigid bureaucracy comes through. The net effect this principal set out to create was more time for teachers to focus on their primary function: "managing classrooms and asking good, intelligent questions" of children.

Two other *administrator*-principals in improving schools garnered significant gains in test scores as a result of a structured focus on test-taking during the years 1984–90. In one case the principal hired a curriculum coordinator to help teachers fine tune their preparation of children for test-taking. The results so pleased the principal that, as a reward for his faculty, he instituted a duty-free lunch time during which he monitored the children. As is the case with the *administrator* in Mitchell's nomenclature, the principal enacted a facilitator's role, supporting and coordinating the work of relatively autonomous teachers with a special-purpose staff person.

In another school that had "closed the gap" (Fillmore Elementary) with its more effective partner, a principal's unrelenting quest for test improvement remedies during the 5-year interval between LSES-III and

-IV appeared to have paid off. Her school's scores on our NRT improved, despite a less strongly middle class student clientele. During interviews she joked about her obsession with finding mechanisms to help her dedicated teachers get the scores she knew their students "deserved." One observer witnessed an exchange between the principal and one of her more energetic teachers in which the principal informed the teacher that yet another test-taking idea had arrived in the principal's mail, to which the teacher replied, "Not another one!" The *administrator* in this principal also came through in her methods of fitting teachers with student groups according to the teachers' apparent strengths. Year in and year out she would move teachers among grade levels and encourage their departmentalization in the upper elementary grades in order to have them teach "from a position of strength." She did little instructional coaching around their weaknesses (a *supervisor's* or *manager's* approach), and she showed no evidence of appreciating the "artfulness" of good teaching (as the *leader* might), yet her coordinating activities for teachers appears to have helped over time with student outcomes.

A principal in a stable more effective school (Truman Elementary) played out the *manager's* orientation. Measured outcomes constituted his "bottom line." Any evidence of slippage, either in classroom climate or test scores, brought quick action. His approach was problem-oriented more than prescriptive; he would give a troublesome situation time to work itself out. While he was "giving a problem time to work out," he would have analytical conversations with the teacher, conduct or arrange for demonstration teaching, and enlist the aid of specialists. On occasion, he was known to "counsel" a teacher out of teaching.

During the 1989–90 observation year, this principal noticed that a new teacher was not managing reading instruction well with a sixth-grade class. The principal viewed the teacher as having potential but would not let her jeopardize the reading development of the sixth graders. Thus, when assistance failed to improve her students' reading scores, the principal restructured the fifth- and sixth-grade schedules so that a veteran fifth-grade teacher would do all the reading instruction and the new teacher would concentrate on math. The principal also compensated for a third-grade weakness when his trusted veteran there broke her leg and needed a long recuperation. Instead of entrusting the student outcomes in reading and math to a long-term, though unpredictable, substitute teacher, he made sure that his certified and proven Chapter 1 teacher conducted the instruction. In making these kinds of modifications in students' instruction, this principal did not institute permanent routines, as did the *administrator*-principal cited above. Instead, he took measures to solve immediate problems, fully expecting that new conditions would arise and require further adjustments in support of teachers' work. In the end, task accomplishment (defined as the highest possible student achievement results) constituted his criterion for executing an intervention.

Only one principal (Ms. Davis at Kennedy) among our 16 reminds us of *Mitchell's leader*. Although there are tangible programs that we can attribute directly to actions by her, this principal worked mostly by fostering an open, problem-solving environment in which teachers were expected (and had learned how) to inquire and innovate. This school was the only one in which the principal and teachers were curious about our classroom observation instruments, not because of a defensive interest in how our measures might catch them up short, but in the hope that our findings might help them improve.

The principal was a key but quiet force in the school. She had established clear rules of decorum and got immediate quiet if ever she encountered students who were in the hallways and talking while classes were in session. The principal played a major role in scheduling and guarded virtually every available minute of instructional time, yet it was her teachers who created three reading groups among their three third-grade classrooms to find the optimal conditions for their students. This principal was blessed with an extraordinarily stable faculty that experienced little turnover during the LSES. Yet between 1984 and 1989, nearly one-third of the middle class students in the school was lost due to economic deterioration in the neighborhood. The new student body seemed to alter the conditions of her work, as the principal defined it, but not its purpose.

BEYOND THE SCHOOL: THE EFFECTS OF CENTRAL OFFICE

This chapter (and most of this book) focuses on the school site, its leadership, and its instructional infrastructure. Although no formal data collection delved into the district contexts in which the schools were set, the effects of central decisions on the working situations in schools emerged over time and, with LSES-IV, became even more apparent.

Incidental findings in earlier phases had prompted us to write about district-level issues (Wimpelberg, 1987b; Wimpelberg et al., 1989). The role of the central office in promoting effective change and supporting both the technical and cultural parts of school development is taking a prominent place in our understanding of schools and change. Similarly, in the case of the successful adoption and implementation of larger curricular programs, Fullan (1991) has noticed that a district-level knowledge base and systematic follow-up are critical. Murphy and Hallinger (1988) have identified a set of California school *districts* that they have dubbed "more effective," where superintendents introduce and promote structured curriculum and achievement-enhancing models.

Central office effects on the conditions in LSES schools were, if anything, detrimental. The strongest form and direction in which central office influence expressed itself was the assignment of inactive or soon-to-retire principal to schools that were in transition or needed assertive leadership. One small-town school with strong community backing had begun to lose its better teachers and failed to attract strong candidates, in part because the instructionally assertive principal died and was replaced by a principal who made his intentions to retire soon evident. There is surely more than one story to be told about central office influence on schools via principalship appointments, and this case probably has to do with a tendency to take for granted the operation of a high-achieving school. Such a setting may be viewed as self-sustaining and invulnerable to managerial style. The small-town example in LSES-IV, however, tells a story of quick decline with the appointment of an inactive principal.

An advocate of public relations mentioned earlier in this chapter (Mr. Lambert at Coolidge), who replaced a principal also famous for her external image building, is known by the research team to carry the high regard of his district's central office administrators. This person is "maintaining," virtually unchanged, a school that was in the less effective category in 1984–85. During the spring visit by our research team, the new principal was on extended leave for medical reasons and a retired principal was called into service to direct the school. At the time of our observations, the substitute principal claimed to know none of the teachers' names.

A new principal in a high-achieving school trying to maintain its effectiveness level, even with a rapidly changing student body, told stories of exercising caution in making changes. She equated "making a school better" with "making trouble" as far as the central office is concerned. "Pressing for change is outside of central office expectations," she explained.

None of the principals noted having significant interaction with district supervisors, although two reported to as many as four central administrators. While we were conducting our research in 1989–90, none of the schools was in overt crisis, and it appears that such a condition allows central office supervisors to stay away. In at least half the schools, declining test scores and teacher dissatisfaction would have been signal enough to prompt more interactions between school supervisors and principals. Yet no such activity was apparent.

SUMMARY: MULTILEVEL INFLUENCES ON SCHOOL EFFECTIVENESS

It is encouraging that more sophisticated analyses of effective schooling by the education research community do not automatically begin and end with school principals. We have gotten used to the idea that school context also matters a lot—the background of the students, the experience and stability of the faculty, the manner in which parents interact with school people, and the support structure in the school district. Studying the roles of teachers as classroom and school leaders, principals as school managers and change facilitators, and central office administrators as supporters creates a nested context for the kinds of effective-school practices that can translate into children's learning and well-being.

The nested concept, with the school principal at the center, allows us to isolate interesting patterns across institutional levels. In the less effective schools studied in LSES, for example, one may detect a kind of conceptual parallel between the isolation of schools from the central office and the distancing of principals from teachers, and teachers from students that takes place in the declining and stable less effective schools. This climate of disconnectedness appears to be modified by individual principals who are active in their work and who focus their energies internally. Without such principals, however, there appears to be scant evidence of a central office "corrective" on which the teachers, children, and parents can rely.

Happily, some newer approaches to developing better school leadership have begun to build multilevel training into their programs. Adaptable school-level change processes in such programs are understood to be embedded in district contexts. A prime example of the multilevel conceptualization is offered by the California School Leadership Academy, which has added a cross-cutting set of programs for school-site teams and for superintendents to its professional development sequence for principals, based on a comprehensive approach to facilitating and maintaining skill development and culture building in schools and districts (Roberts, 1991).

There is no mistaking that the several years of data in the LSES confirm the central, pivotal criticality of the principal. Yet the analytical schemata used to interpret the data in this study—the TSEL and Mitchell's theoretical framework for principals' leadership—lend themselves to making sense of relationships between central structures and schools as much as between principals and teachers, and between teachers and students. Principals happen to find themselves situated in the middle of things.

10 Effective Teaching Within the Context of Effective Schooling

During the past 25 years, the research areas of teacher and school effects emerged separately. Both areas involved study of processes ongoing within elementary and secondary school settings, yet the two fields developed independently. For example, two reviews written in the mid-1980s of the school effects area (Good & Brophy, 1986) and of the teacher effects area (Brophy & Good, 1986) listed a total of 328 references. Of these, only nine overlapped (less than 3% of the total). Most teacher effectiveness studies have been concerned with processes that occur within classrooms, to the exclusion of anything going on schoolwide. Similarly, most school effects studies have involved phenomena that occur in the school, with little emphasis on teaching behaviors within classrooms.

The segregation of these literatures occurred in spite of the logical link between the two. In a recent review of the effective schools literature, Levine and Lezotte (1990) noted that:

> Based on both logic and common sense, educators seem justified in assuming that teachers in effective schools are more likely to use effective teaching and classroom management practices. Unfortunately . . . this conclusion is not well established by systematic research. (p. 30)

This lack of systematic research on teacher behavior within school effects research was succinctly described by Good & Brophy (1986).

> To date not a single naturalistic study of effective schools provides basic data (means and standard deviations for each classroom) to demonstrate that the behavior of individual teachers in one school differs from the behavior of teachers in other schools. (p. 586)

This statement is no longer true, as will be demonstrated by the series of studies (Stringfield & Teddlie, 1991c) described in the rest of this chapter.

187

Before reviewing these studies, however, it is useful to consider why studies nesting teacher effects within school effects have only recently been undertaken. The next section will explore methodological and theoretical biases that led to the lack of such studies.

WHY HASN'T SCHOOL EFFECTS RESEARCH
INCLUDED CLASSROOM DATA?

There are theoretical and methodological blinders that have led teacher and school effects researchers to ignore each other's domains. An overriding difference between researchers in the two areas concerns their intellectual training and the biases associated with these disciplines. Many teacher effects researchers come out of educational psychology, which emphasizes the study of individual differences and student/teacher interactions, while downplaying the role of organizations. Many school effects researchers come from educational administration or sociology of education backgrounds, which emphasize the effect of complex organizations and downplay teacher/student interactions.

From the point of view of the school effects researcher, there have been several reasons to avoid collecting teacher effects data. First, school effects researchers were interested in molar behavior that could be determined to vary across schools, rather than molecular behavior that varies across classrooms. Often, these researchers were interested in determining the characteristics of successful schools that could be manipulated to change the behavior of all classes within a failing school. The quickest way to affect change of that magnitude is to study and manipulate school variables, rather than individual classroom variables.

Second, researchers and reformers in the late 1970s and early to mid-1980s were often committed to the five-factor model of school effects. These factors involved schoolwide processes that superseded individual classroom behavior.

Levine and Lezotte (1990) list two additional reasons why support for effective teaching practices is relatively weak in effective schools research: (1) effective teaching practices are "difficult to assess"; and (2) there are difficulties in "trying to reach generalizable conclusions regarding optimal uses of reinforcement, lesson sequencing, 'wait time' after questions, teacher–student interaction guidelines, and other teaching techniques" (p. 30). Thus, school effects researchers have methodological problems with teacher effects data: The information is hard to gather, and they are unclear what to do with it once it has been collected.

A fifth difficulty that school effects researchers have with teacher effects data concerns their agendas for school improvement. Some school effects/school improvement researchers are reluctant to emphasize teacher effects because they are concerned this would lead to an emphasis on classroom reform, rather than school reform. Such turf guarding between these two areas is unproductive, since true change in elementary/secondary schools must occur at both the school and class level simultaneously.

The two areas of school and teacher effects are vitally linked in terms of both reform efforts and future research. For instance, getting a faculty involved in self-improvement under the umbrella of school effects is a less offensive method of promoting teacher improvement than harping on individual teacher weaknesses. An appeal to superordinate goals (Brown, 1986; Sherif & Sherif, 1953) and team playing is a more attractive reform package to teachers than blaming low achievement solely on poor teaching practices. Blase and Kirby (1992) have recently described methods whereby effective principals improve their teachers' performance.

Finally, there are financial reasons that preclude the gathering of classroom behavior data across entire schools. Gathering such data is labor intensive and quite costly. With the reduction in educational research funds during the Reagan/Bush presidencies, funding for such studies has not been available (Good, 1989).

RECENT STUDIES OF TEACHER/SCHOOL EFFECTS

The rest of this chapter describes a series of studies conducted in Louisiana over the past decade, some associated with the LSES and some not. The commonality for these investigations is their study of teacher effects data within the context of school effects research. These studies revealed consistent mean and standard deviation differences between schools classified as effective or ineffective.

It is our experience that when school effects studies are properly designed, consistent patterns of differences in both mean scores and variances of teaching behaviors in schools will be found. As noted by several authors (e.g., Davis & Thomas, 1989; Gage, 1985), patterns in the variation of behavior, as well as the central tendencies, are important to understanding classroom and school processes.

Stringfield, Teddlie, and Suarez (1985)

As part of LSES-III, we compared a pair of schools designated as effective and ineffective during the 1984–85 school year. The report on these two case studies preceded by 4 years a report on the complete set of 16 schools from LSES-III (Teddlie et al., 1989). The two case studies will be summarized here, since they provide a valuable illustration of the basic issues concerning the interaction of school and teacher effects.

These two LSES-III case studies were of the schools designated as Pair 3 in Chapter 5. This negative and positive outlier pair of schools were from a large, middle class, relatively affluent suburban district. Both schools were majority white, though each had a substantial minority population. Both schools were located in middle class single-family dwelling neighborhoods.

The district had a highly centralized, standardized elementary curriculum. The curriculum included four tracks: 1A (advanced work for gifted students), 1 (a curriculum for students scoring in the top 23% on the Comprehensive Test of Basic Skills or CTBS), 2 (the "regular" curriculum for students scoring between the 23rd and 77th percentiles on the CTBS), and 3 (a slower, remedial track for students scoring in the bottom 23 percentiles).

The principal at Millard Fillmore Elementary School, the negative outlier, was proud of her school and what she believed she had made of it. The printed daily schedule for third grade at Fillmore indicated that school began at 8:25 with a 15-minute homeroom period, followed by the first academic period. All periods were supposed to be 65 minutes long.

The research team noted that in 6 days of observation, no third-grade class began promptly at 8:25. The students and teachers exhibited a tacit understanding that the 8:25 bell meant "begin heading toward your classroom." Not on the schedule was a 5-minute transition between periods, a late beginning after each recess, buses leaving Fillmore 5 minutes before school was "over," and a constant stream of children to and from bathrooms, the office, and the library. The net effect of these downtimes was a loss of at least an hour a day of available academic time.

Of the district's four academic tracking choices, Fillmore had groups in 1, 2, and 3. This relatively affluent school simply did not concern itself with 1A, the most advanced track. As one teacher explained, "I think Piaget was right, you can't push kids to learn before they are ready."

John Adams Elementary School, the positive outlier, was located in a somewhat less affluent, though solidly middle class neighborhood. The minority population at this school was a mix of African-American, Hispanic, and Asian children. Although the school building was not as modern looking as Fillmore, it was clean.

The school experienced a change in principals midway through LSES-III, when the "old" principal was promoted to an administrative position. The "new" principal had been lead teacher at the school for several years and described herself as sharing the philosophy of the former leader. Like the Fillmore principal, both Adams principals described their school as following the Madeline Hunter philosophy.

Through a negotiated agreement with the faculty, Adams Elementary used only curriculum tracks 1A and 2. If a child seemed headed for a low score on the BST or CTBS, he or she was assigned extra work to build skills. The staff assumed that a child who scored in the top 23% could do the advanced, enriched activities of track 1A.

During her tenure, the first Adams principal had felt the need to get rid of two teachers. One transferred while the principal "was documenting a case" to fire her. The second was not recommended for tenure. This principal stated that "I try to work with the faculty. There are many things we can teach teachers."

The academic focus of Adams was visibly present around the school. In the hall that included the third-grade classrooms were eight bulletin boards. At both the fall and spring visits, all eight carried messages either conveying the importance and joy of reading, or exhibiting student achievements. On the wall across from the principal's office was a list of students on the academic honor roll.

Classroom observations confirmed that better teaching was occurring at the effective school (Adams) than at the ineffective school (Fillmore). As indicated in Figure 10.1, no interactive teaching pattern by a Fillmore third-grade teacher reached the lowest percentage of interactive teaching time achieved by an Adams third-grade teacher. The mean percentage of interactive third-grade teaching at Adams, 44.65%, was nearly double the 24.18% mean at Fillmore.

Teaching-performance differences at the third-grade level were repeated throughout the schools. As indicated by Table 5.6, the interactive time-on-task and total time-on-task for all Adams classrooms was considerably higher than that at Fillmore during LSES-III. Adams teachers were rated higher than Fillmore teachers on presentation of new content, teacher expectations, and discipline (see Table 5.5).

In comparing these two schools, one is first struck by their superficial similarity. Both were public and served predominantly middle class children. Both had highly stable staffs, relatively strong parental in-

FIGURE 10.1. Interactive Teaching at the Third-Grade Level
at Adams and Fillmore Elementary Schools

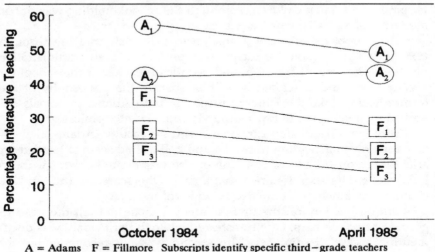

A = Adams   F = Fillmore   Subscripts identify specific third–grade teachers

volvement, and a sense of community during LSES-III. Discipline was not a major problem at either school. Both schools had focused major staff development efforts on attending meetings and implementing strategies from Madeline Hunter seminars.

Beneath the superficial similarity, however, there were schoolwide differences that had an impact on learning at the third-grade level. First, the expectation level for student performance was higher at Adams. While Fillmore had by design no students in the highest track, Adams had a sizable portion of students in it. Students at Adams were not allowed in the lowest track, while some at Fillmore were placed in that track. Adams teachers knew that the administration expected the highest performance from all students, with those eligible for the highest track participating in it and those slated for the lowest track instead placed in a higher track. The high expectation message from the administration was translated into higher expectations by teachers (see Table 5.5).

A second schoolwide difference concerned a clearer focus on present academic expectations at Adams than at Fillmore. The responses of students and faculty at both schools on school effects questionnaires indicated that each had relatively high academic expectations. At Fillmore, these responses took the form of a belief that the students would go to college. At Adams it was expressed as a conviction that *all* students could, and would, learn their third-grade materials *this* year, starting *now*. The emphasis on the here-and-now was beneficial for Adams students.

A third difference involved an active program at Adams for removing teachers who were not performing at a minimum standard. This resulted in the removal of at least two teachers at Adams, while no such dismissals occurred at Fillmore. In the nearly decade-long history of Fillmore at the time of LSES-III, no teacher had asked for a transfer out. The Adams administration would not tolerate the low-interactive teaching recorded by Fillmore teachers, such as F2 or F3 (see Figure 10.1). The Fillmore administration allowed teachers with such subpar performance to continue to teach.

A fourth difference at the schools is related to the third. The Adams administration had more active, direct monitoring and in-servicing of their teachers than the Fillmore administration. The first principal at Adams indicated that "there are many things we can teach teachers," while the Fillmore principal emphasized the family atmosphere at her school. At Adams the administration was more aware of deficiencies in teachers' techniques and were more willing to try to remedy those weaknesses than was the Fillmore administration. More involvement in in-servicing teaching deficiencies directly contributed to higher indices of teacher performance at Adams than at Fillmore.

Teddlie, Kirby, and Stringfield (1989)

Built on the two case studies just described, this study presented data from all 16 schools in the LSES-III sample. This study contained both time-on-task indices and data from field notes gathered using the COI. Also, a pair of schools (designated as Pair 1 in Chapter 5 and described in detail in Chapter 7) was used to illustrate the interaction of school and teacher effects.

Results indicated that teachers in more effective schools consistently outscored those from ineffective schools on all effective teaching indices. Teachers in effective schools were consistently more successful in keeping students on task, spent more time presenting new material, provided more independent practice, demonstrated higher expectations for students, provided more positive reinforcement, experienced fewer classroom interruptions, had fewer discipline problems, generated more consistently friendly classroom ambiences, and provided more pleasant classrooms than did their peers in matched ineffective schools (see Tables 5.3 and 5.4).

In addition to these differences in teaching behaviors between effective and ineffective schools, some interesting differences in patterns of variation were also found. For instance, 9 of the 10 standard deviations reported on effective teaching behaviors were smaller in effective as opposed to ineffective schools (see Table 5.4). These results imply that some formal or informal socialization process is ongoing at effective schools.

The effective school in Pair 1 (designated as Kennedy Elementary School in Chapter 7) is a good example of a systematic socialization experience for teachers, while the ineffective school of that pair (designated as Coolidge Elementary School) provides a good illustration of poor school socialization. The means and standard deviations for the two schools on 10 dimensions of effective teaching are found in Table 10.1. In all cases, Kennedy had higher mean scores and lower standard deviations than Coolidge.

Analysis of field notes from classroom observations and interviews

TABLE 10.1. Teacher Means and Standard Deviations on Dimensions of Effective Teaching for Kennedy and Coolidge Elementary Schools, LSES-III

Teacher Behavior	Kennedy (Effective)		Coolidge (Ineffective)	
	M	SD	M	SD
Time-on-task	1.00	.00	2.91	.29
Presentation of new material	1.07	.26	2.11	1.05
Independent practice	1.13	.35	2.42	.69
High expectations	1.33	.49	1.56	.73
Positive reinforcement	1.00	.00	2.00	.82
Interruptions minimal	2.00	.00	2.40	.75
Discipline	1.13	.35	2.41	.73
Friendly ambience	1.13	.35	2.41	.80
Student work displayed	1.69	.75	2.43	.98
Appearance of room	1.33	.49	1.57	.66

Note: 1 = evidence of effective behavior; 2 = contradictory or weak evidence; 3 = absence of effective behavior.
Source: Teddlie, Kirby, & Stringfield, 1989

suggested possible schoolwide factors contributing to the differences. The schools in this pair were particularly well matched. Both had well integrated student populations. The schools were located a few blocks apart in a middle to lower middle class suburban neighborhood. Both buildings were approximately 20 years old.

Beyond these similarities, however, there were immense differences in school climate that were evident at the time of LSES–III and persisted through LSES–IV. These differences were summarized in Table 7.1, and they all stemmed from the administrative leadership (or lack thereof) at the schools and how that leadership interacted with the faculty.

It was concluded that the effective school principal was the "central figure who guarded the integrity of the classroom" (Teddlie, Kirby, & Stringfield, 1989, p. 234). This guarding of academic integrity resulted in a truncation of the lower end of the range of teaching behaviors through a more organized class day and a greater emphasis on interactive teaching. This emphasis resulted in less variance in time-on-task, classroom instruction, and classroom climate scores, since the lower end of the range of teacher behaviors was not tolerated by the principal.

Virgilio, Teddlie, and Oescher (1991)

This study sought to replicate the LSES–III findings related to teachers' behavior, while involving more types of schools. Teacher behaviors were examined in typical as well as negative and positive outlier schools. The sample included junior high schools as well as elementary schools.

The teacher-behavior variables used in this study were the VTBI and the CS. A MANOVA design was used to analyze the data and included two independent variables: (1) effectiveness status (more effective, typical, less effective); and (2) grade level of school (elementary, junior high school).

Results indicated that teachers from the different school effectiveness levels behaved quite distinctively, as can be seen in Table 10.2. Teachers from more effective schools demonstrated better teaching skills than those from typical schools, who performed better than those from less effective schools. This school effect was more pronounced at the elementary school level, but still persisted at the junior high level on the VTBI indices.

This study replicated and extended the findings on different patterns of variance that were reported from LSES–III. There was less variance in teaching behavior at the more-effective-school level than at the

TABLE 10.2. Comparison of Teacher Means by Levels of School Effectiveness

Teacher Behavior	More Effective Schools		Typical Schools		Less Effective Schools		F values
	M	SD	M	SD	M	SD	
Time-on-task	.79	.20	.74	.18	.58	.19	16.49*
Classroom Managment	3.91	.93	3.26	1.01	2.66	.93	16.31*
Classroom Instruction	3.96	.68	3.43	.76	2.59	.96	26.87*
Classroom Climate	3.51	.72	3.05	.75	2.62	.75	13.50*

Note: Time-on-task scores range from .00 (0%) to 1.00 (100%). The other skills scores range from 1 (low) to 5 (high).
* $p < .0001$
Source: Virgilio, Teddlie, & Oescher, 1991

typical-school level, which in turn had less variance in teaching behavior than that at the less-effective-school level. Table 10.3 contains a summary of these differences in variance patterns for the elementary-school level.

Thus, teachers in more effective schools behaved more similarly than did those in typical or less effective schools. For instance, the range for time-on-task across teachers in more effective elementary schools was only 19%, while for teachers in less effective elementary schools it was 71%. Since both typical and less effective schools had some teachers with very high time-on-task, the difference for more effective elementary schools occurred in the lower end of the range. The lower end of the range of effective-teaching behavior in more effective elementary schools was truncated on both the time-on-task and the VTBI indices.

When examining this range truncation in effective schools, one wonders if teachers are selected or socialized into appropriate teaching behaviors. That is, do principals at effective elementary schools select teachers who can already instruct well, or do they create a school environment in which the weaker teachers learn how to teach? Probably both factors (selection and socialization) are at work in the more effective schools, although faculty stability has a large impact on the role that selection can play.

Emphasis on the selection and removal of teachers probably has its greatest impact as a school is headed toward effectiveness (Stringfield & Teddlie, 1989). During that time, the principal can radically change

TABLE 10.3. Comparison of Variances in Elementary School Teacher Behavior by Levels of School Effectiveness

Teacher Behavior Variable	Lowest Score	Highest Score	Range	Coefficient of Variation
More Effective Schools				
Time-on-Task	.81	1.00	.19	6.62
Classroom Management	2.60	5.00	2.40	16.05
Classroom Instruction	3.63	5.00	1.37	9.60
Classroom Climate	2.38	5.00	2.62	17.57
Typical Schools				
Time-on-Task	.37	.99	.62	23.55
Classroom Management	1.67	5.00	3.33	34.27
Classroom Instruction	2.10	4.67	2.57	23.35
Classroom Climate	1.88	4.00	2.12	18.72
Less Effective Schools				
Time-on-Task	.23	.94	.71	32.56
Classroom Management	1.00	4.33	3.33	37.02
Classroom Instruction	1.06	4.06	3.00	41.39
Classroom Climate	1.38	3.75	2.37	28.96

Note: The coefficient of variation is the standard deviation divided by the mean quantity multiplied by 100.
Source: Virgilio, Teddlie, & Oescher, 1991

the school's overall rates of time-on-task, classroom management, classroom instruction, and classroom climate by encouraging the removal of less effective teachers and carefully selecting teachers to replace them.

The careful selection of teachers who are or have the potential to be effective teachers may be the principal's most important activity in moving his or her school toward effectiveness. Once weaker teachers have been replaced by stronger ones, the faculty will become more stable and the internal socialization process more important. This socialization process will be described in more detail in Chapter 11.

LSES–IV

Results from LSES-IV with regard to teaching behaviors in historically effective and ineffective schools further expand our understanding
of teaching effects within school effects. Data in Tables 5.9 and 5.10
present evidence of differences in teaching behavior on high-inference
and low-inference instruments during LSES-IV.

There was evidence for the persistence of more positive teaching
behaviors within historically effective schools, as opposed to historically
ineffective schools, on the high-inference instruments (see Table 5.9).
Overall, teachers in historically effective schools outperformed those in
historically ineffective schools on classroom management, presentation
and questioning skills, instructional strategies skills, and classroom social psychological climate.

There was greater evidence for the persistence of teacher effects
than school effects. In two of the pairs of schools (Pairs 2 and 3), the
scores on measures of school effectiveness status changed, while teachers' effectiveness did not change. In Pair 3, the historically effective
school became less effective on indices of student achievement, but its
teachers continued to outperform those from its matched school on
high-inference measures of teaching behaviors. In Pair 2, even though
the historically ineffective school improved dramatically on student
achievement, its teachers were still outperformed by those from its
matched school on high-inference teaching behaviors.

The persistence of these teaching effects may have resulted from
the higher retention rate of third-grade teachers in historically effective
schools, as opposed to historically ineffective schools. As noted in Table
5.16, 77% of third-grade teachers in historically effective schools during
LSES-IV had also been there in LSES-III. At the historically ineffective
schools, only 41% of the third-grade teachers remained. Positive teaching processes can persist during school change if the faculty stays. This
may be particularly true in certain grade levels, where a committed
group of teachers remain and create a ''grade-level effectiveness.''

While there was strong evidence for the persistence of teaching
effects on the high-inference data over time, the time-on-task indices
indicated no overall differences between historically effective and ineffective schools in LSES-IV (see Table 5.10). Previous differences in time-
on-task between the two groups of schools had been eroded by school-
level changes.

Thus, there was evidence for both stability and change in teacher
and school effects indices at the time of LSES-IV. While teacher effects
indices appear to be more stable than school effects indices, there were

changes at both levels. The greater instability of school effects, at least in the LSES study, may be partially attributable to the high turnover rate among principals. Fifty percent of the principalships changed from LSES-III to -IV. These principalship changes should have a more immediate effect on school-level variables, with a more gradual effect on teacher behavior.

Case studies from specific pairs of schools further illuminate the effect of the passage of time on school and teacher effects. The remainder of this section will briefly describe three types of processes occurring at the school and teacher levels:

1. Stability at the school level, mirrored by stability at the teacher level
2. Stability at the teacher level, in spite of change at the school level
3. Change at the school level, followed by dramatic change at the teacher level

There was great stability at the effective school in Pair 1, Kennedy Elementary. The principal had been at the school 13 years at the time of LSES-IV, while her third-grade teachers had an average tenure of 20 years. Glenn (1981), along with other researchers, has noted that unusually effective schools tend to have faculties that are relatively experienced and stable. As indicated in the extended case study in Chapter 7, the principal and teachers at this school shared academic leadership, with the teachers exerting a great deal of control. The third-grade teachers at their own initiative had established a method for decreasing time lost during transitions by moving themselves rather than having their classes move. Thus, time-on-task and other indicators of teacher effects remained high from LSES-III to -IV.

The effective school from Pair 3, Adams Elementary School, had experienced a change of leadership at midterm of LSES-III. The current principal, though hardworking and competent, appeared to lack the vision and leadership of the former principal. Thus, the school climate for learning had declined over the period from LSES-III to -IV at Adams relative to its matched school.

Despite this, three of the four LSES-III third-grade teachers were still teaching at that grade during LSES-IV. Fifty-seven percent of the faculty schoolwide remained from LSES-III to -IV. Adams continued to outscore Fillmore on both high- and low-inference indicators of teacher effectiveness, despite a decline at Adams on time-on-task. Schoolwide changes at Adams had apparently begun to erode overall time-on-task, yet the teachers were clearly outperforming Fillmore in overall classroom management, instructional strategies skills, and social psychological and physical climate (see Table 5.9). Despite a perceived loss of vision at the school level, individual teachers were staying at the school and persisting in teaching competently in their classrooms.

Hoover Elementary, the Pair 4 negative outlier described in Chapter 8, is a good example of a school where a change in principalship directly led to better classroom teaching behavior. There are four areas in which school-level behavior can have an impact on teacher behavior:

1. The method of selection and replacement of teachers
2. The type of classroom monitoring and feedback
3. The type of support for individual teacher improvement provided by the administration
4. The instructional leadership provided by the administration, including allocating and protecting academic time

The new principal at Hoover, Mr. Jameson, was radically different from his less effective predecessor in all four of these areas.

With regard to the selection of teachers, Mr. Jameson recruited nine new faculty members in his 4-year tenure. He personally recruited much of the school's academic staff, including all teachers at the third-grade level. Mr. Jameson took great pains to recruit the best teachers possible, especially since his school had a negative reputation.

As for monitoring classrooms, Mr. Jameson intuitively followed the procedure advocated by Deal and Peterson (1990): frequent and short visits to classrooms on an unscheduled basis. Consequently, he could describe the strengths and weaknesses of his teachers, something his predecessor was incapable of doing. Knowledge of each teacher's weaknesses enabled Jameson to focus personal assistance and professional in-service on redressing these problems.

Finally, Mr. Jameson exhibited instructional leadership by actively managing the educational production function. He recaptured valuable academic time by rigorously enforcing the academic schedule and monitoring breaks. As a result of this, the overall time-on-task at Hoover increased from 52% in LSES-III to 84% in LSES-IV, with an increase from 32% to 61% in interactive time-on-task.

NEED FOR FURTHER RESEARCH

Data from the four studies just described confirm that there are mean and variance differences in the behaviors of teachers from more effective and less effective schools. These results indicate that the joint study of school/teacher effects can yield consistent, predictable results, which can generate more probing questions about the processes underlying these effects. The next stage of this research should examine more precisely how school-level variables affect teacher-level behavior, which directly affects student learning (Rowan, Bossert, & Dwyer, 1983).

In the studies just described there was speculation about these processes, with four areas listed in which school policies can positively affect teacher behaviors. A fifth area related to instructional leadership might also be added: promoting a positive academic climate at the school level, which translates to higher expectations and standards at the classroom level (Murphy, 1990). A future research agenda in the joint school/teacher effectiveness area should involve more probing questions about the interaction of school and classroom processes in each of these five areas.

Three of these five areas overlap with the three major categories of the BTQ, which was designed to assess the socialization or induction experience of newcomers to a school. These three areas are monitoring, assistance, and team-building. Team-building is roughly synonymous with the process of promoting a positive academic climate at the school, which includes allowing teachers input into goal formulation and fostering a sense of collegiality.

Chapter 11 presents information on the experiences of beginning teachers in differentially effective schools. This chapter compares historically effective with historically ineffective schools on the three aspects of socialization noted above: monitoring, assistance, and team-building.

11 Teacher Socialization in Effective and Ineffective Schools

Peggy C. Kirby

In LSES–III, Teddlie, Kirby, and Stringfield (1989) demonstrated that teachers' in-class behavior patterns varied significantly among schools with stable, differing levels of student academic achievement (controlling for SES). Teachers in higher-achieving schools demonstrated consistently higher levels of classroom behaviors previously associated with student achievement gains. Of particular interest was the lack of variability in teacher performance in more effective schools. More and less effective schools had similar teacher turnover rates and hiring policies, yet teachers with similar backgrounds appeared to perform differently depending on the school to which they were assigned.

Previous research indicated that induction experiences of beginning teachers vary by district and school. Even in districts with theoretically uniform formal induction programs, significant variations in actual induction programs are likely (Ward & Tikunoff, 1989). Was it possible then that more effective LSES schools were able to maintain high performance levels because they were better at socializing teachers into school norms and expectations? To answer this question, a "Beginning Teacher Study" was included in LSES–IV. Its purpose was to determine whether teachers in more and less effective schools perceived their induction experiences differently and, if so, whether performance over time was associated with varying levels of support. This chapter describes results from that investigation.

TEACHER SOCIALIZATION

Socialization is the process whereby individuals learn the culture and values of a new job setting, adjust to the environment, and develop work skills (Feldman, 1976). Feldman described a four-stage socialization theory: anticipation, accommodation, role management, and outcomes. Individuals first formulate expectations, which may or may not be congruent with organizational demands. Socialization during this pre-employment stage consists of individuals' *anticipation* of their organizational role.

At the *accommodation* stage, roles are defined, the employee and the supervisor evaluate the employee's competence, and interpersonal relationships are established. At the *role management* stage, employees must resolve homelife/worklife conflicts and conflicting demands within the work setting.

Feldman described four *outcomes* of successful socialization: satisfaction, mutual influence, internal work motivation, and job involvement. He proposed that persons who finish activities and resolve conflicts at earlier stages will demonstrate the highest levels on these outcomes.

Higher levels of satisfaction and retention have been reported for teachers in formal induction programs (Varah, Theune, & Parker, 1986). Specific strategies of successful induction programs are designed to guide teachers through the accommodation and role management stages. Generally, these strategies may be grouped into three categories: assistance, monitoring, and team-building.

Assistance

All new teachers have questions about what is to be done, how they are to teach, and where they are to find resources. Strategies such as clarifying expectations, securing resources, limiting workload, or suggesting new discipline strategies provide the support that help to answer these questions.

Perhaps the most popular assistance strategy used in formal induction programs is *mentorship*. An experienced teacher, the mentor, provides professional and psychological support to a less experienced colleague. Some districtwide induction programs combine internal mentor support with external university faculty support (e.g., Varah et al., 1986; Ward & Tikunoff, 1989).

Because *administrative support* seems essential to the success of any induction program, the principal often plays a key role in assisting beginners (Armstrong, 1983; Mickler, 1984). Wildman, Magliaro, McLaughlin, and Niles (1990) found that in the most successful programs, both the principal and at least one teacher functioned as advocates for the beginner. There is great variation in the services provided by principals or mentors. Orientation to school goals and operations may consist of one short meeting or may be ongoing throughout the first year (Armstrong, 1983; Mickler, 1984). Administrators or their designees usually acquaint novices with school goals and operations (Varah et al., 1986) and provide materials related to employment (Hulig-Austin, 1990).

Unfortunately, many beginning teachers receive no more assistance than that given in the initial orientation session. New teachers need to understand school goals and expectations for their role in achieving those goals (Stone, 1987). Most need help with classroom management (Rosenholtz, 1989).

Beginners also need assistance with instruction. Placement in easier classes to optimize the chances of success is often recommended but seldom implemented (Armstrong, 1983; Rosenholtz, 1989). Many teachers begin their careers teaching subjects or grade levels for which they were not trained.

Beginners may benefit from observing effective practice. Although release time to observe other teachers is a desirable aspect of any induction program, it is usually not granted (Hulig-Austin, 1990; Moffett, St. John, & Isken, 1987; Varah et al., 1986). Relatively high retention rates were reported for California programs that allowed beginners release time for observation (Ward & Tikunoff, 1989).

In-service or individualized assistance in classroom instruction is a component of many induction programs. Novices are trained in processes such as Madeline Hunter's clinical teaching model (Moffett et al., 1987), Jane Stallings's Effective Use of Time (Schaffer, Stringfield, & Wolfe, 1990), or development of questioning skills (Mickler, 1984). Due to the lack of well-developed curriculum guides in some districts, beginners often need help with planning instruction (Rog, Donaldson, Quaglia, & Paige, 1990). Forms of direct instructional assistance include newsletters with tips for beginners (Hulig-Austin, 1990), provision of intact instructional products (Rog et al., 1990; Wildman et al., 1990), and funds for securing supplemental materials (Ward & Tikunoff, 1989).

Monitoring

As with assistance strategies, monitoring can be misconstrued as serving for quality control only. In fact, frequent monitoring with feedback is a useful technique for early diagnosis and remedy of instructional and management difficulties. For example, teachers often fear sanctions if they admit to having problems with discipline. An experienced observer can help the novice frame the problem and develop improvement strategies. In such a program, the new teacher can benefit from technical advice as well as liberation from the traditional view of teaching as a solitary, noncollaborative enterprise.

Collaboration can take place, however, only when monitoring is a routine, nonthreatening, and constructive part of the teaching experience. Most authors agree that monitoring and confidential coaching should be provided separate from evaluation (Fox & Singletary, 1986; Hulig-Austin, 1990).

Team-Building

Team-building strategies may also improve the neophyte's sense of belonging and professionalism. A collective vision of the school's future should be discerned easily from the interactions of administrators, faculty, students, and parents. Armstrong (1983) urged administrators to help novices see immediately how their views can be incorporated into decision making. Conscious team-building efforts can help beginning teachers see their role in achieving that vision. Beginners might be included on building-level committees or asked for input on relevant professional issues.

The insecurity that is typical of beginners in any profession may be reduced through opportunities to collaborate with peers who have similar problems (Hulig-Austin, 1990; Fox & Singletary, 1986). Self-confidence also is enhanced by encouragement from administrators or colleagues (Moffett et al., 1987; Stone, 1987) and by a school ethos that allows beginners to seek advice and take risks (Rosenholtz, 1989).

IS THERE A RELATIONSHIP BETWEEN TEACHER SOCIALIZATION AND STUDENT PERFORMANCE?

Lists of recommendations for more positive teacher induction experiences are widely available and generally consistent (e.g., Rosenholtz, 1989; Schlechty, 1985; Stone, 1987). Why then do few novices benefit from knowledge of effective practices? One explanation is the lack of research linking specific induction processes to student outcomes. Perhaps if differences in teacher induction experiences were related to student achievement, districts and schools might be more likely to adopt suggestions from successful programs.

If strategies advocated by induction program designers are effective in socializing teachers into the system, novices who receive these forms of assistance should become better teachers. It was hypothesized in LSES-IV, therefore, that novices in historically more effective schools would perceive their induction experiences more positively and that they would become better teachers than their peers in historically less effective schools. Unlike the studies of formal induction programs that reported evidence of participant-perceived success (Hawk, 1987; Mickler, 1984; Russell, 1986; Varah et al., 1986), this study examined the classroom performance of beginning teachers within a school effects framework. Thus, induction experiences and teacher effectiveness of novices in schools that were identified as differentially effective *on the basis of student achievement* were compared. No prior school effectiveness study specifically examined induction experiences and performance of beginning teachers.

METHODOLOGY OF THE BEGINNING TEACHER STUDY

LSES-IV data in Chapter 5 indicate that teachers in historically more effective schools demonstrated more effective classroom behaviors than teachers in historically less effective schools. One objective of LSES-IV was to identify school processes that might account for the similarity among teachers in more effective schools. One hypothesis was that successful schools utilized specific formal and informal methods to socialize new teachers. These methods may or may not have involved a formal induction program.

In instances where socialization processes had become routine components of the school's culture, experienced teachers and administrators may not have been able to specify all the strategies used with the school's new teachers. For this reason, beginning teachers' experiences in both more and less effective schools were compared. It was hypothesized that successful induction strategies identified through a literature review would be more commonly utilized in effective schools and that teachers receiving higher levels of support would demonstrate more effective teaching behaviors in the areas of time use, classroom management, instruction, and climate than teachers in less supportive environments.

Subjects

Beginning teachers were defined as teachers with less than 3 years total experience. Each LSES-IV school had at least one beginning teacher, but no school had more than four. There were 43 beginning teachers in the 16 schools, 38 of whom (88%) participated in the study. Of these, 20 were from historically less effective schools and 18 from the more effective group; thus, there were no apparent differences in teacher turnover in the two school groups.

During the fall 1989 site visit, the average teaching experience of new teachers in the less effective group was 1.5 years, with a mean of 0.9 year in the current school. New teachers in more effective schools reported similar experience levels—1.7 years overall, with 0.7 year in the present school.

Teachers in the two school groups were also similar with regard to certification and education. All 38 teachers held a bachelor's degree; four had a master's degree. Of these, two were from historically more effective schools and two from historically less effective schools. Eight of the 38 teachers were employed on a temporary certificate. They were equally divided between the more and less effective schools.

The particular university attended by the teachers revealed no differences by school type. Because an equal number of positive and negative outliers were chosen from each of the school districts participating in the study, it is not surprising that teachers within districts (whether in the more effective or less effective school) attended the same universities. Four of the eight state universities attended by the beginning teachers are generally reputed to hold lower admissions and program standards. Six of the teachers graduated from these institutions—three in each of the school effectiveness groups. It seems reasonable to conclude that beginning teachers in the two school groups were quite similar with respect to experience and education.

Instrumentation

Subjects were asked to complete the Beginning Teacher Questionnaire about their teaching experiences at their current schools. The BTQ consists of 14 items related to three areas of socialization: assistance (seven items), monitoring (four items), and team-building (three items). These areas and items were selected on the basis of a review of the recent literature on teacher induction. Discipline was consistently identified as one of the most difficult problems faced by new teachers (Grant & Zeichner, 1981; Veenman, 1984); therefore, one item related to effective *assistance* strategies was

> I have one or more people at this school who are willing and able to help when I have student discipline problems.

In the area of *monitoring*, items included

> My principal visits my classes frequently.
> Feedback from my principal regarding my performance is constructive and helpful.

Finally, sample items under the category of *team-building* were

> I have input in setting school goals.
> I feel that I "fit in" at this school.

Teachers indicated agreement with items by choosing a response from a Likert-like scale on which 1 denoted strong disagreement and 6 denoted strong agreement. Items indicating poor practices (e.g., "I have been assigned to teach some of the most difficult classes in this school") were recoded so that all item scores indicated positive practices. Items within subscales were summed to achieve a subscale score. The total score is the sum of all individual items. Alpha reliability coefficients were high, ranging from .80 to .91 (total scale).

Beginning teachers were also evaluated using the Stallings Classroom Snapshot (CS) and the VTBI (see Chapter 4). Data from these evaluations were used to determine if behavioral differences existed between groups.

Procedure

Beginning teachers completed the BTQ in fall 1989. They also were observed on the VTBI and a modified version of the CS. Each beginning teacher was observed two to five times (45 minutes to 1 hour per observation) over a 3-day period in the fall by a research team member. In addition to using the CS and VTBI, researchers took extensive notes regarding the content and delivery of the day's lesson. Twenty-four of these beginning teachers were observed again in spring 1990. Illness, maternity leave, and time constraints prevented the researchers from observing some teachers from the original group.

RESULTS OF THE STUDY

Induction Experiences

Induction experiences in the 16 LSES–IV schools were perceived as generally positive. Item means for the BTQ ranged from 3.7 to 5.5 on a scale where 6 indicated the highest level of support. The average total score was 67.1 out of a possible 84. However, considerable variability among teachers was noted. An analysis of variance indicated no significant differences in perceived induction experiences among the employing school districts.

A *t*-test was then used to determine whether beginning teachers in more effective schools perceived their induction experiences more positively than teachers in less effective schools. The mean total BTQ score was significantly greater for teachers in the more effective school group ($t_{one-tail} = 1.89$, $p < .05$). Teachers in historically more effective schools rated their schools higher on 13 of the 14 BTQ items and equal on the remaining item. Their scores on assistance, monitoring, and team-building also surpassed scores for novices in historically less effective schools (see Table 11.1).

Less variability in teacher responses for every item and subscale score was noted in the more effective group. Thus, novices in more effective schools consistently reported that they received greater early career support than their peers in historically less effective schools.

Two cases reveal the possible extremes in level of support for beginning teachers. Although only a few years old, an elementary school in the historically less effective group was already overcrowded. The number of students in the fourth grade necessitated the hiring of an additional teacher. An inexperienced teacher arrived in the middle of the school year. Because there was no space available in the elementary school, she was assigned to a windowless room in the gymnasium of the adjoining high school. Her classroom had been intended as a band room, and the cinder block walls made decorating impossible. The incessant dribbling of basketballs outside her door provided a further irritant. Added to the loneliness and impoverished environment was

TABLE 11.1. Descriptive Statistics for Beginning Teacher Questionnaire Items

	More Effective Schools		Less Effective Schools	
	M	*SD*	*M*	*SD*
BTQ sub-scale				
Assistance	34.6	6.0	30.5	6.5
Monitoring	20.2	2.8	18.1	4.4
Team-building	15.3	2.1	14.6	3.4
TOTAL SCORE	70.6	9.9	63.6	12.0

Note: Individual items were rated 1 to 6 with 6 indicating strongest agreement. Item scores within subscales were summed to obtain subscale scores. All item scores were summed to obtain the total score. Highest possible scores are 42 for Assistance, 24 for Monitoring, 18 for Team-building, and 84 for the total BTQ.

her inability to control pranksters from the physical education classes. Several times a day they knocked at her door and ran. The bewildered teacher apologized to her fall visitor for struggling above the noise to give a test orally. Earlier that day, she had been unable to win her battle with the photocopy machine. The teacher's isolation and frustration went unnoticed for the rest of the school year. Distance alone precluded frequent visits by the principal or assistant principal.

Another inexperienced teacher taught kindergarten at a historically more effective school. During a fall visit, she was observed having difficulty with classroom management. She struggled to get the children quieted down to begin work. All students worked on the same activities at the same time. Consequently, much time was lost, especially during oral sight reading of vocabulary words. The 24 five-year-olds simply could not remain attentive while each had a turn to "read."

This teacher was again visited in the spring. By that time, the principal had assigned her an aide. Six separate groups of students now rotated among six different activities. The aide assisted with written exercises and artwork, while the teacher worked with small reading groups and monitored the class. Although no changes were noted for the novice teacher in the historically less effective school, this more fortunate teacher benefited from an astute administration—one that recognized her problem early on and invested additional resources to resolve it.

Teacher Effectiveness

Data from the two instruments used to measure the classroom effectiveness of beginning teachers were analyzed in two ways. First, means were compared for teachers in the two school effectiveness groups to determine whether beginners in historically more effective schools became more successful teachers than beginners in historically less effective schools. Next, teacher effectiveness by level of support was examined. A median split on total BTQ score was used to place teachers into either a high-support group or a low-support group. Teacher effectiveness as measured by the CS and VTBI for the two groups was compared. Because school effects on teacher performance would be evident only after the beginner had spent a reasonable amount of time in the school, only teachers for whom fall and spring data were available were considered in these analyses.

At the beginning of the year, novices in less effective schools outperformed their peers in more effective schools on both interactive teaching time and total time-on-task. By the spring, however, teachers in the more effective school group had surpassed their own fall scores as well as the fall scores for teachers in the less effective schools. Their interactive teaching time rose by 7.5%, and total time-on-task increased by 10%. Teachers in the less effective school group showed decreases on both measures (see Figure 11.1).

Was percent time-on-task related to level of induction support received? Level of support (high or low) had no statistically significant effect on teacher performance during the spring observations; however, spring means were in the predicted direction. Teachers receiving higher support levels began the year with lower interactive teaching rates and approximately equal total time-on-task rates relative to teachers receiving lower support levels. Near the end of the school year, the high-support group showed increases on both measures. Teachers in the low-support group improved only slightly on total time-on-task and declined in interactive teaching time (see Figure 11.2).

Management, instruction, and climate subscale scores on the VTBI were used to test differences in teacher performance in more and less effective schools and in high- and low-support groups. Beginning teachers in historically more effective schools scored lower on the management and instruction subscales and higher on the climate subscale than

FIGURE 11.1. Percentages of Interactive Teaching and Time-on-Task, by School Effectiveness Group

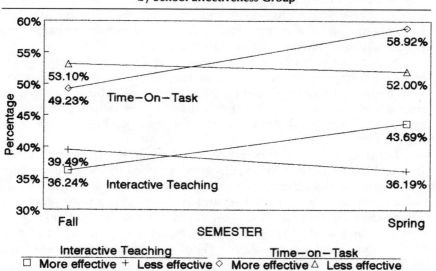

FIGURE 11.2. Percentages of Interactive Teaching and Time-on-Task,
by Level of Support

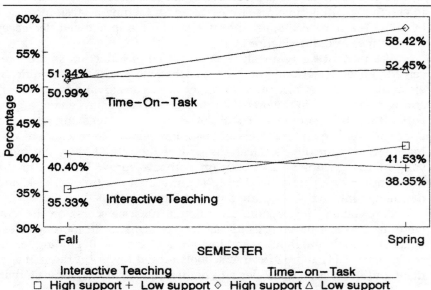

teachers in the historically less effective school group in the fall. By the spring, they scored higher on all subscales. Teachers in the historically less effective group showed declines in all areas, while teachers in the historically more effective group stayed the same.

Support level did not have a significant impact on changes in classroom performance on the VTBI from the fall to the spring. Teachers with higher support levels during the academic year did score higher in instruction and climate in the spring than teachers with lower support levels, but their spring performance in all areas declined slightly from the fall scores.

Isolating school factors related to teacher development is confounded by teachers' prior experiences. In order to add to our understanding of school effects, data for 14 teachers in their first year at the current school were examined separately. Correlations revealed moderate positive relationships between support level received during the first year and teacher effectiveness as measured by the CS and VTBI. Correlations ranged from .22 to .51 for first-year teachers (see Table 11.2).

TABLE 11.2. Correlations Between Level of Support and Teacher Effectiveness (Spring Observation) for First-Year Teachers

	Inter. Tchng.	T.O.T.	Mgmt.	Instr.	Climate
BTQ Total	.51	.48	.35	.22	.51
Interactive teaching		.83	.61	.68	.73
Time-on-task			.65	.57	.55
Management				.45	.32
Instruction					.86

IMPLICATIONS FOR TEACHER INDUCTION

Due to difficulty in attracting and retaining good teachers, efforts to ensure successful socialization of beginning teachers would seem prudent. What role does the school play in this process? Based on results from this study, it appears that the principal and other school personnel in effective schools positively influence socialization at the accommodation and role management stages.

Rosenholtz (1989) recommended that novice teachers be given clear, frequent feedback about their performance and regular encouragement. Teachers in historically more effective schools in this study stated that principals visited their classes more regularly and provided more constructive feedback. They also reported that they knew how their principal felt about their performance. This indicates a clarity of expectations, which is necessary for success at the accommodation stage of socialization (Feldman, 1976).

New teachers in effective schools also reported receiving more technical assistance than their peers in less effective schools. They felt that specific individuals within the school (the principal, a mentor, or other more experienced teacher) were available and willing to help with professional matters. Discipline problems, for example, are often quite challenging for beginners; teachers in effective schools perceived high levels of support in their discipline efforts. It probably helped that they did not feel that they had been assigned the most difficult classes.

Beginners also need opportunities for collaboration. Rosenholtz (1989) endorsed a "school ethos that specifically encourages [beginners] to ask for advice when needed and feel non-threatened when others offer their help" (p. 437). Collaborative decision making and problem solving also are part of Feldman's (1976) orientation. He proposes that individuals at the role management stage must learn to resolve conflicts among work groups over priorities and methods for accomplishing tasks. Facilitating collaboration among teachers is consistent with this proposal.

The team-building/collaboration subscale did not differentiate between historically effective and ineffective schools, although scores for one item ("I feel that I 'fit in' at this school") did reveal significant differences ($t = 2.0$, $p < .05$). Teachers in effective schools did not feel isolated from their co-workers. This suggests that outcome measures of satisfaction and mutual influence are higher in historically more effective schools; that is, teachers in these schools felt that they were accepted and contributing faculty members.

The results of this study of induction processes lend empirical support to Rosenholtz's (1989) practical suggestions for improving teacher commitment and to Feldman's (1976) model of socialization. Teddlie and colleagues' (1989) conclusions regarding the similarities of teachers and classrooms in effective schools, and higher variability in less effective schools, are reinforced.

Schools appear to play a major role in teacher socialization. The induction experiences of new teachers with similar training and experience, and even employed within the same district, are partially dependent on the school to which they are assigned. Schools that exceeded expectations for student achievement had teachers who demonstrated superior teaching skills, and these schools tended to use strategies and resources to ensure that novices had a reasonable chance also to become effective teachers.

Findings with regard to the relationship between teacher effectiveness and induction experiences are less conclusive. Although no significant differences were found in beginning teacher effectiveness in schools providing different support levels, novices in high-support schools outperformed their peers in low-support schools on four of five measures (interactive teaching time, time-on-task, instruction, classroom climate) by the end of the year. For the 14 teachers who were new to their schools (i.e., in their first year), support level was positively associated with all teacher effectiveness variables. These results constitute one step in moving induction research beyond the bounds of conveniently measured outcomes.

Our data indicate that historically more effective schools are more supportive of beginning teachers, and document activities perceived by these teachers as associated with higher support levels. Schools can positively affect teacher development through active administrative support, assistance with classroom management and instruction, actions to include beginners in decision processes and encourage their efforts, and frequent monitoring with corrective feedback. It appears that schools remain stable outliers in no small part through the more or less careful, thoughtful, effective induction of teachers into their cultures.

Lessons Learned from a Decade-Long Study of School Effects

In any study in an emerging field, the lessons learned tend to be methodological as well as substantive. This is particularly the case with school effects research, given the methodological criticisms that were leveled against studies in this area during the early to mid-1980s.

The LSES also addressed several substantive issues. Information on those issues could have implications for school improvement projects, although the generation of such implications was not a planned part of this research study.

The information gleaned from the LSES can be divided into the following four categories, which we will discuss in turn.

1. What we learned about school effects
2. What we learned that may inform school improvement projects
3. What we learned about the methods of school effects research
4. What we learned about the practical conduct of school effects research

WHAT WE LEARNED ABOUT SCHOOL EFFECTS

The Existence of School Effects

The LSES is the fourth major study (Brookover et al., 1979; Mortimore et al., 1988a; Rutter et al., 1979; Teddlie et al., 1984, 1989) to clearly identify school effects as important influences on school-level student achievement. These effects occur at a single point in time, but are especially pronounced over time.

The school climate factors presented in the multiple regression analyses reported in Chapter 2 and the Appendix match closely those identified by Brookover and colleagues (1979). The effect of these LSES-II factors held up using the more sophisticated HLM analyses that are now standard.

It has been noted (Bosker & Scheerens, 1989; Mortimore et al., 1988b; Reynolds, 1992) that school effects at any given point in time explain 8–15% of the variance in individual-level student achievement. In LSES-II, school effects predicted 13% of individual-level student achievement, while teacher effects accounted for another 11% of the variance. The cumulative effect of such contributions is substantial especially if a student stays in a school that retains its effectiveness status and teachers over time.

The Stability of School Effects

About one-half of the LSES-III and -IV schools retained their effectiveness status over an 8-year period. Stability was about the same for both historically effective and ineffective schools.

These results disagree with Reynolds's (1992) conclusion that schools do not remain effective or ineffective over considerable time periods. Reynolds based his conclusion largely on the work of Nutall, Goldstein, Prosser, and Rasbash (1989), who looked at examination performance of secondary students in London across a 3-year period. One reason why such studies demonstrate less stability of school effects is their overreliance on achievement scores alone as indices of schools' effectiveness. Such narrowly defined school effects measures can be greatly affected by many factors across time, thus indicating less stability in school effects than may actually exist.

In longitudinal case studies, on the other hand, data are gathered on a variety of indices of school effectiveness, such as student attendance and faculty retention over time. The validity of school effectiveness classification is greatly enhanced with multiple measures. The more valid the initial and subsequent classifications of a school's effectiveness status are, the more likely that classifications will remain stable.

The Dramatic Effects of School Context

The results of LSES-II confirmed research indicating that student SES has a profound effect on the success of strategies employed to make schools more effective. LSES-III and -IV results indicated the importance of urbanicity as a context variable, while the Virgilio and colleagues (1991) study confirmed grade-level configuration as another context factor.

School effects research in the 1990s will hopefully define context in more dynamic ways than just the impact of SES, urbanicity, and grade level. Nevertheless, by studying these basic contextual factors, the LSES, in conjunction with other investigations of the late 1980s and early 1990s, has firmly established context as one of the major areas in the school effects research field.

The Importance of School Leadership

The importance of the principal throughout all LSES phases was more pronounced than we expected. Of the 16 schools in LSES-III and -IV, only four were experiencing mandated restructuring programs in which leadership was formally shared with teachers and other individuals. Of these four restructured schools, only one appeared to have a viable sharing of leadership among the principal, faculty, and others interested in the school.

While the case study of Hoover Elementary School (see Chapter 8) contained an excellent example of a strong instructional leader moving a school toward effectiveness, we were equally impressed with the behavior of the principal at Kennedy Elementary School (see Chapter 7). This individual displayed what we call "stable adaptability." As the context changed at her school, she was able to make adjustments that resulted in continuing excellence.

The Differences Between Naturally Occurring and Externally Imposed School Improvement

Four naturally occurring school improvement efforts were observed in LSES-III (Stringfield & Teddlie, 1990). We were surprised that as many as one-half of the schools designated as ineffective in LSES-III were actively trying to improve. This indicates the pressures from the community and local governing boards on unsuccessful schools to improve.

Some of these naturally occurring efforts involved only technical changes designed to raise achievement test scores, while others were more comprehensive attempts to move the school toward excellence. We concluded that there were several areas of difference between naturally occurring and externally developed school improvement (Huberman & Miles, 1984), including setting, early implementation, and change in user practice. Naturally occurring school improvement is an area that warrants further investigation.

The Relationship Between Teacher and School Effects

The barriers between the fields of teacher and school effects are dissolving, as more researchers are embedding teacher effects within school effects studies. While such research is labor intensive, there is a growing recognition that school effects research must take into account what happens in classrooms. As several researchers have noted (e.g., Creemers, 1992; Reynolds, 1992; Scheerens, Vermeulen, & Pelgrum, 1989), a large percentage of the variation among schools is due to classroom variation.

The research reported in Chapter 10 indicates that there are consistent mean and variance differences between differentially effective schools across grade levels. The variance differences are particularly intriguing and represent a potentially fruitful line of research (e.g., Crone, 1992; Crone & Tashakkori, 1992).

The Impact on Teacher Socialization Experiences

The areas of teacher induction/socialization have received attention recently, partially because of the excessively high turnover rate of teachers (e.g., Schlechty & Vance, 1983). As demonstrated in Chapter 11, there are continued differences between socialization experiences of teachers in historically effective and ineffective schools. This is particularly interesting since about one-half of the schools in the sample studied changed effectiveness status over time. This indicates the persistence of a teacher ethos for functional or dysfunctional behavior (Teddlie & Stringfield, 1989), even after school changes have occurred.

These results were recently replicated by Ter Haar (1992), who focused on induction experiences for newcomers using the Rosenholtz (1988, 1989) framework. The differing induction and socialization experiences of teachers in differentially effective schools is an area that needs more study.

The Effect of District Offices

Across all LSES phases, we were struck by the lack of meaningful influence from the district offices on school effectiveness. In fact, the only influences we saw were negative and were of little import to overall school effectiveness. We (Stringfield & Teddlie, 1991b) recently concluded that the major impact of districts concerns the absence of resources in economically disadvantaged areas, which places restrictions on the effectiveness status of schools in those districts.

This is distressing, since several authors (e.g., Hill, Wise, & Shapiro, 1989; Lezotte, 1990) have contended that district support significantly enhances the likelihood of positive school change. Research needs to be done exploring why most superintendents do not employ what is now known about school effects. An essential issue in this line of study is the peculiar method whereby school administrators are selected.

It appears that more thought is put into the selection and training of managers for businesses than into the selection and training of principals for some schools. One recent study that did find district effects (Pollack, Chrispeels, Watson, Brice, & McCormick, 1988) noted that some superintendents directly participated in the selection and hiring of principals. More qualitative investigations of district-level behavior with regard to principal selection and other important school effects issues are needed.

The Gradual Development of a Theory of School Effects

While there is general consensus that the five-factor model of school effects is inadequate, further theory development has progressed very slowly. In a recent article, Mortimore (1991) concluded that "my own view is that the most productive use of theory would be to begin to construct a set of postulates to be tested empirically, and for these postulates to be focused on . . . school improvement" (p. 224). Mortimore then listed six postulates that could be tested, such as "Schools are more likely to improve if an outside agent is involved" (p. 224).

While the testing of postulates with regard to school improvement constitutes a useful direction for further research, others have argued that a comprehensive theory of school effects, rather than improvement, would be more valuable at this time. Reynolds (1992) concluded that middle-range school effects theories, linking sets of findings in ways that would structure the field, are currently needed. Such school effects theories do not currently exist, although recent formulations are pointing in that direction.

For instance, Scheerens and Creemers (1989, 1990) propose a school effects conceptualization that looks at cross-level relations among school variables, school context, the classroom, and the background of students. This context emphasis is reiterated in the TSEL described earlier (Slater & Teddlie, in press). In addition to context, the TSEL also emphasizes the process of schooling and conceptualizes schools as constantly moving within a cycle from ineffectiveness to effectiveness and vice versa.

The overall point, however, is that while school effects theories are emerging, no major study of school effects has ever been theoretically driven, and it is likely that future studies will only partially be theory driven. While our knowledge base has increased to the point of supporting theories that can explain some recurrent school effects, it is unlikely that a comprehensive theory encompassing the area will be developed soon. Gradual theory development characterizes most scientific pursuits.

For instance, Cronbach (1982), drawing on the philosophy of Mackie (1974), asserted that progress in causal knowledge occurs through "gappy" knowledge. Such partial or "gappy" knowledge about a phenomenon is gradually increased as uncertainties about the phenomenon decrease through empirical investigations. Hence, knowledge in an area is gained through progressive localization of the phenomenon's causes. If student achievement alone is considered the operational definition of school effects, then the following progress in knowledge has occurred:

1. During the 1960s Coleman and others demonstrated that student SES predicts much of the variance in school-level student achievement.
2. During the 1970s and 1980s Brookover, Mortimore, Rutter, Teddlie, and their colleagues demonstrated that school climate (or ethos or community) explains additional variance in school-level student achievement beyond SES.
3. During the 1980s and early 1990s researchers simultaneously studying teacher/school-level variables have demonstrated that teacher behaviors account for additional variance in school-level student achievement beyond SES and school climate.

This progression of incremental knowledge, and accompanying theoretical work, will probably characterize school effects research into the twenty-first century.

WHAT WE LEARNED THAT MAY INFORM SCHOOL IMPROVEMENT

Our experiences included several cases of schools improving dramatically or becoming less effective. This naturally occurring school change can be used to inform the process of enacting an external innovation to improve a school.

At the District Level

Get More Involved. While some authors (e.g., Hord, Jolly, & Méndez-Morse, 1992) have documented instances of central offices supporting improvement, we saw little of that in the LSES. Central office behavior toward school improvement was either benign neglect or interference. Organizationally speaking, this lack of involvement is debilitating since school leadership assignments are made at the district level.

Enough information has now been gathered to characterize the type of principal who might be more successful at middle- or low-SES schools, elementary or secondary schools, and rural or urban schools. Planned school improvement might begin at a central office with the thoughtful assignment of a specific principal with a certain set of characteristics to a particular school with its own context.

The quickest way to engender improvement across a number of schools is thoughtful matching of principals with schools by the central office. Moving principals from their current schools to other schools where they might be successful is another way to promote improvement. These changes can happen only in situations where the superintendent is aware of contextually sensitive school effects research, has restructured her or his office, has the backing of the governing board, and has a sufficient talent pool from which to select leaders. Also, someone in the central office needs the personnel skills required to identify potential school leaders for different types of schools.

Capitalize on Naturally Occurring School Improvement. With modern management information systems, superintendents should be able to identify improving schools from achievement, attendance (teacher, student), retention (teacher, student), and other school data. Fullan (1991) has noted that such databases and superintendent follow-up are critical for improved school effectiveness. Superintendents should know which schools are improving or "moving" at any point in time.

There are two ways that a district can capitalize on naturally occurring school improvement: by identifying the sources of the change and then supporting that emerging leadership team, and by studying the school's change in its context and then trying to transfer that improvement process to other "stuck" (Rosenholtz, 1989) schools with similar contextual characteristics. This means that the central office wouldn't adopt one externally developed improvement program and apply it to all schools in the district, but would instead nurture and create improvement processes that are indigenous to particular school contexts.

At the School Level

Perform a Context Analysis. Once a leadership team has emerged, it should conduct a school context inventory, including these questions.

- What are the SES backgrounds of parents of the children? Are these backgrounds mixed or homogeneous?
- Is the school equally effective for all students, or are some students adequately served while others are not? If inequities exist, how can they be rectified?
- What is the school's geographic context and how might it affect the improvement plan? Is the district poor relative to others in the state, and, if so, what can be done to creatively merge community and school resources? Is the school located in a neighborhood with many negative influences, and, if so, what kind of buffers can be created to shield the students?
- What is the grade configuration of the school? Does departmentalization exist? Are there different academic tracks? Is the institution maximally organized for learning at the school, class, and student levels? If not, what changes can be made to maximize learning?
- What are the major sociological and historical factors that have led to failure at the school? Are these factors still at work and, if so, how can they be eradicated? On the other hand, what positive sociological and historical factors exist, and how can variations in these factors be exploited?

In most formulaic improvement plans, these context issues are not addressed up front. A principal, frustrated by continued failure of her or his school, adopts an external change model, complete with a multistep process and appropriate videos. One school prescription cures all schools, to paraphrase an old saying.

Our research indicates that a much more effective way to improve schools is to spend more time gaining a thorough understanding of the school's context, current social organization, and history. Once this contextual framework is understood, then basic principles from the school effects literature can be adapted to the particular school.

Develop a Plan Unique to the School. An ineffective school did not get that way overnight—each has a unique history. As Reynolds (1992) stated:

Such schools have an abnormal staff culture and exhibit a disturbed set of interpersonal relations, and the introduction into them of improvement programs and/or effective schools knowledge needs to be handled with particular sensitivity. (p. 83)

While the school leadership team will develop the goals for the improvement process, it may be technically or psychologically incapable of assessing the school culture and personal relationships to which Reynolds (1992) referred. An external consultant could construct a sociogram of the interpersonal and professional relationships among staff members (e.g., Teddlie & Kochan, 1991) using nonreactive, unobtrusive measures. The sociogram might then be very informative to a school leadership team trying to improve the school culture and personal relationships.

As for the school improvement plan, Brookover and his colleagues (1984) have outlined a generic method for its development, while Taylor (1990) has presented several case histories of successful improvement plans. The adaptation of generic school effects principles, together with information gleaned from contextually sensitive studies, to a particular situation will result in a plan unique to the school.

Implement Instructional and School Improvement Plans Simultaneously. The two fields of teacher and school effects have been estranged for too long. Since the teacher is more proximate to the student, teacher change must occur as the school changes. Assessment of the school entails not only current school climate, but also individual teachers' characteristics.

When the school improvement plan is developed, there should be specific goals for improving classroom teaching, as well as overall school climate. A differentiated teacher development plan, based on general needs across classes and specific needs within classes, should be part of the school improvement plan. This requires much more time up front to painstakingly assess each teacher individually and the staff as a whole. Without this assessment, however, targeted staff development, a critical part of any school improvement project, cannot be accomplished.

An essential part of staff development should occur internally, with teachers getting to "know how to use other teachers as resources" (Good, 1989, p. 38). In some reform districts, teachers have been given more planning time, with the expectation that they would develop collegial relationships. Some districts, however, have failed to provide training aimed at altering the norm of autonomy that is so prevalent among teachers. An effective school improvement plan would not only tell teachers they should work together, but provide structured and unstructured opportunities to do so, so that teachers can learn specifically how to work together.

Assess Improvement Plans Using Many Indicators. A methodological lesson from the LSES and other school effects studies is that multiple measures are necessary to create stable school effects indices. Similarly, several indicators (attitudinal, behavioral, cognitive) should be used to evaluate school improvement. Multiple indicators not only provide greater validity for the school effectiveness classification, but also allow assessment of the various goals of the school improvement plan.

For instance, a school improvement program might include attitudinal, behavioral, and cognitive goals. In most cases, the school leadership team would first stress changes in students' and teachers' attitudes (e.g., higher expectations), followed by behavior changes (e.g., higher attendance, time-on-task), and finally changes in cognitive indices (e.g., NRTs and CRTs). As the improvement effort progresses, the number of indicators increases (first, attitudinal only; second, behavioral added; third, cognitive added).

School improvement programs almost always take a minimum of 3 years to affect student achievement. Most school improvement programs should probably be conceived as 5-year processes, since that is about the length of time it takes for naturally occurring school improvement to happen. Moreover, school improvement efforts never cease, since schools are always headed toward greater or lesser effectiveness.

Include a Teacher Induction Process. The LSES indicates that a teacher-level ethos for behavior exists in each school (Teddlie & Stringfield, 1989). This teacher ethos has an effect on the socialization experiences of newcomers even after significant changes at the school level have occurred. Given the resistance of this teacher ethos to change, it is important that novices experience an induction process designed to encourage positive teacher behavior.

This induction process is especially important as a school moves toward effectiveness, since new teachers are more likely to be recruited at that time as veteran teachers retire or decide to leave the school. In ineffective schools, the ethos for teacher behavior is either negative (poor attitudes, low time-on-task, etc.) or nonexistent (teachers subscribe to the norm of autonomy). In order to make the induction experience more successful, the school leadership team should encourage newcomers to participate in shared goal setting, shared student management procedures, and so forth (Rosenholtz, 1989; Ter Haar, 1992).

WHAT WE LEARNED ABOUT THE METHODS
OF SCHOOL EFFECTS RESEARCH

The LSES was always methodologically driven. We wanted to respond to as many of the criticisms of school effects research as possible. While we were conducting the research, several new methodological issues, or nuances on old issues, emerged.

Addition of a Typical School Level

In both LSES–II and Virgilio and colleagues (1991), a third level of effective school classification (typical) was added to the other levels (effective, ineffective). Purkey and Smith (1983) argued that typical schools would be a better comparison group for effective schools than would ineffective schools.

Results from both these studies followed what was predicted: Effective schools outperformed typical schools, which outperformed ineffective schools. In the Virgilio study, effective schools had less variance in teacher behaviors than typical schools, which had less variance than ineffective schools.

The addition of the typical level enhances results by allowing investigators to compare across the whole range of school effectiveness status. When conducting labor-intensive case studies, however, investigators must weigh the cost of adding 50% more schools to their outlier school sample against the benefits to be gained from another comparison level.

Collection of Classroom Process Data

Comprehensive studies of school effects must involve classroom observations because too much variance between schools is due to variations in teachers' behaviors. This conclusion greatly affects the conduct of school effects research, due to the labor-intensive nature of collecting classroom data. These data are necessary, however, if the field is to move beyond collection of archived and survey data into the actual study of class and school processes.

The selection of instruments for classroom observation is an important consideration in that the investigator wants to collect the maximum amount of information in the most efficient manner. The observation instruments should be appropriate for research purposes, not for personnel evaluation. Fortunately, research instruments are simpler than those used to make certification decisions. We used simple, easily coded teacher observation instruments. The COI, for instance, consisted of 13 open-ended questions, while the VTBI had 35 closed-ended items.

Careful consideration of the appropriateness of instruments for specific contexts should be made. For example, time-on-task measures may not be good indicators of effective teaching at the secondary level, while they work quite well at the elementary level (Virgilio et al., 1991).

Additionally, to minimize costs and maximize information, the research team should devise a sampling scheme for classroom observations. It is important, however, when doing school effects research that all teachers be observed, even if investigators are unable to visit a particular classroom more than once.

Contributions of Longitudinal Studies

It is necessary to conduct longitudinal studies to understand the processes whereby school effects emerge and change. The classification schemata for schools in such studies change from fixed levels (effective, typical, ineffective) to variable levels (stable effective, stable ineffective, improving, declining).

Combined, LSES-III and -IV constituted a longitudinal study in the sense that we examined 16 schools over four points in time (fall 1984, spring 1985, fall 1989, spring 1990). While the physical facilities typically remained the same, almost all the students and about 50% of the teachers and principals changed over that period. In LSES-III and -IV, we were struck by the constancy of some school processes in the face of great change, a phenomenon we call "stable adaptability." At other schools, chaotic school and classroom climates and processes seemed to reflect the student and staff upheavals.

Validity of Multiple Indicators

In LSES-III and -IV, we had time to construct the multilevel databases described in Chapter 4. As a result, we had many indicators of school effects: NRTs, CRTs, student attendance, faculty retention over time (stability of staff), and so on. Like Mortimore and colleagues (1988a), we found considerable variance across indices within any given school.

The process of assigning school effectiveness status using several indicators, some of which are contradictory, is more complicated than simply looking at residualized school-level achievement scores. Despite these complications, a school effectiveness index based on multiple indicators has inherently greater validity than one based on student achievement alone.

We have been discouraged by some studies that apply the most sophisticated mathematical models available to archived data that are ill suited to inform us about school processes. It is ironic, when such investigations yielded marginal results, that the investigators concluded that school effects were not found. Since the investigators did not collect the necessary data (e.g., classroom observations, faculty interviews, other proximal indicators of school effects), it should not be surprising that they were unable to explain their results (Geske & Teddlie, 1990).

Independent Administration of Achievement Measures

Somewhat related to the issue of the validity of school effects classification is what has been euphemistically labeled "testing irregularities." Cheating on achievement tests has increased with greater demands for school/teacher accountability, together with school "report cards" that are made available to the public (Mandeville & Anderson, 1987; Myers, 1991, 1992). The demand on classroom teachers to produce appropriate achievement scores from their students has been chronicled, especially in educational "reform" states.

These "testing irregularities" cause thorny problems for investigators trying to establish accurate school effects indices. One method for dealing with, or at least determining the extent of, this problem is to administer study-specific tests after the initial school effectiveness classifications have been made and during later phases of the study. These data can be used to verify the validity of the initial school classifications and later classification changes.

Utilization of Multilevel Analyses

It is no longer feasible to conduct school effects studies without using multilevel analyses that consider the effects of the student, teacher, and school simultaneously. Previous analysis strategies that aggregated data to the school level are no longer appropriate: These analyses may underestimate school effects; estimates of the importance of variables tend to be unstable and inefficient; and conclusions about students are subject to the risk of cross-level inference problems (Knapp, 1977).

Currently HLM is the preferred statistical tool for assessing multi-level schooling. Researchers wishing to have their results treated seriously by the educational establishment must employ this analytical technique.

Financial Implications

All of these methodological lessons have a price tag. If a research team adds a typical school level, collects classroom process data, conducts a longitudinal study, gathers multiple school effects indicators, administers its own achievement tests, and conducts multilevel analyses, the resulting research study will be very expensive in 1990s dollars. We have estimated that the LSES cost $300,000, plus a decade of labor from teams of researchers. A study of its size in the 1990s would probably cost a half million dollars. Additionally, the research team for such a study would have to consist of investigators willing to invest their own time, at very low rates of pay, in order to learn more about school/teacher effects. As Good (1989) has noted, the U.S. federal expenditure for educational research has plummeted during the Reagan/Bush administrations, with no end in sight. It is ironic that just as we are learning how to do school effects research, there is little money to do it, at least in the United States.

WHAT WE LEARNED ABOUT THE PRACTICAL CONDUCT OF SCHOOL EFFECTS RESEARCH

As the LSES research began in 1980, the two principal investigators were in their early thirties and just out of graduate schools in social and educational psychology. Over a decade later, it is apparent that we matured as educational researchers as the study itself evolved. We have both used LSES examples in our educational research methods courses as good ways to approach problems inherent in school and classroom research. Along the way, we have learned several lessons about the conduct of school effects research.

The Publicizing of School Effects Data

In his book on evaluating educational and social programs, Cronbach (1982) referred to the multiple roles played by the educational evaluator, including teacher and journalist. When the school effects researcher plays those roles, he or she risks the danger of being typecast as a "reformer" rather than a "scientist" (Ralph & Fennessey, 1983). In earlier phases of the LSES (LSES–II in particular), we were put in a position of reporting our results directly to a larger audience through the local media. The results were a mixed blessing.

The initial LSES–II results were released by the LDE in 1984 in the forms of an executive summary and an extensive research report (Teddlie et al., 1984). The executive summary was disseminated to the press, as well as numerous other institutions. The study results, which replicated the Brookover and colleagues (1979) research, were positive, indicating that school climate could have an effect on student outcomes.

We were approached by reporters from the two largest daily newspapers in the state to do stories about the importance of positive school climate. Several supportive articles appeared, as indicated by the following headlines:

"High expectations said part of successful schools" (LaPlante, 1984a)
"Schools' attitudes linked to learning" (LaPlante, 1984b)
"Children respond to expectations" (1984)
"Teachers' expectations basic clue to learning" (1984)
"Proper educational climate a must for production of achievers" (McDonnell, 1985)
"School study: Attitude can spell success" (Siegel, 1986)

Because the LSES has been the major study of school effects in Louisiana to date, it is safe to say that these articles, and radio reports on the Louisiana Radio Network, publicized school effects research more than any other mass media effort.

Utilization of the mass media to publicize school effects results is a double-edged sword, however, as will be described in the next section.

The Potential Abuses of School Effects Data

Information as powerful as that gathered from school effects research can be very damaging. One misuse of the information, the application of one school improvement model to all schools, has been discussed throughout this book. Another misuse, the identification of school effects research with a particular point of view, such as the "back-to-basics" orientation or the "equity-in-schools" movement (Teddlie, Stringfield, & Wimpelberg, 1986), is also potentially dangerous. School effects data should be treated as scientific evidence, not grist for the mill of those who consider themselves to be politically correct.

Another abuse of school effects data was painfully discovered by the LSES team. As the first LSES newspaper reports were going to press, the project director was contacted by a reporter from the major newspaper in the state's largest city. She wanted to do an article on an effective school in her region and asked for the name of such a school. I referred her to the local district, which, as a matter of policy, refused to release the name of any school in the study.

At this point, the forces of freedom of the press and the public's right to know were unleashed. In a suit brought against the LDE (*LaPlante* v. *Stewart*), a local newspaper demanded that we release names of all schools involved in the study and their effectiveness status. This caused grave concerns for us since release of that information implied evaluation of the schools, their principals, and staffs. Also, we had guaranteed anonymity of this information in our verbal contracts with the districts.

The headlines were not so supportive now, as the LDE lost the case from the local court to the appeals court to the State Supreme Court. Our arguments concerning the nature of the analyses performed, the less than adequate level of model refinement, the instability of the data, and the potential harm to dedicated professionals fell on deaf ears. As Judge William Brown stated in his opinion:

> I don't believe the effectiveness or ineffectiveness of the schools reflects on the teachers. It points the finger at the person who accumulates the information and what he feels is an effective or ineffective school. (Chandler, 1985a, p. 6–A)

It was hard for us to communicate to the schools in question that their ineffective status was to be judged our fault as researchers, and not theirs as educators, by the public.

The attitude of the newspaper establishment in this case can be summarized in the words of its attorney: "War is too important to be left for the generals, and education is too important to be left to the so-called experts in the Education Department" (Chandler, 1985b). The "so-called experts," thus, had to inform the superintendents and principals who participated in LSES-II that the effectiveness status of their schools had to be released to the two largest daily newspapers in the state.

The nature of the U.S. justice system worked in our favor in this case, however. It was 1986 before the State Supreme Court handed down its opinion. Both newspapers felt that the schools' effectiveness status, now 3 years old, was no longer newsworthy. In fact, after the State Supreme Court ruling, one newspaper ran an article on the study identifying the schools, but not their effectiveness status (Siegel, 1986).

Of course, we learned a lot about the conduct of school effects research during this prolonged episode. First, community entities will use research data for other purposes, such as personnel evaluation, for which they were never intended. Second, school effects researchers should code their data in such a manner that retrieval by school name or number is impossible. While such a method is standard operating procedure for evaluation studies (Joint Committee, 1981), researchers often do not heed the guideline, since their data are supposedly intended for "research purposes only." We will never make that mistake again.

The "Obviousness" of School Effectiveness Classifications

In spite of a double blind research design, LSES–III observers correctly identified the effectiveness classification of all 16 schools in the study. We (Stringfield & Teddlie, 1991a) concluded that these results at least partially validated the oft-repeated belief that "you can identify a good school just by looking at it." If "looking at it" consists of extended, structured observations of the school, its classrooms, and its students, then that belief is correct.

For example, a member of one of our research teams had received several days training on the observation instruments, but had never taught or worked in a school. The first school her team visited was a very attractive school serving affluent, suburban children. By noon of the team's first day on site, she had correctly identified the school as being one in which students' academic achievement was falling well below reasonable expectations. We later learned that the district testing office had, for several years, informed the administration that this school was performing below expectation on district-administered NRTs and CRTs. There are obvious ethical imperatives for professional educators when existing problems are so obvious that a noneducator can discern them during an initial visit.

There is also an ethical issue for school effects researchers with regard to schools' classification status. Should researchers inform a district of the effectiveness classifications of its schools when the study is over? From a scientific point of view, the answer is obviously no, because such behavior would violate norms of researcher/subject trust, anonymity of the research unit, and confidentiality of sensitive results. On the other hand, shouldn't district superintendents and supervisors be informed if evidence indicates that one of their schools is ineffective in educating its students? This question is an intriguing one, especially if the researcher also aims to improve schools.

The Dilemma of Following an Ineffective School over Time

Related to the previous issue is one that concerns following a "stable ineffective" school over time. At a presentation in which we were reporting the initial LSES–IV results (Teddlie, Stringfield, Wimpelberg, & Kirby, 1990), a member of the audience asked if the stable ineffective schools were still failing. Her question had a tone of accusation—how could we allow such obvious failure to continue? What were we doing to improve the failing schools?

The question, and its tone, caught us by surprise. Never having been active in the school improvement movement, we assumed that the audience would share our enthusiasm for having discovered a stable ineffective school, which could inform us about the processes whereby schools continue to fail over time. Again the values of the researcher and the reformer were in conflict.

We never informed a district that their School X was an ineffective school. We never tried to improve School X. We must admit, however, that when a School X teacher stopped her class (as a few did during the study) and asked us, "Am I doing this right," it was difficult not to intervene.

Students are very aware of a school's failure and will easily tell you about it. Teachers may be aware, but it is very hard for them to talk to an outsider about it. Principals always claim that their school is successful, and it's hard to tell if they are simply deluding themselves. In the face of these behaviors, we believe it is the researcher's job only to record, even though it often hurts immeasurably to do so.

CONCLUSION

In this chapter, we have summarized information from the LSES in four areas: what we have learned about school effects, how that knowledge might inform the school improvement process, what we have learned about school effects methods, and what we have learned about conducting school effects research. We believe that the LSES has been useful in further defining several emerging topics in the study of school effects.

The existence and magnitude of school effects.
The multilevel nature of school effects.
The context of school effects.
The stability of school effects across time.
The consistency of school effects across measures.
The variance of school effects.
Naturally occurring school improvement.
The interaction of teacher and school effects.
The role of the principal in school effects.
The impact of school effects on teacher induction/socialization.
Methodological issues in school effects research.
The role of theory in school effects research.

As evidence with regard to these areas is accumulated by a new generation of international scholars, the science of school effects will continue to develop. The prospects for that development are now brighter than ever before.

EPILOGUE

As this book was going to press, the Carnegie Foundation for the Advancement of Teaching released a survey of parents regarding proposed voucher systems (Ross, 1992). A large majority of the parents indicated that they would rather see the public school in their neighborhood become more effective than see the voucher system enacted in their community.

The results of this survey illustrate the continued importance of research into school effects. School improvement, based on this research, remains a most economical and popular method for reform, since it typically involves making best use of existing school site and community resources. The study of school effects is thus likely to remain a relevant topic long after the voucher system and other school-reform vogues have passed.

Statistical Analyses of the LSES–II Data

INITIAL STATISTICAL ANALYSES

Analysis Strategy

The steps involved in the initial statistical analyses were as follows. Separate factor analyses were performed on each of the five separate nonachievement datasets. In each case the factors were obliquely (promax) rotated. Factors were chosen for further analysis if they met three criteria: possessed an eigenvalue greater than 1.00, passed a scree test, and appeared interpretable and substantively interesting. Correlation analysis was used to determine the extent to which first-order factors from each dataset were related to school mean achievement. A regression analysis of all related factors against mean EDS scores was conducted to determine the extent to which, under maximizing conditions, the first-order factors could predict school mean achievement.

All first-order factors related to achievement were then entered into a second-order, orthogonal, varimax rotated factor analysis, and the results of that procedure were regressed against school mean scores. In second-order factor analysis, oblique factors from one or more first-order analyses are entered as variables into a second analysis (Cattell, 1965; Rummel, 1970). By forcing an orthogonal solution at the second level, researchers simultaneously address multicollinearity issues and increase parsimony.

Results of First-Order Factor Analyses

One of the major reasons for these analyses was to compare our results with those reported by Brookover and colleagues (1979). These comparisons are shown in Table A.1. LSES–II factors not comparable to those of Brookover and colleagues are not included in the table.

TABLE A.1. Comparison of Brookover et al. (1979) School Climate Factors with LSES-II First Order Factors[1]

Brookover et al. (1979) Factors[2]		LSES-II Factors[3]	
Factor	(Pearson r with achievement)	Factor	(Pearson r with achievement)
Data Source (Student)			
I Student Sense of Academic Futility	(.769)	S5 Absence of Negative Peer Pressure	(.541)
		S6 Students and Teachers Care About Grades	(.582)
		S10 Teachers Care/Students Work	(N.S.)
II Future Evaluations and Expectations	(.218)	S2 Students Future Education Expectation	(.311)
III Perceived Present Evaluations and Expectations	(−.568)	S1 Students' Relative Productivity	(N.S.)
IV Perception of Teacher Push and Teacher Norms	(−.090)	S3 Negative School Climate	(N.S.)
		S4 Teachers Do Not Push	(.297)
V Student Academic Norms	(−.080)	S8 Students Don't Work Hard	(N.S.)
		S10 Teachers Care/Students Work	(N.S.)
Comparable data not gathered		S7 Internal Locus of Control	(−.255)
Comparable data not gathered		S9 Negative Self Image	(−.228)

238

Data Source (Teacher)

I	Ability, Evaluations, Expectations, & Quality of Education for College	(.228)	T1 College Expectation	(.292)
			T2 Student Academic Ability	(.547)
II	Present Evaluations and Expectations for High School Completion	(.664)	T6 High School Expectation	(.228)
III	Teacher-Student Commitment to Improve	(−.105)	T3 Students Try Hard	(N.S.)
IV	Perception of Principal's Expectations	(.198)	T1 (Partial Overlap) College Expectation	(.292)
V	Teacher Academic Futility	(−.129)	No comparable factor	

Data Source (Principal)

I	Parent Concern and Expectation for Quality of Education	(.320)	P3 Parent Concern About Grades and Education	(.331)
II	Efforts to Improve	(−.237)	P5 Principal Rarely Works With Teachers	(.284)
III	Evaluations (Principal and Parents) of Present School Quality	(.365)	P2 School Success	(.495)
IV	Present Evaluations and Expectations of Students	(.377)	P1 Future Academic Expectations	(.401)
	Comparable data not gathered		P8 Absence of the Principal and Teacher	(−.306)
	Comparable data not gathered		P10 Parental Support	(.263)

[1] LSES-II Factors not comparable to Brookover, et al. factors and not significantly correlated with achievement not presented

[2] State random sample, $N = 68$

[3] Stratified, random sample, $N = 76$

239

Student Questionnaire. The first factor analysis was performed on 33 items from the student questionnaire. These items were 29 questions from the modified Brookover instrument plus scores on the negative self-concept scale, positive self-concept scale, external locus of control scale, and internal locus of control scale.

Ten interpretable factors (S1–S10) emerged from these initial analyses, as shown in Table A.1. Two of the factors were related to educational expectations. One of them was composed of present academic expectations and comparison of work with that of classmates, that is, students' relative productivity (S1 in Table A.1). The other involved future educational expectations (S2). The students apparently responded differently to questions about how well they were currently doing in school than they did to items concerning how far they expected to go in school.

Correlations between factors and school mean EDS scores were computed to determine the relationship between the student questionnaire factors and student achievement. As can be seen in Table A.1, there were significant correlations between six student questionnaire factors and student achievement.

It is interesting that students' future educational expectations (S2) were significantly related to student achievement, while students' present educational expectations relative to their peers (S1) were not. A problem with the students' present educational expectations factor was that almost all students reported thinking they were better scholars than most other students. The students were more discriminating in assessing their long-term educational expectations.

The factor most highly correlated with achievement was the students' perception of how much students and teachers care about grades (S6). As the perception of caring increased, so did achievement. Students at schools in which other students and their teachers cared about grades scored higher on achievement tests.

The more negative the students' perceptions of the academic environment in the school, the more likely the schools' academic achievement was to be low. Students from the lower-achieving schools were more likely to say that other students teased those who did well and that other students didn't do as well as they could because they were afraid others would not like them as much (S5).

Teacher Questionnaire. The factor analysis on the teacher questionnaire was performed on 71 items. These items were 67 questions from the Brookover instrument plus scores on four scales (negative self-concept, positive self-concept, internal locus of control, and external locus of control).

Ten interpretable factors emerged from these analyses; the four that are shown in Table A.1 are comparable to the teacher factors from Brookover and colleagues (1979). Three factors were related to expectations. Teachers responded differently when describing the general academic reputation of their schools (T2), the number of students that they expected to finish high school (T6), and the number of students they expected to go to college (T1). For teachers, expectations for their students were multifaceted. As can be seen in Table A.1, there were significant correlations between these three teacher factors and achievement. As might be expected, when teacher expectations increased so did students' performance.

Principal Questionnaire. Fifty-five items were included in the factor analysis of the principal data. Of those variables, 51 were questionnaire items and four were the same scales as those for the teacher analysis.

Ten factors were retained from the factor analysis of the principal questionnaire data; the six that are shown in Table A.1 are comparable to the principal factors from Brookover and colleagues (1979). Several factors similar to those from the teacher analysis were found in the analysis of principal data. School success (P2) was similar to T2 on the teacher factor analysis. Future academic expectations (P1) was similar to a combination of T1 and T6. The principal analysis produced two factors related to parents' concern and support, while the teacher analysis produced none.

Similar kinds of relationships occurred between principal perception of student academic ability and student achievement as were obtained from the teacher analysis. As principals' academic expectations and perceptions of student ability increased (P1, P2), so did achievement. Principals from the lower-achieving schools reported being more actively involved with teachers in trying to raise achievement (P5).

The more the principal perceived strong parental support (P10), the more likely the school's academic achievement was to be high. Parental support was measured by PTA participation and average daily attendance.

School Context. Nine demographic and school characteristic variables were examined in a separate factor analysis. The variables were students' mothers' and fathers' mean levels of education and level of professional employment, percentage of students and faculty who were white, mean success rate on the National Teachers Examination for colleges from which a school's teachers graduated, mean total years teaching experience of the faculty, and the average amount of post-baccalaureate work completed by faculty.

Factor analysis of these nine variables yielded three clear factors. The first (SES1) was a simple SES factor. The second (SES2) measured racial composition of schools (percentage of white students correlated highly with percentage of white faculty). Factor 3 (SES3) was a measure of faculty experience. SES1 and SES2 were significantly correlated with student achievement and were included in subsequent analyses.

Predicting Student Achievement. Seventeen factors from the initial factor analyses of demographic, student, teacher, and principal databases were significantly correlated with achievement. Following Brookover and colleagues (1979), these 17 factors were entered into multiple and stepwise regressions to examine the factors' importance as contributors to school mean student achievement.

The 17 factors explained about 70% of the variance (adjusted) in school scores on the EDS test. Three factors were significant contributors to the model: students' SES, students' perception of how much teachers and students care about grades, and students' future educational expectations. None of the teacher or principal factors were significant contributors.

The ratio of cases (76) to predictor variables (17) in these analyses produces an inherently unstable model. We present this analysis for two reasons. First, it is similar to, and hence a partial replication of, the Brookover and colleagues analysis, and second, it will contrast in interesting ways with the more stable second-order factor prediction model.

Results of Second-Order Factor Analysis

The initial analyses produced 17 factors that were significantly correlated with school mean achievement. While these analyses were interesting, because of the large number of factors (17), second-order factor analyses were undertaken to overcome the instability in analyses with high ratios of predictor variables to number of cases and to address the problem of multicollinearity in the interpretation of results.

The factor analysis of the 17 initial factors reduced this number to five new latent variables, which in this instance are called second-order factors. Six of the initial factors were associated with the first second-order factor (SOF1). Principals' and teachers' expectations for students' future academic success, and teachers' ratings of students' ability and school success were highly related to students' SES. We interpret this factor to be SES/school personnel expectations. Of greatest interest in SOF1 was the fact that principals' and teachers' future educational expectations were tied to student SES (SES1). By contrast, students' future educational expectations (S2) were not highly related to SOF1.

The only student factor associated with SOF1 was S4, teacher push. The direction of the association was such that students in low-SES schools in which teachers and principals had lower future expectations reported that their teachers pushed them harder. Both informal data gathered from LSES–II and classroom process observations from LSES–III suggested that children in low-SES schools were not being pushed harder by teachers in an absolute sense. We concluded that relative to the rest of these children's experiences, they perceived school as being more rigorous.

Two of the initial 17 factors were associated with the next second-order factor (SOF2). These were SES2, student and faculty racial composition, and P5, principals' reporting of frequency of working with teachers to improve achievement. In schools with a low percentage of white students and teachers, a more hierarchical administrative system may have existed. Within that system, the principal may have felt more comfortable intervening in classrooms than a principal in a majority white school would have. We interpret SOF2 to reflect school racial composition.

The third second-order factor (SOF3) comprised S6 (students' perception that peers/teachers care about grades), S5 (student perception of the absence of a negative academic environment), and P2 (principal perception of school success). The nature of the relationship was such that in schools where students felt that peers/teachers cared about grades, and students didn't tease each other for making good grades, principals reported feeling moderately successful. We interpret SOF3 as measuring positive academic climate.

Both P10 (principal perception of actual parental support) and S2 (students' future educational expectations) were associated with the fourth second-order factor (SOF4). Interestingly, while principals' rating of expressed parental concern (P3) was associated with the SES second-order factor (SOF1), the measure of parental action was associated with students' future educational expectations. This factor measures family commitment to education.

The fifth second-order factor was composed of P8 (principal estimate of principal/teacher absence from building) and S9 (student negative self-image). SOF5 presents a climate in which students feel bad about themselves, and principals/teachers absent themselves from the school. We interpret this factor as describing generally negative school climate.

The next step in these analyses was to regress the five second-order factors on school mean student achievement. A stepwise multiple regression analysis was used for this purpose. The adjusted r^2 (amount of variance explained) for the five-factor model was .69, or 69% of the total school-level variance. This compares favorably with the adjusted r^2 of .71 for the model based on the initial 17 factors. SOF3 (positive academic climate) was the best single predictor of achievement, accounting for 27% of the variance. SOF1 (students' SES/principals' and teachers' expectations) entered the equation second, accounting for an additional 23.5% of the achievement variance. SOF4 (family commitment to education) entered third and added 9.3%. SOF2 (school racial composition and principals' intervention rate) added 6.2%. SOF5 (general negative climate) added a final 5%.

HLM REANALYSIS

Prediction with First-Order Factor Analysis

For the HLM analyses, we began with a within-school model, wherein the achievement of students in a particular school is considered a function of various student-level characteristics. In LSES-II, we limited consideration to a within-school model that posited achievement as a function of student SES, defined as a composite of parents' education and occupation.

Our multilevel analyses involved specification of the school-level predictors that could be used to predict the school-to-school variation in the intercept (mean EDS achievement) and the regression slope relating student achievement to SES background. The climate and context predictors that yielded significant correlations from the first-order factor analysis were selected for this purpose. Data for each school were centered so that the within-school intercepts represented mean school achievement. Our analysis strategy involved adding and deleting predictors until only statistically significant predictors remained in the model.

The multilevel reanalysis of LSES-II was accomplished with a computer program developed by Bryk, Raudenbush, Seltzer, and Congdon (1986). The program generates a residual file that can be used to assess the tenability of the normality assumption needed for this technique.

Toward this end, the so-called Q–Q plots were examined for the various analyses, and they did not show any drastic departures from normality.

The final HLM model is presented in Table A.2. First, as expected, the model is much more relevant to variation in mean achievement (intercept) than in the SES-achievement slope. The amount of parameter variation in means explained is generally twice that associated with the slope. With respect to the predictors present, the final HLM model for school means is essentially identical to that for the school-level regression analysis presented in the previous section. However, it is interesting that these same predictors are not particularly effective at explaining the school-to-school variation in the achievement/SES regression slope. In the current results, only the SES factors appear to have any relevance to slope variability. The model explains approximately 66% of the estimated parameter variance in school mean student achievement—a result very similar to the earlier analyses.

TABLE A.2. HLM Results for First-Order Factor Analysis

	Achievement Composite	Standard Error	Z
School Mean Achievement			
SES1	3.66	0.78	4.69*
SES2	2.36	0.66	3.54*
S6	3.11	0.73	4.26*
S2	2.46	0.68	3.58*
SES-Achievement Slope			
SES1	1.88	0.54	3.48*
Percent Observed Variation Explained			
School Mean Achievement	58.27%		
SES-Achievement Slope	11.37%		
Percent Parameter Variation Explained			
School Mean Achievement	65.83%		
SES-Achievement Slope	28.33%		

* $p < 0.05$

We interpret the analyses in Table A.2 as follows. Across the SES, student, teacher, and principal datasets, four factors provided the most efficient explanation of differences between schools on mean achievement. Not surprisingly, two of them related to socioeconomic status: SES1 (with which father's occupation and mother's education were highly associated), and SES2 (with which the racial mix of each school's student body was highly associated). Interestingly, the other two predictors were not from the teacher or principal questionnaires, but from school averages on the student questionnaires. These were S6 (students' estimation of the extent to which students and teachers care about grades) and S2 (students' future educational expectations). This would indicate that if future school researchers were interested in finding the "school climate" factors that mattered most in predicting achievement, they might begin by asking students, even third graders, before teachers and principals.

Second-Order Factor Analysis

In this part of the reanalyses of LSES–II with HLM, the second-order factors became the school characteristics under consideration. The same within-school model was used as in the previous analyses, and a similar model-fitting strategy was employed. The results are presented in Table A.3. Again, the model is much more relevant to variation in school mean achievement than school-to-school variation in regression slopes. Also, the predictors for school means are very similar to those in the previous analysis, with the exception that SOF5 was dropped. Additionally, the percentage of parameter variability explained is not dramatically different. Data in Table A.3 indicate that SES and its correlates, such as teachers' and principals' long-term academic expectations for students, matter in predicting student achievement (SOF1 and SOF2). The higher the mean SES and percentage of white population in these schools, the higher the mean student achievement.

Interestingly, in the second-order analyses, two composite variables emerge as predicting mean achievement. The first of these, SOF3, is positive academic climate, which included student factors S6 (students' perceptions that their peers and teachers care about grades) and S5 (students' perception that their school does not have a negative academic environment), and principal factor P2 (principals' perceptions of their schools' success). While confirming the importance of student variables noted in Table A.2, the SOF3 data indicate that principals' sense of school academic success may have some statistical validity. SOF4 (family commitment to education) was also a significant predictor in this analysis.

TABLE A.3. HLM Results for Second-Order Factor Analysis

	Achievement Composite	Standard Error	Z
School Mean Achievement			
SOF1	4.01	0.719	5.58*
SOF2	2.76	0.722	3.84*
SOF3	4.40	0.734	5.99*
SOF4	2.73	0.741	3.70*
SES-Achievement Slope			
SOF1	1.31	0.635	2.07*
Percentage Observed Variation Explained			
School Mean Achievement	53.51%		
SES-Achievement Slope	3.63%		
Percentage Parameter Variation Explained			
School Mean Achievement	60.43%		
SES-Achievement Slope	8.88%		

* $p < 0.05$

The second-order results also indicate that SOF4 is significantly related to school-to-school variation in the SES-achievement slope. Unlike
the earlier HLM analyses, a composite climate variable significantly affects the slope, explaining approximately 9% of the estimated parameter
variation. Students' future educational expectations (S2) and principals'
perceptions of parental support (P10) combine to generate SOF4. Apparently, in schools where more students anticipate completing high school
and attending college, and where their parents tend to be actively involved in school, the linkage between SES and achievement grows
stronger.

The HLM analyses of the initial 17 factors found that in the higher-
mean SES schools, SES had some value in predicting the SES-achievement
slope. This may have been, in part, a function of having a fuller range
of students along this dimension in some schools than in others. In
LSES–II there were only a few schools serving exclusively upper middle
class communities, and several serving relatively impoverished commu-

nities. Therefore, the presence of a mix of students in the sample probably brought with it a range of achievement levels. That SOF4 predicted
the SES-achievement slope is not as easily explained, but the explanation
may again have to do with a truncated range of parental support. That
is, it may be that in schools where a significant percentage of parents,
but not all, were actively perceived by principals as supporting education, the result was greater differentiation. The contrast would be that
in schools with virtually inactive parental support, there was less SES
differentiation.

References

Aitkin, M., & Longford, N. (1986). Statistical modeling issues in school effectiveness studies. *Journal of the Royal Statistical Society, Series A, 149*(1), 1–43.

Armor, D., Conry-Oseguera, P., Cox, M., King, N., McDonnell, L., Pascal, A., Pauly, E., & Zellman, G. (1976). *Analysis of the school preferred reading program in selected Los Angeles minority schools.* Santa Monica, CA: Rand Corporation.

Armstrong, D. (1983, April). *Evaluating teacher induction processes associated with the conditions of practice.* Paper presented at the annual meeting of the National Council of Teachers of English, Seattle, WA. (ERIC Document Reproduction Service No. ED 231 799)

Bayless, D. (1983). *Louisiana school effectiveness study: Sample design.* Research Triangle Park, NC: Research Triangle Institute.

Blase, J., & Kirby, P. C. (1992). *Bringing out the best in teachers: What effective principals do.* Newbury Park, CA: Corwin Press.

Blumberg, P. (1972). *The impact of social class.* New York: Thomas Y. Cromwell.

Bolman, L. G., & Deal, T. E. (1984). *Modern approaches to understanding and managing organizations.* San Francisco: Jossey-Bass.

Bolman, L. G., & Deal, T. E. (1991). *Reframing organizations: Artistry, choice, and leadership.* San Francisco: Jossey-Bass.

Bosker, R. J., & Scheerens, J. (1989). Issues in the interpretation of the results of school effectiveness research. *International Journal of Educational Research, 13,* 741–751.

Brandt, R. S. (1982). On school improvement: A conversation with Ron Edmonds. *Educational Leadership, 40*(12), 13–15.

Bridge, R. G., Judd, C. M., & Moock, P. R. (1979). *The determinants of educational outcomes—The impact of families, peers, teachers, and schools.* Cambridge, MA: Ballinger Publishing.

Bridges, E. (1986). *The incompetent teacher.* Philadelphia: Falmer.

Brookover, W. B., Beady, C., Flood, P., Schweitzer, J., & Wisenbaker, J. (1979). *Schools, social systems and student achievement: Schools can make a difference.* New York: Praeger.

Brookover, W. B., Beamer, L., Efthim, H., Hathaway, D., Lezotte, L., Miller, S., Passalacqua, J., & Tornatzky, L. (1984). *Creating effective schools: An in-service program for enhancing school learning climate and environment.* Holmes Beach, FL: Learning Publications.

Brookover, W. B., & Lezotte, L. W. (1979). *Changes in school characteristics coinci-*

dent with changes in student achievement. East Lansing: Institute for Research on Teaching, College of Education, Michigan State University.

Brookover, W. B., Schweitzer, J. H., Schneider, J. M., Beady, C. H., Flood, P. K., & Wisenbaker, J. M. (1978). Elementary school social climate and school achievement. *American Educational Research Journal, 15,* 301–318.

Brophy, J. E., & Good, T. L. (1986). Teacher behavior and student achievement. In M. Wittrock (Ed.), *Third handbook of research on teaching* (pp. 328–375). New York: Macmillan.

Brown, R. (1986). *Social psychology.* New York: The Free Press.

Bryk, A. S., & Raudenbush, S. W. (1992). *Hierarchical linear models.* Newbury Park, CA: Sage.

Bryk, A. S., Raudenbush, S. W., Seltzer, M., & Congdon, R. T. (1986). *An introduction to HLM: Computer program and users' guide.* University of Chicago, Department of Education.

Burns, J. M. (1978). *Leadership.* New York: Harper & Row.

Buttram, J. L., & Carlson, R. V. (1983). Effective schools research: Will it play in the country? *Research in Rural Education, 2*(2), 73–78.

Campbell, D. T., & Stanley, J. (1966). *Experimental and quasi-experimental design for research.* Chicago: Rand McNally.

Cattell, R. (1965). Higher-order factor structures and reticular-vs-hierarchical formulae for their interpretation. In C. Banks & P. Broadhurst (Eds.), *Studies in psychology* (pp. 223–266). London: University of London Press.

Chandler, L. (1985a, April 11). Arguments heard on release of public school rankings. *Baton Rouge Morning Advocate,* p. 6-A.

Chandler, L. (1985b, April 13). Judge rules schools survey be made public. *Baton Rouge Morning Advocate,* p. 1-B.

Children respond to expectations. (1984, July 16). *Monroe News-Star-World,* p. 1-A.

Chrispeels, J., & Pollack, S. (1989). Equity schools and equity districts. In B. Creemers, T. Peters, & D. Reynolds (Eds.), *School effectiveness and school improvement: Selected proceedings of the Second International Congress for School Effectiveness* (pp. 295–308). Amsterdam: Swets & Zeitlinger.

Clark, T. A., & McCarthy, D. P. (1983). School improvement in New York City: The evolution of a project. *Educational Researcher, 12*(4), 17–24.

Coleman, J. S. (1968). The concept of equality of educational opportunity. *Harvard Educational Review, 38,* 7–22.

Coleman, J. S., Campbell, E., Hobson, C., McPartland, J., Mood, A., Weinfeld, R., & York, R. (1966). *Equality of educational opportunity.* Washington, DC: U.S. Government Printing Office.

Coleman, J. S., Hoffer, T., & Kilgore, S. (1982). Cognitive outcomes in public and private schools. *Sociology of Education, 55,* 65–76.

Conklin, N. F., & Olson, T. A. (1988). *Toward more effective education for poor, minority students in rural areas: What the research suggests.* Portland, OR: Northwest Regional Educational Laboratory.

Crandall, V. C., Katkovsky, W., & Crandall, V. J. (1965). Children's beliefs in their own control of reinforcements in intellectual-academic situations. *Child Development, 36,* 91–109.

Creemers, B. (1992). School effectiveness and effective instruction: The need for a further relationship. In J. Bashi & Z. Sass (Eds.), *School effectiveness and improvement: Selected proceedings of the Third International Congress for School Effectiveness* (pp. 105–132). Jerusalem, Israel: Magnes Press.

Creemers, B., & Reynolds, D. (1990). School effectiveness and school improvement: A mission statement. *School Effectiveness and School Improvement, 1*(1), 1–3.

Cronbach, L. J. (1982). *Designing evaluations of educational and social programs.* San Francisco: Jossey-Bass.

Crone, L. J. (1992). *The methodological issues of variance in teacher behavior and student achievement: The relationship of variance to school and teacher effectiveness.* Unpublished doctoral dissertation, Louisiana State University, Baton Rouge.

Crone, L. J., & Tashakkori, A. (1992, April). *Variance of student achievement in effective and ineffective schools: Inconsistencies across SES categories.* Paper presented at the annual meeting of the American Educational Research Association, San Francisco.

Cuban, L. (1983). Effective schools: A friendly but cautionary note. *Phi Delta Kappan, 64,* 695–696.

Cuban, L. (1984). Transforming the frog into a prince: Effective schools research, policy, and practice at the district level. *Harvard Educational Review, 54,* 129–151.

Curtis, R., & Jackson, E. (1977). *Inequality in American communities.* New York: Academic Press.

Davis, G. A., & Thomas, M. A. (1989). *Effective schools and effective teachers.* Boston: Allyn & Bacon.

Deal, T. E., & Peterson, K. D. (1990). *The principal's role in shaping school cultures.* Washington, DC: U.S. Department of Education.

DeYoung, A. (1987). The status of American rural education research: An integrated review and commentary. *Review of Educational Research, 57*(2), 123–148.

Edmonds, R. R. (1979a). Effective schools for the urban poor. *Educational Leadership, 37*(10), 15–24.

Edmonds, R. R. (1979b). Some schools work and more can. *Social Policy, 9*(2), 28–32.

Edmonds, R. R. (1981). Making public schools effective. *Social Policy, 12,* 56–60.

Eisner, E. W. (1991). *The enlightened eye: Qualitative inquiry and the enhancement of educational practice.* New York: Macmillan.

Evans, R. L. (1988). *Teachers' perceptions of principals' change facilitator styles in schools that differ according to effectiveness and socioeconomic context.* Unpublished doctoral dissertation, University of New Orleans.

Feldman, D. C. (1976). A contingency theory of socialization. *Administrative Science Quarterly, 21,* 433–443.

Fiedler, F. E. (1967). *A theory of leadership effectiveness.* New York: McGraw-Hill.

Firestone, W. A., & Herriott, R. (1982). Prescriptions for effective elementary schools don't fit secondary schools. *Educational Leadership, 40*(12), 51–52.

Firestone, W. A., & Wilson, B. (1985). Using bureaucratic and cultural linkages to improve instruction: The principal's contribution. *Educational Administration Quarterly, 21,* 7–30.

Forsythe, R. A. (1973). Some empirical results related to the stability of performance indicators in Dyer's student change model of an educational system. *Journal of Educational Measurement, 10,* 7–12.

Fox, S., & Singletary, T. (1986). Deductions about supportive induction. *Journal of Teacher Education, 37*(1), 12–15.

Fullan, M. G. (1991). *The new meaning of educational change* (2nd ed.). New York: Teachers College Press.

Gage, N. L. (1985). *Hard gains in the soft sciences.* Bloomington, IN: Phi Delta Kappa.

General Accounting Office. (1989). *Effective schools programs: Their extent and characteristics.* (GAO Publication No. HRD-89–132BR). Washington, DC: U.S. Government Printing Office.

Geske, T. G., & Teddlie, C. (1990). Organizational productivity of schools. In P. Reyes (Ed.), *Teachers and their workplace: Commitment, performance, and productivity* (pp. 191–221). Berkeley, CA: McCutchan.

Glasman, N. S., & Biniaminov, I. (1981). Input-output analyses of schools. *Review of Educational Research, 51*(4), 509–539.

Glenn, B. (1981). *What works? An examination of effective schools for poor black children.* Cambridge, MA: Center for Law and Education, Harvard University.

Goldstein, H. I. (1986). Efficient statistical modeling of longitudinal data. *Annals of Human Biology, 13,* 129–142.

Good, T. L. (1989). *Classroom and school research: Investments in enhancing schools.* Columbia, MO: Center for Research in Social Behavior.

Good, T. L., & Brophy, J. E. (1986). School effects. In M. Wittrock (Ed.), *Third handbook of research on teaching* (pp. 570–602). New York: Macmillan.

Good, T. L., & Weinstein, R. (1986). Schools make a difference: Evidence, criticisms, and new directions. *American Psychologist, 41,* 1090–1097.

Grant, C., & Zeichner, K. (1981). Inservice support for beginning teachers: The state of the scene. *Journal of Research and Development in Education, 14*(2), 99–111.

Greer, C. (1976). *The great school legend.* New York: Penguin.

Hall, G. E., Rutherford, W. L., Hord, S. M., & Huling, L. L. (1984). Effects of three principalship styles on school improvement. *Educational Leadership, 41,* 22–29.

Hallinger, P., & Murphy, J. (1985, April). *Instructional effectiveness and school socioeconomic status: Is what's good for the goose, good for the gander?* Paper presented at the annual meeting of the American Educational Research Association, Chicago.

Hallinger, P., & Murphy, J. (1986). The social context of effective schools. *American Journal of Education, 94,* 328–355.

Hanson, M., Gardner, W., & McNamara, J. (1986). Edological inference in administrative reporting and decision-making. *Educational Administration Quarterly, 22,* 63–89.

Hanushek, E. A., & Kain, J. F. (1972). On the value of Equality of Educational Opportunity as a guide to public policy. In F. Mosteller & D. P. Moynihan (Eds.), *On equality of educational opportunity* (pp. 116–145). New York: Vintage.

Hawk, P. (1987). Beginning teacher programs: Benefits for the experienced educator. *Action in Teacher Education, 8*(4), 59–63.

Hill, P. T., Wise, A. E., & Shapiro, L. (1989). *Educational progress: Cities mobilize to improve their schools*. Santa Monica, CA: Rand Center for the Study of the Teaching Profession.

Hord, S. M., Jolly, D. V., & Méndez-Morse, S. E. (1992). The superintendent's leadership in school improvement: A rural perspective. *School Effectiveness and School Improvement, 3*(2), 110–130.

Hubel, K., & Baker, B. (1986). *Rural Education Association research agenda report*. Fort Collins: Colorado State University.

Huberman, A. M., & Miles, M. B. (1984). *Innovation up close*. New York: Plenum.

Hulig-Austin, L. (1990). Teacher induction programs and internships. In W. R. Houston (Ed.), *Handbook of research on teacher education* (pp. 535–548). New York: Macmillan.

Jencks, C. S., Smith, M., Acland, H., Bane, M. J., Cohen, D., Ginter, H., Heyns, B., & Michelson, S. (1972). *Inequality: A reassessment of the effect of the family and schooling in America*. New York: Basic Books.

Joint Committee on Standards for Educational Evaluation. (1981). *Standards for evaluations of educational programs, projects, and materials*. New York: McGraw-Hill.

Kennedy, E., Teddlie, C., & Stringfield, S. (January, 1991). *A multilevel analysis of Phase II of the Louisiana School Effectiveness Study*. Paper presented at the fourth annual meeting of the International Congress for School Effectiveness and Improvement, Cardiff, Wales.

Kim, J., & Mueller, C. Q. (1978). *Factor analysis: Statistical methods and practical issues*. Newbury Park, CA: Sage.

King, R. L. (1992). Implementing and assessing a large-scale school improvement project. In J. Bashi & Z. Sass (Eds.), *School effectiveness and improvement: Selected proceedings of the Third International Congress for School Effectiveness* (pp. 323–343). Jerusalem, Israel: Magnes Press.

Klitgaard, R. E., & Hall, G. R. (1974). Are there unusually effective schools? *Journal of Human Resources, 74*, 90–106.

Knapp, T. R. (1977). The unit-of-analysis problem in applications of simple correlation analysis to educational research. *Journal of Educational Statistics, 2*, 171–186.

Lang, M. H. (1991). *Effective school status: A methodological study of classification consistency*. Unpublished doctoral dissertation, Louisiana State University, Baton Rouge.

LaPlante, J. (1984a, July 9). High expectations said part of successful schools. *The Baton Rouge State Times*, p. 1-B.

LaPlante, J. (1984b, July 10). Schools' attitudes linked to learning. *The Baton Rouge Morning Advocate*, p. 1-A.

Leadership Frameworks. (1988). *Leadership orientations* (questionnaire, principal's form). Brookline, MA: Author.

Lee, V. E. (1986, April). *Multi-level causal models for social class and achievement.* Paper presented at the annual meeting of the American Educational Research Association, San Francisco, CA.

Levine, D. (1991). Creating effective schools: Findings and implications from research and practice. *Phi Delta Kappan, 72*(1), 389–393.

Levine, D. U., & Eubanks, E. E. (1989). Instructional and organizational arrangements that improve achievement in inner-city schools. *Educational Leadership, 40*(3), 41–46.

Levine, D. U., Levine, R. F., & Eubanks, E. E. (1984). Characteristics of effective inner-city intermediate schools. *Phi Delta Kappan, 65,* 707–711.

Levine, D. U., & Lezotte, L. W. (1990). *Unusually effective schools: A review and analysis of research and practice.* Madison, WI: The National Center for Effective Schools Research and Development.

Lezotte, L. W. (1990). Lessons learned. In B. O. Taylor (Ed.), *Case studies in effective schools research* (pp. 195–199). Madison, WI: National Center for Effective Schools Research and Development.

Lezotte, L. W., & Bancroft, B. (1985). Growing use of effective schools model for school improvement. *Educational Leadership, 42*(3), 23–27.

Lightfoot, S. L. (1983). *The good high school: Portraits of character and culture.* New York: Basic Books.

Lomotey, K., & Swanson, A. (1990). Restructuring school governance: Learning from the experiences of rural and urban schools. In S. L. Jacobson & J. A. Conway (Eds.), *Educational leadership in an age of reform* (pp. 65-82). White Plains, NY: Longman.

Louisiana Department of Education. (1990). *Louisiana Educational Assessment Program, annual program report, 1988–89 school year.* Baton Rouge: Author.

Mackie, J. L. (1974). *The cement of the universe: A study of causation.* Oxford, England: Clarendon Press.

Mandeville, G. K. (1988). School effectiveness indices revisited: Cross-year stability. *Journal of Educational Measurement, 25,* 349–365.

Mandeville, G. K., & Anderson, L. W. (1987). The stability of school effectiveness indices across grade levels and subject areas. *Journal of Educational Measurement, 24,* 203–216.

Mandeville, G. K., & Kennedy, E. (1991). The relationship of effective schools indicators and changes in the social distribution of achievement. *School Effectiveness and School Improvement, 2*(1), 14–33.

Mason, W. M., Wong, G. Y., & Entwisle, B. (1983). Contextual analysis through the multi-level linear model. In S. Leinhardt (Ed.), *Sociological methodology* (pp. 72–103). San Francisco: Jossey-Bass.

McCarthy, D., Canner, J., & Pershing, A. (1983). *Local school development project: Third annual process evaluation.* New York: Office of Educational Evaluation.

McCormack-Larkin, M. (1985). Ingredients in a successful school effectiveness project. *Educational Leadership, 42*(6), 31–37.

McCormack-Larkin, M., & Kritek, W. J. (1982). Milwaukee's project RISE. *Educational Leadership*, *40*(3), 16–21.

McDill, E. L., & Rigsby, L. C. (1973). *Structure and process in secondary schools: The academic impact of educational climates*. Baltimore: Johns Hopkins University Press.

McDonnell, J. (1985, April 27). Proper educational climate a must for production of achievers. *Lafayette Advertiser*, p. 1.

McIntosh, R. G. (Chairman, Board of Editors). (1968). Equal educational opportunity [Special issue]. *Harvard Educational Review*, *38*(1).

Michael, W. B., & Smith, R. A. (1976). *Dimensions of Self-Concept, Form E, Grades 4–6*. Form developed for the Los Angeles Unified School District, Programs for the Gifted.

Mickler, W. (1984, November). *The Beginning Teacher Program: A model local induction system and school improvement program*. Paper presented at the meeting of the National Council of States on In-Service Education, Orlando, FL. (ERIC Document Reproduction Service No. ED 274 647)

Miles, M., & Huberman, M. (1984). *Qualitative data analysis*. Beverly Hills, CA: Sage.

Mills, C. N., Teddlie, C., & Falkowski, C. K. (1984). The relationship between the Louisiana basic skills test and the Educational Development Series lower primary test. *Louisiana Education Research Journal*, *11*(2), 31–43.

Mitchell, D. (1990). *Principal leadership: A theoretical framework for research*. Urbana-Champaign: National Center for School Leadership, University of Illinois at Urbana-Champaign.

Moffett, K., St. John, J., & Isken, J. (1987). Training and coaching beginning teachers: An antidote to reality shock. *Educational Leadership*, *44*, 34–36.

Mortimore, P. (1991). School effectiveness research: Which way at the crossroads? *School Effectiveness and School Improvement*, *2*(3), 213–229.

Mortimore, P., & Sammons, P. (1987). New evidence on effective elementary schools. *Educational Leadership*, *45*(2), 4–8.

Mortimore, P., Sammons, P., Stoll, L., Lewis, D., & Ecob, R. (1988a). *School matters: The junior years*. Somerset, England: Open Books.

Mortimore, P., Sammons, P., Stoll, L., Lewis, D., & Ecob, R. (1988b). *The junior school project: Technical appendices*. London: ILEA Research and Statistics Branch.

Mosteller, F., & Moynihan, D. P. (1972). *On equality of educational opportunity*. New York: Vintage.

Murphy, J. (1990). Principal instructional leadership. In P. Thurston & L. Lotto (Eds.), *Advances in educational leadership* (pp. 163–200). Greenwich, CT: JAI Press.

Murphy, J., & Hallinger, P. (1988). Characteristics of instructionally effective school districts. *Administrator's Notebook*, *33*(10), 1–4.

Myers, D. (1991, August 18). Cody wants "report cards" accurate. *The Baton Rouge Sunday Advocate*, p. 1-B.

Myers, D. (1992, February 19). Education officials taking care to ensure "report card" credibility. *The Baton Rouge Morning Advocate*, p. 3-C.

Nachtigal, P. (1982). *Rural education: In search of a better way*. Boulder, CO: Westview.

Nutall, D. L., Goldstein, H., Prosser, R., & Rasbash, J. (1989). Differential school effectiveness. *International Journal of Educational Research, 13*, 769–776.

Olthof, A. L., & Lugthart, E. (1992). Effectiveness of various types of secondary school organization: A contingency approach. In J. Bashi & Z. Sass (Eds.), *School effectiveness and improvement: Selected proceedings of the Third International Congress for School Effectiveness* (pp. 344–369). Jerusalem, Israel: Magnes Press.

Patton, M. Q. (1990). *Qualitative evaluation and research methods*. Newbury Park, CA: Sage.

Pechman, E. (1985, April). *Morality play: Psychometrics, and ethics in testing*. Symposium presented at the American Educational Research Association, Chicago.

Pollack, S., Chrispeels, J., Watson, D., Brice, R., & McCormick, S. (1988, April). *A description of district factors that assist in the development of equity schools*. Paper presented at the annual meeting of the American Educational Research Association, New Orleans, LA.

Purkey, S. C., & Smith, M. S. (1983). Effective schools: A review. *Elementary School Journal, 83*, 427–452.

Ralph, J. H., & Fennessey, J. (1983). Science or reform: Some questions about the effective schools model. *Phi Delta Kappan, 64*, 689–694.

Raudenbush, S. W., & Bryk, A. S. (1986). A hierarchical model for studying school effects. *Sociology of Education, 59*, 1–17.

Raudenbush, S. W., & Bryk, A. S. (1987). *Quantitative models for estimating teacher and school effectiveness*. Paper presented at the Invitation Conference of the Center for Student Testing, Evaluation, and Standards, Princeton, NJ.

Raudenbush, S. W., & Bryk, A. S. (1989). Methodological advances in analyzing the effects of schools and classrooms on student learning. In E. Z. Rothokopf (Ed.), *Review of research in education* (Vol. 15, pp. 423–475). Washington, DC: American Educational Research Association.

Reynolds, D. (1992). School effectiveness and school improvement. In J. Bashi & Z. Sass (Eds.), *School effectiveness and improvement: Selected proceedings of the Third International Congress for School Effectiveness* (pp. 67–87). Jerusalem, Israel: Magnes Press.

Reynolds, D., Jones, D., & St. Leger, S. (1976). Schools do make a difference. *New Society, 37*, 223–225.

Riverside Publishing Company. (1983). *The 3-R's test*. Chicago: Riverside.

Roberts, L. M. (1991, April). *Constructing a practical framework for the superintendent's leadership role in school reform*. Paper presented at the annual meeting of the American Educational Research Association, Chicago.

Rog, J., Donaldson, G., Quaglia, R., & Paige, J. (1990, April). *Learning the ropes: How beginning teachers develop pedagogical knowledge*. Paper presented at the annual meeting of the American Educational Research Association, Boston.

Rosenberg, M. (1963). Parental influence in children's self-conceptions. *Sociometry, 26*, 35–49.

Rosenholtz, S. J. (1988). Workplace conditions that affect teacher quality an commitment: Implications for teacher induction programs. *Elementary School Journal, 89,* 421–439.

Rosenholtz, S. J. (1989). *Teachers' workplace: The social organization of schools.* New York: Longman.

Rosenshine, B. (1983). Teaching functions in instructional programs. *Elementary School Journal, 83,* 335–351.

Ross, S. (1992, October 26). Foundation finds most parents reject school-choice idea. *Baton Rouge Advocate,* p. 1-A.

Roussel, D. M. (1988). *Managerial frames of mind among school principals: A construct validation study.* Unpublished doctoral dissertation, University of New Orleans, New Orleans.

Rowan, B., Bossert, S. T., & Dwyer, D. C. (1983). Research on effective schools: A cautionary note. *Educational Researcher, 12*(4), 24–31.

Rowan, B., & Denk, C. E. (1982). *Modeling the academic performance of schools using longitudinal data: An analysis of school effectiveness measures and school and principal effects on school-level achievement.* San Francisco: Far West Laboratory.

Rummel, R. (1970). *Applied factor analysis.* Evanston, IL: Northwestern University Press.

Russell, D. (1986, March). *Collaboration: The key to teacher induction programs.* Paper presented at the annual meeting of the American Association of Colleges for Teacher Education, Chicago.

Rutter, M. (1983). School effects on pupil progress: Research findings and policy implications. In L. Shulman & G. Sykes (Eds.), *Handbook of teaching and policy* (pp. 3–41). New York: Longman.

Rutter, M., Maughan, B., Mortimore, P., & Ouston, J., with Smith, A. (1979). *Fifteen thousand hours: Secondary schools and their effect on children.* Cambridge, MA: Harvard University Press.

Schaffer, G., Stringfield, S., & Wolfe, D. (1990, April). *Two year effects on classroom interactions of a sustained beginning teacher induction program.* Paper presented at the annual meeting of the American Educational Research Association, Boston.

Scheerens, J., & Creemers, B. (1989). Towards a more comprehensive conceptualization of school effectiveness. In B. Creemers, T. Peters, & D. Reynolds (Eds.), *School effectiveness and school improvement: Proceedings of the Second International Congress for School Effectiveness* (pp. 265–278). Amsterdam: Swets & Zeitlinger.

Scheerens, J., & Creemers, B. (1990). Conceptualizing school effectiveness. *International Journal of Educational Research, 13*(7), 691–706.

Scheerens, J., Vermeulen, C. J., & Pelgrum, W. J. (1989). Generalizability of instructional and school effectiveness indicators across nations. *International Journal of Educational Research, 13*(7), 789–799.

Schlechty, P. (1985). A framework for evaluating induction into teaching. *Journal of Teacher Education, 36*(1), 37–41.

Schlechty, P., & Vance, V. (1983). Recruitment, selection, and retention: The shape of the teaching force. *Elementary School Journal, 83,* 469–487.

Scholastic Testing Service. (1978). *Educational development series technical report, Lower primary level, Forms A, S.* Bensonville, IL: Author.

Sherif, M., & Sherif, C. W. (1953). *Groups in harmony and tension.* New York: Harper.

Siegel, S. (1986, April 14). School study: Attitude can spell success. *New Orleans Times-Picayune*, p. A-15.

Sirotnik, K. A., & Burstein, L. (1985). Measurement and statistical issues in multilevel research on schooling. *Educational Administration Quarterly, 21,* 169–185.

Slater, R. O., & Teddlie, C. (in press). A theory of school effectiveness and leadership. *School Effectiveness and School Improvement, 4*(4).

Stallings, J. A. (1980). Allocated academic learning time revisited, or beyond time on task. *Educational Researcher, 9*(11), 11–16.

Stallings, J. A., & Freiberg, H. J. (1991). Observation for improvement of teaching. In H. C. Waxman & H. J. Walberg (Eds.), *Effective teaching: Current research* (pp. 107–134). Berkeley, CA: McCutchan.

Stallings, J. A., & Kaskowitz, D. (1974). *Follow through classroom observation evaluation (1972–1973).* Menlo Park, CA: SRT International.

Stogdill, R. M., & Coons, A. E. (Eds.). (1957). *Leader behavior: Its description and measurement* (Research Monograph No. 88). Columbus: Bureau of Business Research, Ohio State University.

Stone, B. (1987). Why beginning teachers fail—and what you can do about it. *Principal, 67*(1), 33–35.

Stringfield, S., & Hartman, A. (1985). *Irregularities in testing: Ethical, psychometric, and political issues.* Paper presented at the annual meeting of the American Educational Research Association, Chicago.

Stringfield, S., & Teddlie, C. (1988). A time to summarize: The Louisiana School Effectiveness Study. *Educational Leadership, 46*(2), 43–49.

Stringfield, S., & Teddlie, C. (1989). The first three phases of the Louisiana School Effectiveness Study. In B. Creemers, T. Peters, & D. Reynolds (Eds.), *School effectiveness and school improvement: Proceedings of the Second International Congress for School Improvement* (pp. 281–294). Amsterdam: Swets & Zeitlinger.

Stringfield, S., & Teddlie, C. (1990). School improvement efforts: Qualitative and quantitative data from four naturally occurring experiments in phases III and IV of the Louisiana School Effectiveness Study. *School Effectiveness and School Improvement, 1*(2), 139–162.

Stringfield, S., & Teddlie, C. (1991a). Observers as predictors of schools' effectiveness status. *Elementary School Journal, 91*(4), 357–376.

Stringfield, S., & Teddlie, C. (1991b). School, classroom, and student level indicators of rural school effectiveness. *Journal of Research in Rural Education, 7*(3), 15–28.

Stringfield, S., & Teddlie, C. (1991c). Schools as affectors of teacher effects. In H. C. Waxman & H. J. Walberg (Eds.), *Effective teaching: Current research* (pp. 161–180). Berkeley, CA: McCutchan.

Stringfield, S., Teddlie, C., & Suarez, S. (1985). Classroom interaction in effective and ineffective schools: Preliminary results from phase III of the Louisiana School Effectiveness Study. *Journal of Classroom Interaction,* 20(2), 31–37.

Stringfield, S., Teddlie, C., Wimpelberg, R., & Kirby, P. (1990, January). *Design and first analyses from a five year follow-up of more and less effective schools in the Louisiana School Effectiveness Study.* Paper presented at the International Congress for School Effectiveness, Jerusalem, Israel.

Stringfield, S., Teddlie, C., Wimpelberg, R. K., & Kirby, P. C. (1992). A five-year follow-up of schools in the Louisiana School Effectiveness Study. In J. Bashi & Z. Sass (Eds.), *School effectiveness and improvement: Selected proceedings of the Third International Congress for School Effectiveness* (pp. 381–414). Jerusalem, Israel: Magnes Press.

Taylor, B. O. (Ed.). (1990). *Case studies in effective schools research.* Madison, WI: National Center for Effective Schools Research and Development.

Taylor, R. C., Sadowski, C. J., & Peacher, R. K. (1981). *Development of a Likert-type locus of control scale for teachers.* Paper presented at the annual meeting of the Southeastern Psychological Association, Atlanta.

Teachers' expectations basic clue to learning. (1984, August 20). *Education USA,* p. 381.

Teddlie, C. (1992). *Quantitative results from LSES-III and -IV: Technical manual* (Technical Report No. 4). Baton Rouge: Louisiana State University, Department of Administrative and Foundational Studies, Louisiana School Effectiveness Project.

Teddlie, C., Falkowski, C., & Falk, W. (1982). *The Louisiana School Effectiveness Study: Phase one, 1980–82.* Baton Rouge: Louisiana Department of Education.

Teddlie, C., Falkowski, C., Stringfield, S., Desselle, S., & Garvue, R. (1984). *The Louisiana School Effectiveness Study: Phase two, 1982–84.* Baton Rouge: Louisiana Department of Education. (ERIC Document Reproduction Service No. ED 250 362)

Teddlie, C., Kirby, P. C., & Stringfield, S. (1989). Effective versus ineffective schools: Observable differences in the classroom. *American Journal of Education,* 97(3), 221–236.

Teddlie, C., & Kochan, S. (1991, April). *Evaluation of a troubled high school: Methods, results, and implications.* Paper presented at the annual meeting of the American Educational Research Association, Chicago.

Teddlie, C., & Stringfield, S. (1985). A differential analysis of effectiveness in middle and lower socioeconomic status schools. *Journal of Classroom Interaction,* 20(2), 38–44.

Teddlie, C., & Stringfield, S. (1989). Ethics and teachers: Implications of research on effective schools. *Ethics in Education,* 9(2), 12–14.

Teddlie, C., & Stringfield, S. (1992). *Case histories from a longitudinal study of school effectiveness.* Paper presented at the annual meeting of the American Educational Research Association, San Francisco.

Teddlie, C., Stringfield, S., & Desselle, S. (1985). Methods, history, selected findings, and recommendations from the Louisiana School Effectiveness Study: 1980–85. *Journal of Classroom Interaction,* 20(2), 22–30.

Teddlie, C., Stringfield, S., & Wimpelberg, R. (1986). Equity in school effectiveness research: Examples from a study in Louisiana. *Journal of Educational Equity and Leadership, 6*(2), 171–176.

Teddlie, C., Stringfield, S., Wimpelberg, R. K., & Kirby, P. C. (1989). Contextual differences in models for effective schooling in the USA. In B. Creemers, T. Peters, & D. Reynolds (Eds.), *School effectiveness and school improvement: Selected proceedings of the Second International Congress for School Effectiveness* (pp. 117–130). Amsterdam: Swets & Zeitlinger.

Teddlie, C., Stringfield, S., Wimpelberg, R. K., & Kirby, P. C. (1990, April). *Phase four of the Louisiana School Effectiveness Study: Results from a longitudinal study.* Paper presented at the annual meeting of the American Educational Research Association, Boston.

Teddlie, C., Virgilio, I., & Oescher, J. (1990). Development and validation of the Virgilio Teacher Behavior Inventory. *Educational and Psychological Measurement, 50*(2), 421–430.

Ter Haar, C. S. (1992). *A study of the differences in induction experiences for teachers in differentially effective schools.* Unpublished doctoral dissertation, Louisiana State University, Baton Rouge.

U.S. Bureau of the Census. (1988). *County statistics file 3 (CO-STAT3)* [machine-readable data file]. Washington, DC: Author.

Varah, L., Theune, W., & Parker, L. (1986). Beginning teachers: Sink or swim? *Journal of Teacher Education, 37*(1), 30–34.

Veenman, S. (1984). Perceived problems of beginning teachers. *Review of Educational Research, 54*(2), 143–178.

Venezky, R. L., & Winfield, L. F. (1979). *Schools that succeed beyond expectations in reading* (Studies on Education Technical Report No. 1). Newark: University of Delaware. (ERIC Document Reproduction Service No. ED 177 484)

Virgilio, I., Teddlie, C., & Oescher, J. (1991). Variance and context differences in teaching at differentially effective schools. *School Effectiveness and School Improvement, 2*(2), 152–168.

Ward, B., & Tikunoff, W. (1989). *New teacher retention project: External study—Year two project implementation and outcomes.* Larkspur, CA: Southwest Regional Educational Laboratory.

Weber, G. (1971). *Inner city children can be taught to read: Four successful schools.* Washington, DC: Council for Basic Education.

Weber, M. (1946). *From Max Weber: Essays in sociology* (H. H. Gerth & C. W. Mills, Eds. & Trans.). New York: Oxford University Press.

Wildman, T., Magliaro, S., McLaughlin, R., & Niles, J. (1990, April). *Roles, procedures, and conditions in the development of mentor teacher programs.* Paper presented at the annual meeting of the American Educational Research Association, Boston.

Willett, J. B., & Singer, J. D. (1991). From whether to when: New methods for studying student dropout and teacher attrition. *Review of Educational Research, 61*(4), 407–450.

Wimpelberg, R. K. (1987a). Managerial images and school effectiveness. *Administrator's Notebook, 32*(4), 1–4.

Wimpelberg, R. K. (1987b). The dilemma of instructional leadership and a central role for central office. In W. Greenfield (Ed.), *Instructional leadership: Concepts and controversies* (pp. 100–117). Boston: Allyn & Bacon.

Wimpelberg, R. K., Teddlie, C., & Stringfield, S. (1989). Sensitivity to context: The past and future of effective schools research. *Educational Administration Quarterly, 25*(1), 82–107.

Witte, J. F., & Walsh, D. J. (1990). A systematic test of the effective schools model. *Educational Evaluation and Policy Analysis, 12,* 188–212.

About the Authors

CHARLES TEDDLIE is Associate Professor of Educational Research Methodology at the Louisiana State University College of Education. Dr. Teddlie received the Ph.D. in Social Psychology from the University of North Carolina at Chapel Hill in 1979. Since that time, he has directed the Division of Research and Development at the Louisiana Department of Education and taught at the University of New Orleans. He has over 45 articles in refereed journals, including *Educational Leadership, American Journal of Education, Educational Administration Quarterly, Educational and Psychological Measurement, Journal of Personality and Social Psychology,* and *Elementary School Journal.* He has received grants and/or contracts from numerous sources, including the American Broadcasting Corporation, the Carnegie Corporation, the Kellogg Foundation, and the U.S. Department of Education. His current research focuses on school and teacher effects.

SAM STRINGFIELD is Principal Research Scientist at the Johns Hopkins University Center for Social Organization of Schools. Dr. Stringfield completed the Ph.D. in Educational Psychology from Temple University in 1983. Before coming to Johns Hopkins, he worked as a teacher, a program evaluator, a Tulane University faculty member, and coordinator of the Denver field office of Northwest Regional Educational Laboratory. As a Kellogg Fellow, Dr. Stringfield studied school improvement practices in the United States, Asia, Africa, and Europe. He is the author or coauthor of more than 40 publications, most of which focus on school and teacher effectiveness, and compensatory education. Currently he is the director of the Suburban/Rural Study of Special Strategies for Educating Disadvantaged Children and serves as a senior researcher on *Prospects: The Congressionally Mandated Study of Educational Growth and Opportunity.*

ROBERT K. WIMPELBERG is Interim Dean and Professor of Education in the College of Education at the University of New Orleans. Dr. Wimpelberg completed the Ph.D. in Administrative, Institutional, and Policy

Studies at the University of Chicago in 1981, where he was also editor of the *Administrator's Notebook*. His recent writing about principals, school effectiveness, and school restructuring has appeared in *Educational Administration Quarterly* (with Charles Teddlie and Sam Stringfield) and *Planning and Changing* (with William Boyd). His work on national reform commissions with Rick Ginsberg has appeared in *Educational Evaluation and Policy Analysis* and *Education and Urban Society*. He has also researched and written about the central office role in school change and about equity issues in school finance. For his research on schooling in New Orleans and Louisiana and his community service in education, Dr. Wimpelberg was awarded the University of New Orleans DeBlois Faculty Fellowship in 1990.

PEGGY C. KIRBY is Chair and Associate Professor of Education, Department of Educational Leadership, Counseling, and Foundations at the University of New Orleans. Since receiving the Ph.D. from the University of New Orleans in Educational Administration in 1987, she has taught school administration, educational foundations, and educational research at both the University of Georgia and the University of New Orleans. Her research has focused on school-level factors, particularly leadership and governance, that influence teacher and student outcomes. She recently coauthored *Bringing Out the Best in Teachers: What Effective Principals Do*, a Corwin Press publication.

EUGENE KENNEDY is Assistant Professor of Educational Research Methodology at Louisiana State University (LSU). Since receiving the Ph.D. in Educational Research from the University of South Carolina in 1990, he has taught psychometrics and educational research at LSU. His research has focused on longitudinal issues in school effects and analysis of item responses in achievement and aptitude testing.

Index